Network Programming with Go

Essential Skills for Using and Securing Networks

Jan Newmarch

Network Programming with Go: Essential Skills for Using and Securing Networks

Jan Newmarch
Oakleigh, Victoria
Australia

ISBN-13 (pbk): 978-1-4842-2691-9   ISBN-13 (electronic): 978-1-4842-2692-6
DOI 10.1007/978-1-4842-2692-6

Library of Congress Control Number: 2017941517

Managing Director: Welmoed Spahr
Editorial Director: Todd Green
Acquisitions Editor: Steve Anglin
Development Editor: Matthew Moodie
Technical Reviewer: Ronald Petty
Coordinating Editor: Mark Powers
Copy Editor: Kezia Endsley
Compositor: SPi Global
Indexer: SPi Global
Artist: SPi Global
Cover image designed by Freepik

Distributed to the book trade worldwide by Springer Science+Business Media New York, 233 Spring Street, 6th Floor, New York, NY 10013. Phone 1-800-SPRINGER, fax (201) 348-4505, e-mail orders-ny@springer-sbm.com, or visit www.springeronline.com. Apress Media, LLC is a California LLC and the sole member (owner) is Springer Science + Business Media Finance Inc (SSBM Finance Inc). SSBM Finance Inc is a **Delaware** corporation.

For information on translations, please e-mail rights@apress.com, or visit http://www.apress.com/rights-permissions.

Apress titles may be purchased in bulk for academic, corporate, or promotional use. eBook versions and licenses are also available for most titles. For more information, reference our Print and eBook Bulk Sales web page at http://www.apress.com/bulk-sales.

Any source code or other supplementary material referenced by the author in this book is available to readers on GitHub via the book's product page, located at www.apress.com/9781484226919. For more detailed information, please visit http://www.apress.com/source-code.

Printed on acid-free paper

Contents at a Glance

About the Author xvii

About the Technical Reviewer xix

Preface xxi

▮Chapter 1: Architecture 1

▮Chapter 2: Overview of the Go Language 21

▮Chapter 3: Socket-Level Programming.. 29

▮Chapter 4: Data Serialization 57

▮Chapter 5: Application-Level Protocols 87

▮Chapter 6: Managing Character Sets and Encodings 107

▮Chapter 7: Security.. 121

▮Chapter 8: HTTP 137

▮Chapter 9: Templates.. 161

▮Chapter 10: A Complete Web Server... 175

▮Chapter 11: HTML 193

▮Chapter 12: XML 199

▮Chapter 13: Remote Procedure Call... 209

▮Chapter 14: REST 221

▮Chapter 15: WebSockets... 247

Afterword.. 267

Index.. 269

Contents

About the Author xvii

About the Technical Reviewer xix

Preface xxi

Chapter 1: Architecture 1

Protocol Layers...1

    ISO OSI Protocol..2

    OSI Layers..2

    TCP/IP Protocol 3

    Some Alternative Protocols 3

Networking...3

Gateways..4

Packet Encapsulation 4

Connection Models..5

    Connection Oriented 5

    Connectionless 5

Communications Models..5

    Message Passing..5

    Remote Procedure Call 6

Distributed Computing Models...7

Client-Server System 8

Client-Server Application..8

Server Distribution 9

Communication Flows 9
    Synchronous Communication 10
    Asynchronous Communication 10
    Streaming Communication 10
    Publish/Subscribe 10

Component Distribution 10
    Gartner Classification 11
    Three-Tier Models 13
    Fat versus Thin 14

Middleware Model 14
    Middleware Examples 14
    Middleware Functions 15

Continuum of Processing 15

Points of Failure 16

Acceptance Factors 16

Transparency 17
    Access Transparency 17
    Location Transparency 17
    Migration Transparency 17
    Replication Transparency 17
    Concurrency Transparency 17
    Scalability Transparency 17
    Performance Transparency 18
    Failure Transparency 18

Eight Fallacies of Distributed Computing 18
    Fallacy: The Network Is Reliable 18
    Fallacy: Latency Is Zero 19
    Fallacy: Bandwidth Is Infinite 19
    Fallacy: The Network Is Secure 19

Fallacy: Topology Doesn't Change 19

Fallacy: There Is One Administrator 19

Fallacy: Transport Cost Is Zero.. 20

Fallacy: The Network Is Homogeneous.. 20

Conclusion.. 20

■Chapter 2: Overview of the Go Language 21

Types 22

Slices and Arrays... 22

Structures.. 22

Pointers 23

Functions 23

Maps.. 24

Methods.. 24

Multi-Threading... 25

Packages 25

Type Conversion 25

Statements... 25

GOPATH.. 25

Running Go Programs 26

Standard Libraries... 26

Error Values 26

Conclusion... 27

■Chapter 3: Socket-Level Programming.. 29

The TCP/IP Stack 29

IP Datagrams 30

UDP... 30

TCP 30

Internet Addresses 30

IPv4 Addresses 31

IPv6 Addresses 31

IP Address Type 32

    The IPMask Type 33

    The IPAddr Type 36

    Host Lookup 37

Services.. 38

    Ports 38

    The TCPAddr Type 39

TCP Sockets 40

    TCP Client 40

    A Daytime Server.. 42

    Multi-Threaded Server... 44

Controlling TCP Connections 46

    Timeout.. 46

    Staying Alive 46

UDP Datagrams 47

Server Listening on Multiple Sockets... 49

The Conn, PacketConn, and Listener Types 49

Raw Sockets and the IPConn Type 52

Conclusion... 55

Chapter 4: Data Serialization... 57

Structured Data... 57

Mutual Agreement... 59

Self-Describing Data 59

ASN.1.. 60

    ASN.1 Daytime Client and Server 66

JSON... 68

    A Client and Server... 72

The Gob Package... 75

    A Client and Server... 78

Encoding Binary Data as Strings 81

Protocol Buffers 83

    Installing and Compiling Protocol Buffers 84

    The Compiled personv3.pb.go File 84

    Using the Compiled Code 85

Conclusion 86

■Chapter 5: Application-Level Protocols 87

Protocol Design 87

Why Should You Worry? 88

Version Control 88

    The Web 89

Message Format 90

Data Format 91

    Byte Format 91

    Character Format 92

A Simple Example 92

    A Standalone Application 93

    The Client-Server Application 94

    The Client Side 94

    Alternative Presentation Aspects 95

    The Server Side 95

    Protocol: Informal 95

    Text Protocol 96

    Server Code 97

    Client Code 99

    Textproto Package 101

State Information 101

    Application State Transition Diagram 103

    Client State Transition Diagrams 104

Server State Transition Diagrams 105

Server Pseudocode 105

Conclusion 106

■Chapter 6: Managing Character Sets and Encodings 107

Definitions 108

Character 108

Character Repertoire/Character Set 108

Character Code 108

Character Encoding 108

Transport Encoding 109

ASCII 109

ISO 8859 111

Unicode 111

UTF-8, Go, and Runes 112

UTF-8 Client and Server 112

ASCII Client and Server 113

UTF-16 and Go 113

Little-Endian and Big-Endian 113

UTF-16 Client and Server 114

Unicode Gotchas 116

ISO 8859 and Go 117

Other Character Sets and Go 119

Conclusion 119

■Chapter 7: Security 121

ISO Security Architecture 121

Functions and Levels 122

Mechanisms 123

Data Integrity 124

Symmetric Key Encryption 126

Public Key Encryption 127

X.509 Certificates 129

TLS 132

   A Basic Client.. 132

   Server Using a Self-Signed Certificate 133

Conclusion... 136

■Chapter 8: HTTP 137

URLs and Resources 137

   I18n... 137

   HTTP Characteristics 138

   Versions 138

   HTTP 0.9 138

   HTTP 1.0 139

   HTTP 1.1 140

   HTTP/2 141

Simple User Agents 141

   The Response Type.. 141

   The HEAD Method.. 142

   The GET Method 143

Configuring HTTP Requests... 145

The Client Object 147

Proxy Handling 149

   Simple Proxy... 149

   Authenticating Proxy 151

HTTPS Connections by Clients.. 153

Servers 155

   File Server 155

   Handler Functions... 156

   Bypassing the Default Multiplexer.. 158

HTTPS.. 159

Conclusion... 160

■Chapter 9: Templates **161**

Inserting Object Values 161

    Using Templates 162

Pipelines 164

Defining Functions 165

Variables 167

Conditional Statements 168

The HTML / Template Package 173

Conclusion 173

■Chapter 10: A Complete Web Server **175**

Browser Site Diagram 175

Browser Files 177

Basic Server 177

The listFlashCards Function 179

The manageFlashCards Function 181

The Chinese Dictionary 181

    The Dictionary Type 182

Flashcard Sets 183

Fixing Accents 184

The ListWords Function 187

The showFlashCards Function 189

Presentation on the Browser 191

Running the Server 191

Conclusion 191

■Chapter 11: HTML **193**

The Go HTML/Template Package 194

Tokenizing HTML 195

XHTML/HTML 197

JSON..198

Conclusion...198

■**Chapter 12: XML** **199**

Parsing XML 200

The StartElement Type...200

The EndElement Type 200

The CharData Type...200

The Comment Type 200

The ProcInst Type 201

The Directive Type 201

Unmarshalling XML 203

Marshalling XML..206

XHTML 207

HTML 207

Conclusion...207

■**Chapter 13: Remote Procedure Call**...**209**

Go's RPC 210

HTTP RPC Server 212

HTTP RPC Client...213

TCP RPC Server 214

TCP RPC Client...216

Matching Values 217

JSON..217

JSON RPC Server...218

JSON RPC Client 219

Conclusion...220

■**Chapter 14: REST** **221**

URIs and Resources 221

Representations 222

REST Verbs 223

    The GET Verb 223

    The PUT Verb 223

    The DELETE Verb 224

    The POST Verb 224

No Maintained State 224

HATEOAS 224

Representing Links 225

Transactions with REST 226

The Richardson Maturity Model 227

Flashcards Revisited 228

    URLs 228

The Demultiplexer (Demuxer) 229

Content Negotiation 230

    GET / 232

    POST / 233

Handling Other URLs 234

The Complete Server 234

Client 240

Using REST or RPC 245

Conclusion 245

■Chapter 15: WebSockets 247

WebSockets Server 248

The Go Sub-Repository Package 248

    The Message Object 248

    The JSON Object 251

    The Codec Type 254

    WebSockets Over TLS 257

    WebSockets in an HTML Page 259

The Gorilla Package 263

    Echo Server 264

    Echo Client 265

Conclusion 266

Afterword 267

Index 269

About the Author

Jan Newmarch is head of ICT (higher education) at Box Hill Institute, adjunct professor at Canberra University, and adjunct lecturer in the School of Information Technology, Computing and Mathematics at Charles Sturt University. He is interested in more aspects of computing than he has time to pursue, but the major thrust over the last few years has developed from user interfaces under UNIX into Java, the Web, and then into general distributed systems. Jan developed a number of publicly available software systems in these areas. For the last few years, he has been looking at sound for Linux systems and programming the Raspberry Pi's GPU. He is now exploring aspects of the IoT. He lives in Melbourne, Australia and enjoys the food and culture there, but is not so impressed by the weather.

About the Technical Reviewer

Ronald Petty, M.B.A., M.S. is the founder of Minimum Distance LLC, a management consulting firm based in San Francisco. He spends his time helping technology-based startups do the right thing. He is also an instructor at UC Berkeley Extension.

Preface

It's always fun to learn a new programming language, especially when it turns out to be a major one. Prior to the release of Go in 2009, I was teaching a Master's level subject in network programming at Monash University. It's good to have a goal when learning a new language, but this time, instead of building yet another wine cellar program, I decided to orient my lecture notes around Go instead of my (then) standard delivery vehicle of Java.

The experiment worked well: apart from the richness of the Java libraries that Go was yet to match, all the programming examples transferred remarkably well, and in many cases were more elegant than the original Java programs.

This book is the result. I have updated it as Go has evolved and as new technologies such as HTTP/2 have arisen. But if it reads like a textbook, well, that is because it is one. There is a large body of theoretical and practical concepts involved in network programming and this book covers some of these as well as the practicalities of building systems in Go.

In terms of language popularity, Go is clearly rising. It has climbed to 16th in the TIOBE index, is 18th in the PYPL (Popularity of Programming Language), and is 15th in the RedMonk Programming Language rankings. It is generally rated as one of the fastest growing languages.

There is a growing community of developers both of the core language and libraries and of the independent projects. I have tried to limit the scope of this book to the standard libraries only and to the "sub-repositories" of the Go tree. While this eliminates many excellent projects that no doubt make many programming tasks easier, restricting the book to the official Go libraries provides a clear bound.

This book assumes a basic knowledge of Go. The focus is on using Go to build network applications, not on the basics of the language. Network applications are different than command-line applications, are different than applications with a graphical user interface, and so on. So the first chapter discusses architectural aspects of network programs. The second chapter is an overview of the features of Go that we use in this book. The third chapter on sockets covers the Go version of the basics underlying all TCP/IP systems. Chapters 4, 5, and 6 are more unusual in network programming books. They cover the topics of what representations of data will be used, how a network interaction will proceed, and for text, which language formats are used. Then in Chapter 7, we look at the increasingly important topic of security. In Chapter 8, we look at one of the most common application layer protocols in use, HTTP. The next four chapters are about topics related to HTTP and common data formats carried above HTTP—HTML and XML. In Chapter 13, we look at an alternative approach to network programming, remote procedure calls. Chapters 14 and 15 consider further aspects of network programming using HTTP.

CHAPTER 1

Architecture

This chapter covers the major architectural features of distributed systems. You can't build a system without some idea of what you want to build. And you can't build it if you don't know the environment in which it will work. GUI programs are different than batch processing programs; games programs are different than business programs; and distributed programs are different than standalone programs. They each have their approaches, their common patterns, the problems that typically arise, and the solutions that are often used.

This chapter covers the high-level architectural aspects of distributed systems. There are many ways of looking at such systems, and many of these are dealt with.

Protocol Layers

Distributed systems are *hard*. There are multiple computers involved, which have to be connected in some way. Programs have to be written to run on each computer in the system and they all have to cooperate to get a distributed task done.

The common way to deal with complexity is to break it down into smaller and simpler parts. These parts have their own structure, but they also have defined means of communicating with other related parts. In distributed systems, the parts are called *protocol layers* and they have clearly defined functions. They form a stack, with each layer communicating with the layer above and the layer below. The communication between layers is defined by protocols.

Network communications requires protocols to cover high-level application communication all the way down to wire communication and the complexity handled by encapsulation in protocol layers.

© Jan Newmarch 2017
J. Newmarch, *Network Programming with Go*, DOI 10.1007/978-1-4842-2692-6_1

ISO OSI Protocol

Although it was never properly implemented, the OSI (Open Systems Interconnect) protocol has been a major influence in ways of talking about and influencing distributed systems design. It is commonly given as shown in Figure 1-1.

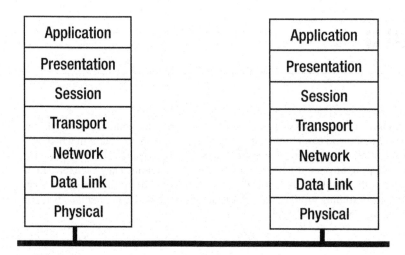

Figure 1-1. *The Open Systems Interconnect protocol*

OSI Layers

The function of each layer from bottom to top is as follows:

- The Physical layer conveys the bit stream using electrical, optical, or radio technologies.

- The Data link layer puts the information packets into network frames for transmission across the physical layer, and back into information packets.

- The Network layer provides switching and routing technologies.

- The Transport layer provides transparent transfer of data between end systems and is responsible for end-to-end error recovery and flow control.

- The Session layer establishes, manages, and terminates connections between applications.

- The Presentation layer provides independence from differences in data representation (e.g., encryption).

- The Application layer supports application and end-user processes.

TCP/IP Protocol

While the OSI model was being argued, debated, partly implemented, and fought over, the DARPA Internet research project was busy building the TCP/IP protocols. These have been immensely successful and have led to *The Internet* (with capitals). This is a much simpler stack, as shown in Figure 1-2.

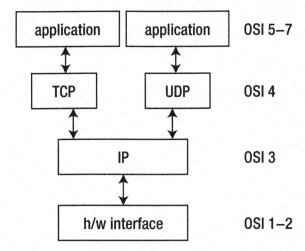

Figure 1-2. *The TCP/IP protocols*

Some Alternative Protocols

Although it almost seems like it, the TCP/IP protocols are not the only ones in existence and in the long run may not even be the most successful. Wikipedia's list of network protocols (see https://en.wikipedia. org/wiki/List_of_network_protocols_(OSI_model)) has a huge number more, at each of the ISO layers. Many of these are obsolete or of little use, but due to advances in technology in all sorts of areas—such as the Internet in Space and the Internet of Things—there will always be room for new protocols.

The focus in this book is on the TCP/IP (including UDP) layer, but you should be aware that there are other ones.

Networking

A *network* is a communications system for connecting end systems called hosts. The mechanisms of connection might be copper wire, Ethernet, fiber optic, or wireless, but that won't concern us here. A local area network (LAN) connects computers that are close together, typically belonging to a home, small organization, or part of a larger organization.

A Wide Area Network (WAN) connects computers across a larger physical area, such as between cities. There are other types as well, such as MANs (Metropolitan Area Network), PANs (Personal Area Networks), and even BANs (Body Area Network).

An internet is a connection of two or more distinct networks, typically LANs or WANs. An intranet is an internet with all networks belonging to a single organization.

There are significant differences between an internet and an intranet. Typically, an intranet will be under a single administrative control, which will impose a single set of coherent policies. An internet, on the other hand, will not be under the control of a single body, and the controls exercised over different parts may not even be compatible.

A trivial example of such differences is that an intranet will often be restricted to computers by a small number of vendors running a standardized version of a particular operating system. On the other hand, an internet will often have a smorgasbord of different computers and operating systems.

The techniques of this book are applicable to internets. They are also valid with intranets, but there you will also find specialized, non-portable systems.

And then there is the "mother" of all internets: The Internet. This is just a very, very large internet that connects us to Google, my computer to your computer, and so on.

Gateways

A *gateway* is a generic term for an entity used to connect two or more networks. A repeater operates at the physical level and copies information from one subnet to another. A bridge operates at the data link layer level and copies frames between networks. A router operates at the network level and not only moves information between networks but also decides on the route.

Packet Encapsulation

The communication between layers in either the OSI or the TCP/IP stacks is done by sending packets of data from one layer to the next, and then eventually across the network. Each layer has administrative information that it has to keep about its own layer. It does this by adding header information to the packet it receives from the layer above, as the packet passes down. On the receiving side, these headers are removed as the packet moves up.

For example, the TFTP (Trivial File Transfer Protocol) moves files from one computer to another. It uses the UDP protocol on top of the IP protocol, which may be sent over Ethernet. This looks like the diagram shown in Figure 1-3.

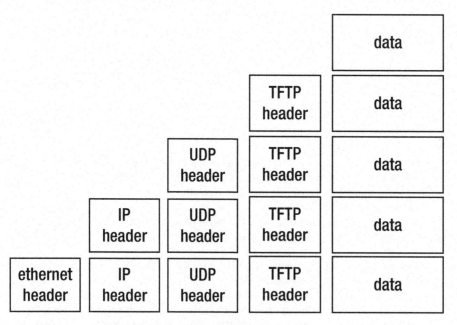

Figure 1-3. *The TFTP (Trivial File Transfer Protocol)*

The packet transmitted over Ethernet is of course the bottom one.

Connection Models

In order for two computers to communicate, they must set up a path whereby they can send at least one message in a session. There are two major models for this:

- Connection oriented
- Connectionless

Connection Oriented

A single connection is established for the session. Two-way communications flow along the connection. When the session is over, the connection is broken. The analogy is to a phone conversation. An example is TCP.

Connectionless

In a connectionless system, messages are sent independent of each other. Ordinary mail is the analogy. Connectionless messages may arrive out of order. An example is the IP protocol. UDP is a connectionless protocol above IP and is often used as an alternative to TCP, as it is much lighter weight.

Connection-oriented transports may be established on top of connectionless ones—TCP over IP. Connectionless transports may be established on top of connection-oriented ones—HTTP over TCP.

There can be variations on these. For example, a session might enforce messages arriving, but might not guarantee that they arrive in the order sent. However, these two are the most common.

Communications Models

In a distributed system there will be many components running that have to communicate with each other. There are two primary models for this, message passing and remote procedure calls.

Message Passing

Some non-procedural languages are built on the principle of *message passing*. Concurrent languages often use such a mechanism, and the most well known example is probably the UNIX pipeline. The UNIX pipeline is a pipeline of bytes, but this is not an inherent limitation: Microsoft's PowerShell can send objects along its pipelines, and concurrent languages such as Parlog can send arbitrary logic data structures in messages between concurrent processes.

Message passing is a primitive mechanism for distributed systems. Set up a connection and pump some data down it. At the other end, figure out what the message was and respond to it, possibly sending messages back. This is illustrated in Figure 1-4.

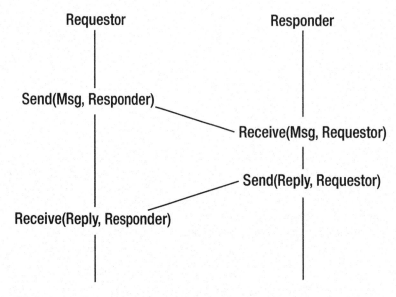

Figure 1-4. *The message passing communications model*

Event-driven systems act in a similar manner. At a low level, node.js runs an event loop waiting for I/O events, dispatching handlers for these events and responding. At a higher level, most user interface systems use an event loop waiting for user input, while in the networking world, Ajax uses the XMLHttpRequest to send and receive requests.

Remote Procedure Call

In any system, there is a transfer of information and flow control from one part of the system to another. In procedural languages, this may consist of the procedure call, where information is placed on a call stack and then control flow is transferred to another part of the program.

Even with procedure calls, there are variations. The code may be statically linked so that control transfers from one part of the program's executable code to another part. Due to the increasing use of library routines, it has become commonplace to have such code in dynamic link libraries (DLLs), where control transfers to an independent piece of code.

DLLs run in the same machine as the calling code. it is a simple (conceptual) step to transfer control to a procedure running in a different machine. The mechanics of this are not so simple! However, this model of control has given rise to the remote procedure call (RPC), which is discussed in much detail in a later chapter. This is illustrated by Figure 1-5.

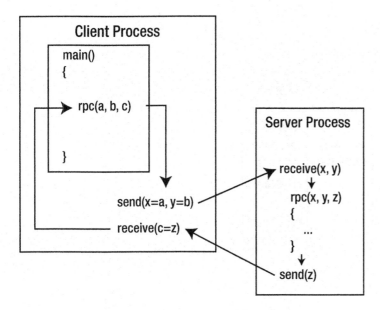

Figure 1-5. *The remote procedure call communications model*

There are many examples of this: some based on particular programming languages such as the Go rpc package (discussed in Chapter 13) or RPC systems covering multiple languages such as SOAP and Google's grpc.

Distributed Computing Models

At the highest level, we could consider the equivalence or the non-equivalence of components of a distributed system. The most common occurrence is an asymmetric one: a client sends requests to a server, and the server responds. This is a *client-server* system.

If both components are equivalent, both able to initiate and to respond to messages, then we have a *peer-to-peer* system. Note that this is a logical classification: one peer may be a 16,000 core supercomputer, the other might be a mobile phone. But if both can act similarly, then they are peers.

These are illustrated as shown in Figure 1-6.

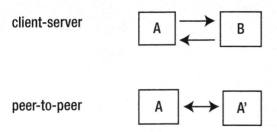

Figure 1-6. *Client-sever versus peer-to-peer systems*

Client-Server System

Another view of a client-server system is shown in Figure 1-7.

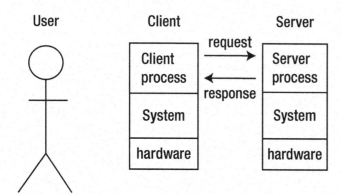

Figure 1-7. *The client-server system*

This view may be held by a developer who needs to know the components of a system. It is also the view that may be held by a user: a user of a browser knows it is running on her system but is communicating with servers elsewhere.

Client-Server Application

Some applications may be seamlessly distributed, with the user unaware that it is distributed. Users will see their view of the system, as shown in Figure 1-8.

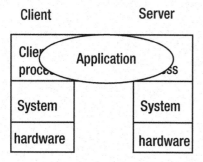

Figure 1-8. *The user's view of the system*

Server Distribution

A client-server system need not be simple. The basic model is a single client, single server system, as shown in Figure 1-9.

Figure 1-9. *The single client, single server system*

However, you can also have multiple clients, single server, as illustrated in Figure 1-10.

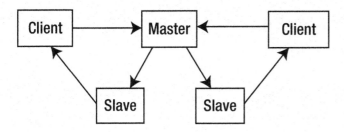

Figure 1-10. *The multiple clients, single server system*

In this system, the master receives requests and instead of handling them one at a time itself, it passes them to other servers to handle. This is a common model when concurrent clients are possible.

There are also single client, multiple servers, as shown in Figure 1-11.

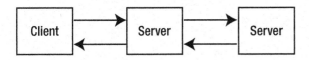

Figure 1-11. *The single client, multiple servers system*

This type of system occurs frequently when a server needs to act as a client to other servers, such as a business logic server getting information from a database server. And of course, there could be multiple clients with multiple servers.

Communication Flows

The previous diagrams have shown the connection views between high-level components of a system. Data will flow between these components and it can do so in multiple ways, discussed in the following sections.

Synchronous Communication

In a synchronous communication, one party will send a message and block, waiting for a reply. This is often the simplest model to implement and is just relies on blocking I/O. However, there may need to be a timeout mechanism in case some error means that no reply will ever be sent.

Asynchronous Communication

In asynchronous communication, one party sends a message and instead of waiting for a reply carries on with other work. When a reply eventually comes, it is handled. This may be in another thread or by interrupting the current thread. Such applications are harder to build but are much more flexible to use.

Streaming Communication

In streaming communication, one party sends a continuous stream of messages. Online video is a good example. The streaming may need to be handled in real time, may or may not tolerate losses, and can be one-way or allow reverse communication as in control messages.

Publish/Subscribe

In pub/sub systems, parties subscribe to topics and others post to them. This can be on a small or massive scale, as demonstrated by Twitter.

Component Distribution

A simple but effective way of decomposing many applications is to consider them as made up of three parts:

- Presentation component

- Application logic

- Data access

The *presentation component* is responsible for interactions with the user, both displaying data and gathering input. It may be a modern GUI interface with buttons, lists, menus, etc., or an older command-line style interface, asking questions and getting answers. It could also encompass wider interaction styles, such as the interaction with physical devices such as a cash register, ATM, etc. It could also cover the interaction with a non-human user, as in a machine-to-machine system. The details are not important at this level.

The *application logic* is responsible for interpreting the users' responses, for applying business rules, for preparing queries, and for managing responses from the third component.

The *data access* component is responsible for storing and retrieving data. This will often be through a database, but not necessarily.

Gartner Classification

Based on this threefold decomposition of applications, Gartner considered how the components might be distributed in a client-server system. They came up with five models, shown in Figure 1-12.

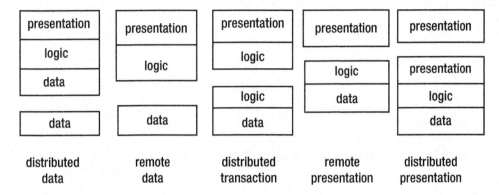

Figure 1-12. *Gartner's five models*

Example: Distributed Database

- Gartner classification: 1 (see Figure 1-13)

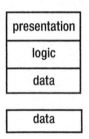

Figure 1-13. *Gartner example 1*

Modern mobile phones make good examples of this. Due to limited memory, they may store a small part of a database locally so that they can usually respond quickly. However, if data is required that is not held locally, then a request may be made to a remote database for that additional data.

Google maps is another good example. All of the maps reside on Google's servers. When one is requested by a user, the "nearby" maps are also downloaded into a small database in the browser. When the user moves the map a little bit, the extra bits required are already in the local store for quick response.

Example: Network File Service

Gartner classification 2 allows remote clients access to a shared file system, as shown in Figure 1-14.

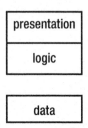

Figure 1-14. *Gartner example 2*

There are many examples of such systems: NFS, Microsoft shares, DCE, etc.

Example: Web

An example of Gartner classification 3 is the Web with Java applets or JavaScript, and CGI scripts or similar (Ruby on Rails, etc.) on the server side. This is a distributed hypertext system, with many additional mechanisms, as illustrated in Figure 1-15.

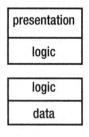

Figure 1-15. *Gartner example 3*

Example: Terminal Emulation

An example of Gartner classification 4 is terminal emulation. This allows a remote system to act as a normal terminal on a local system, as shown in Figure 1-16.

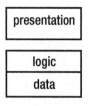

Figure 1-16. *Gartner example 4*

Telnet is the most common example of this.

Example: Secure Shell

The secure shell on UNIX allows you to connect to a remote system, run a command there, and display the presentation locally. The presentation is prepared on the remote machine and displayed locally. Under Windows, remote desktop behaves similarly. See Figure 1-17.

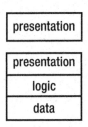

Figure 1-17. Gartner example 4

Three-Tier Models

Of course, if you have two tiers, then you can have three, four, or more. Some of the three-tier possibilities are shown in Figure 1-18.

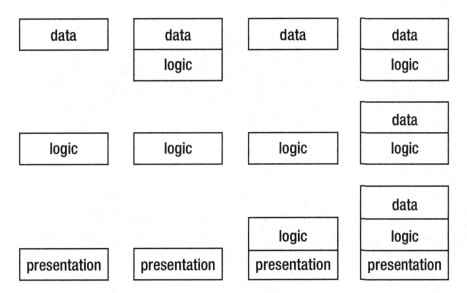

Figure 1-18. Three-tier models

The modern Web is a good example of the rightmost of these. The backend is made up of a database, often running stored procedures to hold some of the database logic. The middle tier is an HTTP server such as Apache running PHP scripts (or Ruby on Rails, or JSP pages, etc.). This will manage some of the logic and will have data such as HTML pages stored locally. The frontend is a browser to display the pages, under the control of some JavaScript. In HTML 5, the frontend may also have a local database.

Fat versus Thin

A common labeling of components is "fat" or "thin". Fat components take up lots of memory and do complex processing. Thin components on the other hand, do little of either. There don't seem to be any "normal" size components, only fat or thin!

Fatness or thinness is a relative concept. Browsers are often labeled as thin because all they do is display web pages. However, Firefox on my Linux box takes nearly half a gigabyte of memory, which I don't regard as small at all!

Middleware Model

Middleware is the "glue" connecting components of a distributed system. The middleware model is shown in Figure 1-19.

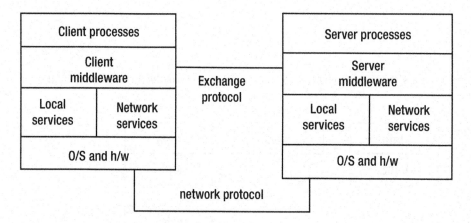

Figure 1-19. *The middleware model*

Components of middleware include the following:

- The network services such as TCP/IP

- The middleware layer is application-independent software using the network services

- Database access

- Managers of services such as identity

- Security modules

Middleware Examples

Examples of middleware include the following:

- Primitive services such as terminal emulators, file transfer, and e-mail

- Basic services such as RPC

- Integrated services such as DCE (Distributed Computing Environment)

- Distributed object services such as CORBA and OLE/ActiveX

- Mobile object services such as RMI and Jini

- The World Wide Web

Middleware Functions

The functions of middleware can include these:

- Initiation of processes at different computers

- Session management

- Directory services to allow clients to locate servers

- Remote data access

- Concurrency control to allow servers to handle multiple clients

- Security and integrity

- Monitoring

- Termination of processes, both local and remote

Continuum of Processing

The Gartner model is based on a breakdown of an application into the components of presentation, application logic, and data handling. A finer grained breakdown is illustrated in Figure 1-20.

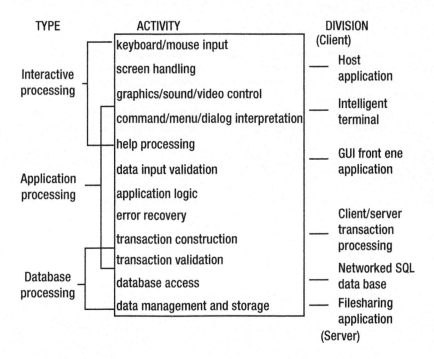

Figure 1-20. *Breakdown of an application into its components of presentation*

Points of Failure

Distributed applications run in a complex environment. This makes them much more prone to failure than standalone applications on a single computer. The points of failure include:

- Client-side errors

  - The client side of the application could crash

  - The client system may have hardware problems

  - The client's network card could fail

- Network errors

  - Network contention could cause timeouts

  - There may be network address conflicts

  - Network elements such as routers could fail

  - Transmission errors may lose messages

- Client-server errors

  - The client and server versions may be incompatible

- Server errors

  - The server's network card could fail

  - The server system may have hardware problems

  - The server software may crash

  - The server's database may become corrupted

Applications have to be designed with these possible failures in mind. Any action performed by one component must be recoverable if failure occurs in some other part of the system. Techniques such as transactions and continuous error checking need to be employed to avoid errors. It should be noted that while a standalone application may have a lot of control over the errors that can occur, that is not the case with distributed systems. For example, the server has no control over network or client errors and can only be prepared to handle them. In many cases, the cause of an error may not be available: did the client crash or did the network go down?

Acceptance Factors

The acceptance factors of a distributed system are similar to those of a standalone system. They include the following:

- Reliability

- Performance

- Responsiveness

- Scalability

- Capacity

- Security

Currently users often tolerate worse behavior than from a standalone system. "Oh, the network is slow" seems to be an acceptable excuse. Well, it isn't really, and developers should not get into the mindset of assuming that factors under their control can have ignorable effects.

Transparency

The "holy grails" of distributed systems are to provide the following:

- Access transparency
- Location transparency
- Migration transparency
- Replication transparency
- Concurrency transparency
- Scalability transparency
- Performance transparency
- Failure transparency

Access Transparency

The user should not know (or need to know) if access to all or parts of the system are local or remote.

Location Transparency

The location of a service should not matter.

Migration Transparency

If part of the system moves to another location, it should make no difference to a user.

Replication Transparency

It should not matter if one or multiple copies of the system are running.

Concurrency Transparency

There should be no interference between parts of the system running concurrently. For example, if I am accessing the database, then you should not know about it.

Scalability Transparency

It shouldn't matter if one or a million users are on the system.

Performance Transparency

Performance should not be affected by any of the system or network characteristics.

Failure Transparency

The system should not fail. If parts of it fail, the system should recover without the user knowing the failure occurred.

Most of these transparency factors are observed more in the breach than in the observance. There are notable cases where they are almost met. For example, when you connect to Google, you don't know (or care) where the servers are. Systems using Amazon Web Services are able to scale up or down in response to demand. Netflix has what almost seems cruel testing strategies, regularly and deliberately breaking large sections of its system to ensure that the whole still works.

Eight Fallacies of Distributed Computing

Sun Microsystems was a company that performed much of the early work in distributed systems, and even had a mantra" "The network is the computer." Based on their experience over many years, a number of the scientists at Sun came up with the following list of fallacies commonly assumed:

1. The network is reliable.

2. Latency is zero.

3. Bandwidth is infinite.

4. The network is secure.

5. Topology doesn't change.

6. There is one administrator.

7. Transport cost is zero.

8. The network is homogeneous.

Fallacy: The Network Is Reliable

A paper by Bailis and Kingsbury entitled "The Network is Reliable" (see http://queue.acm.org/detail.cfm?id=2655736) examines this fallacy. It finds many instances, such as Microsoft reporting on their datacenters giving 5.2 device failures per day and 40.8 link failures per day.

The Chinese government uses "DNS poisoning" as one of its techniques to censor what it considers to be undesirable web sites. China also runs one of the DNS root servers. In 2010, this server was misconfigured and poisoned the DNS servers of many other countries. This made many non-Chinese web sites inaccessible outside of China as well as inside (see http://www.pcworld.com/article/192658/article.html).

There are many other possible cases, such as DDS (distributed denial of service) attacks making web sites unavailable. At Box Hill Institute, a contractor once put a back hoe through the fiber cable connecting our DHCP server to the rest of the network, and so we went home for the rest of the day.

The network is *not* reliable. The implications are that any networked program must be prepared to deal with failure. This led to the design choices of Java's RMI and most later frameworks, with application design allowing for each network call possibly failing.

Fallacy: Latency Is Zero

Latency is the delay between sending a signal and getting a reply. In a single-process system, latency can depend on the amount of computation performed in a function call before it can return, but on the network, it is usually caused by simply having to traverse transports and be processed by all sorts of nodes such as routers on the way.

The ping command is a good way of showing latency. A ping to Google's Australia server takes about 20 milliseconds from Melbourne. A ping to Baidu's Chinese servers takes about 200 msecs[1].

By contrast, Williams (see http://www.eetimes.com/document.asp?doc_id=1200916) discusses the latency of the Linux scheduler and comes up with a mean latency of 88 *micro*seconds. The latency of network calls is thousands of times greater.

Fallacy: Bandwidth Is Infinite

Everyone who goes to make a cup of tea or coffee while a download takes place knows this is a fallacy. I run my own web server, and on ADSL2 get an upload speed of 800 Kbps. I am unfortunate enough to have HFC to my home, and the disastrous Australian National Broadband Network will upgrade this to 1000 Kbps perhaps. In three years time, by 2020.

In the meantime, I use a local wireless connection to give me 75 Mbps up and down and it still isn't fast enough!

Fallacy: The Network Is Secure

There is a strong push by technology companies for strong crypto to be used for all network communications, and an equally strong push by governments all over the world for weaker systems or for backdoors "only for particular governments". This seems to apply equally well to *demoncratic* (my accidental misspelling may be accurate!) as well as totalitarian governments.

In addition, of course, there are the general "baddies," stealing and selling credit card numbers and passwords by the millions.

Fallacy: Topology Doesn't Change

Well it does. Generally this may affect latency and bandwidth. But the more hard-coding of routes, or of IP addresses, the more prone to failure network applications will become.

Fallacy: There Is One Administrator

So what? No problem when everything is working fine. It's when it goes wrong that problems start—who to blame, who to fix it?

---

[1]From my Melbourne, Australia location I see the ping time by
ping www.google.com.au
PING google.com.au (216.58.203.99) 56(84) bytes of data.
64 bytes from syd09s15-in-f3.1e100.net (216.58.203.99): icmp_seq=1 ttl=50 time=27.1 ms
64 bytes from syd09s15-in-f3.1e100.net (216.58.203.99): icmp_seq=2 ttl=50 time=19.7 ms

A major research topic for years was *grid computing,* which distributed computing tasks across typically many university and research organizations to solve huge scientific problems. This had to resolve many complex issues due to not only multiple administrators but also different access and security problems, different maintenance schedules, and so on. The advent of cloud computing has *solved* many of these issues, reducing the number of administrators and systems, so that cloud computing is more resilient than many grid systems.

Fallacy: Transport Cost Is Zero

Once I've bought my PC, the transport cost from CPU to monitor is zero (well, minor electricity!). But we all pay our IP providers money each month because they have to build server rooms, lay cables, and so on. It's just a cost that has to be factored in.

Fallacy: The Network Is Homogeneous

The network isn't homogenous and neither are the endpoints—your and my PCs, iPads, Android devices, and mobile phones for example. Let alone with the IoT bringing a myriad of connected devices into the picture. There are continual attempts by vendors for product lockin, and continually restrictive work environments trying to simplify their control systems, which succeed to some extent. But when they fail, systems dependent on homogeneity fail too.

Conclusion

This chapter has tried to emphasize that distributed computing has its own unique features compared to other styles of computing. Ignoring these features can only lead to failure of the resultant systems. There are continual attempts to simplify the architectural model, with the latest being "microservices" and "serverless" computing, but in the end the complexities still remain.

These have to be addressed using any programming language, and subsequent chapters consider how Go manages them.

CHAPTER 2

■ ■ ■

Overview of the Go Language

There is a continual stream of programming languages being invented. Some are highly specialized, others are quite generic, while a third group is designed to fill broad but to some extent niche areas. Go was created in 2007 and released publically in 2009. It was intended to be a systems programming language, augmenting (or replacing) C++ and other statically compiled languages for production network and multiprocessing systems.

Go joins a group of modern languages including Rust, Swift, Julia, and several others. Go's particular features are a simple syntax, fast compilation of multiple program units, a form of O/O programming based on "structural" typing, and of course the benefit of lessons learned from large-scale programs in C, C++, and Java.

The language popularity listings in early 2017 such as TIOBE (see `http://www.tiobe.com/tiobe-index/`) rank Go as currently the 14th most popular language. PYPL (see `http://pypl.github.io/PYPL.html`) places it at number 19. This is alongside the 20+ year old languages of Java, Python, C, C++, JavaScript, and more.

This book assumes you are an experienced programmer with some or extensive knowledge of Go at some level. This could be by an introductory text such as *Introducing Go* by Caleb Doxsey (O'Reilly) or *The Little Go Book* by Karl Seguin, or by reading the more formal documentation such as The Go Programming Language Specification at `https://golang.org/ref/spec`.

If you are an experienced programmer, you can skip this chapter. If not, this chapter points out the bits of Go that are used in this book, but you should go elsewhere to get the necessary background. There are several tutorials on the Go web site at `http://golang.org`:

- Getting started

- A tutorial for the Go programming language

- Effective Go

- GoLang tutorials

Installing Go is best done from the Go programing language web site. At the time of writing, Go 1.8 has just been released. Most of the examples in this book will run using Go 1.6, with a few pointers to Go 1.8. You don't actually need to install Go to test the programs: Go has a "playground" accessible from the main page which can be used to run code. There are also several REPL (Read–Eval–Print Loop) environments, but these are third party.

The book predominantly uses libraries and packages from the Go Standard Library (`https://golang.org/pkg/`). The Go team also built a further set of packages as "sub-repositories," which often do not have the same support as the Standard Library. These are occasionally used. They will need to be installed using the go get command. These have package names including an "x," such as `golang.org/x/net/ipv4`.

© Jan Newmarch 2017
J. Newmarch, *Network Programming with Go*, DOI 10.1007/978-1-4842-2692-6_2

Types

There are pre-defined types of Boolean, numeric, and string types. The numeric types include uint32, int32, float32, and other sized numbers, as well as bytes (uint8) and runes. Runes and strings are dealt with extensively in Chapter 7, as issues of internationalization can be significant in distributed programs.

There are more complex types, discussed next.

Slices and Arrays

Arrays are sequences of elements of a single type. Slices are segments of an underlying array. Slices are often more convenient to deal with in Go. An array can be created statically:

```
var x [128]int
```

Or dynamically as a pointer:

```
xp := new([128]int)
```

A slice may be created along with its underlying array:

```
x := make([]int, 50, 100)
```

or

```
x := new([100]int)[0:50]
```

These last two are both of type []int (as shown by reflect.TypeOf(x)).

Elements of an array or slice are accessed by their index:

```
x[1]
```

The indices are from 0 to len(x)-1.

A slice may be taken of an array or slice by using the lower (inclusive) and upper (exclusive) indices of the array or slice:

```
a := [5]int{-1, -2, -3, -4, -5}
s := a[1:4]  // s is now [-2, -3, -4]
```

Structures

Structures are similar to those in other languages. In Chapter 4, we consider serialization of data and use the example of the following structs:

```
type Person struct {
        Name   Name
        Email  []Email
}
```

```go
type Name struct {
        Family   string
        Personal string
}

type Email struct {
        Kind    string
        Address string
}
```

A compound struct can be declared as follows:

```go
person := Person{
                Name: Name{Family: "Newmarch", Personal: "Jan"},
                Email: []Email{Email{Kind: "home",
                                     Address: "jan@newmarch.name"},
                        Email{Kind: "work",
                                     Address: "j.newmarch@boxhill.edu.au"}}}
```

The *visibility* of a structure's fields is controlled by the case of the first character of the field's name. If it is uppercase, it is visible outside of the package it is declared in; if it is lowercase, it is not. In the previous example, all the fields of all the structures are visible.

Pointers

Pointers behave similarly to pointers in other languages. The * operator dereferences a pointer, while the & operator takes the address of a variable. Go simplifies the use of pointers so that most of the time you don't have to worry about them. The most we do in this book is check if a pointer value is nil, which will usually signify an error, or conversely, if a possible error value is not nil, as described in the next section.

Functions

Functions are defined using a notation unique to Go. Why the familiar C syntax (or any other for that matter) is not used is explained in the Go's Declaration Syntax blog (see https://blog.golang.org/gos-declaration-syntax). We leave it to the textbooks to explain the details of the syntax.

Every Go program must have a main function declared as follows:

```go
func main() { ... }
```

We will frequently use a function checkError defined as follows:

```go
func checkError(err error) {
        if err != nil {
                fmt.Fprintf(os.Stderr, "Fatal error: %s", err.Error())
                os.Exit(1)
        }
}
```

It takes one parameter and has no return value. It starts with a lowercase letter, so it is local to the package in which it is declared.

23

Functions that return values will often return an error status as well as a substantive value, as in this function from Chapter 3:

```
func readFully(conn net.Conn) ([]byte, error) { ... }
```

It takes net.Conn as a parameter and returns an array of bytes and an error status (nil if no error occurred).

In this book, no more complex definitions than this are used.

Maps

A *map* is an unordered group of elements of one type, indexed by a key of another type. We do not use maps much in this book, although one place is in Chapter 10, where the values of fields of an HTTP request may be accessed through a map using the field name as key.

Methods

Go does not have classes in the sense that languages like Java do. However, *types* can have *methods* associated with them, and these act similar to methods of more standard O/O languages.

We will make heavy use of the methods defined for the various networking types. This will happen from the very first programs of the next chapter. For example, the type IPMask is defined as an array of bytes:

```
type IPMask []byte
```

A number of functions are defined on this type, such as:

```
func (m IPMask) Size() (ones, bits int)
```

A variable of type IPMask can have the method Size() applied, as follows:

```
var m IPMask
...
ones, bits := m.Size()
```

Learning how to use methods of the network-related types is a principal aim of this book.

We won't be defining our own methods much in this book. That's because to illustrate the Go libraries we don't need many of our own complex types. A typical use will be pretty-printing a type like the Person type defined previously:

```
func (p Person) String() string {
        s := p.Name.Personal + " " + p.Name.Family
        for _, v := range p.Email {
                s += "\n" + v.Kind + ": " + v.Address
        }
        return s
}
```

There is more extensive use in Chapter 10, where a number of types and methods on these types, are used. This is because we *do* need our own types when we are building more realistic systems.

Multi-Threading

Go has a simple mechanism for starting additional threads using the go command. In this book, that is all we will need. Complex tasks such as synchronizing multiple threads are not needed here.

Packages

Go programs are built from linked packages. The packages used by any block of code have to be imported, by an `import` statement at the head of the code file. Our own programs are declared to be in package `main`.

Apart from Chapter 10 again, nearly all of the programs in this book are in the `main` package.

Most packages are imported from the Standard Library. Some are imported from the sub-repositories such as `golang.org/x/net/ipv4`.

Type Conversion

The only one we need to worry about in this book is conversion of strings to byte arrays and vice versa. To convert a string to a byte array, you do:

```
var b []byte
b = []byte("string")
```

To convert the whole of an array/slice to a string, use this:

```
var s string
s = string(b[:])
```

Statements

A function or method will be composed of a set of statements. These include assignments, `if` and `switch` statements, `for` and `while` loops, and several others.

Apart from syntax, these have essentially the same meaning as in other programming languages. Nearly all of the statements types will be used in later chapters.

GOPATH

There are two ways of organizing workspaces for projects: put every project in a shared workspace or have a separate workspace for each project. My preference is for the second, whereas apparently the preference by most Go programmers is for the first.

Either way is supported by the go tool by the environment variable GOPATH. This can be set to a list of directories (a : separated list in Linux/UNIX a ; separated list on Windows, and a list on Plan9). It defaults to the directory go in the user's home directory if it's unset.

For each directory in GOPATH, there will be three sub-directories—src, pkg, and bin. The directory src will typically contain one directory per package name, and under that will be the source files for that package. For example, in Chapter 10 we have a complete web server that uses packages we define of dictionary and flashcards. The src/flashcards directory contains the file FlashCards.go.

Running Go Programs

A Go program must have a file defining the package main. Most of the programs in this book are defined in a single file, such as the program IP.go in Chapter 3. The simplest way to run it is from the directory containing the file:

```
go run IP.go <IP address>
```

Alternatively, you can build an executable and then run it:

```
go build IP.go
./IP <IP address>
```

Programs that require packages other than the standard ones will require GOPATH to be set. For example, the programs in Chapter 10 require (under Linux):

```
export GOPATH=$PWD
go run Server.go <port>
```

Standard Libraries

Go has an extensive set of Standard Libraries. Not as large as C, Java, or C++, for example, but those languages have been around for a *long* time. The Go packages are documented at https://golang.org/pkg/ We will use these extensively in this book, particularly the net, crypto, and encoding packages.

In addition, there is a sub-repositories group of packages available from the same page. These are less stable, but sometimes have useful packages, which we will use occasionally.

As well as these, there is a large set of user-contributed packages. They will not be used in the body of this book which deals with principles, but in practice you may find many of them very useful. Some are discussed in the concluding chapter.

Error Values

We discussed in the last chapter that a major difference between distributed and local programming is the greatly increased likelihood of errors occurring during execution. A local function call may fail because of simple programming errors such as divide by zero; more subtle errors may occur such as out-of-memory errors, but their possible occurrences are generally predictable.

On the other hand, almost any function that utilizes the network can fail for reasons beyond the application's control. Networking programs are consequently riddled with error checks. This is tedious, but necessary. Just like operating system kernel code is always error checking—errors need to be managed.

In this book, we generally exit a program with errors with appropriate messages on the client side, and for servers, attempt to recover by dropping the offending connection and carrying on.

Languages like C generally signal errors by returning "illegal" values such as negative integers, null pointers, or by raising a signal. Languages like Java raise exceptions, which can lead to messy code and are often slow. The standard Go functions give an error in an extra parameter return from a function call.

For example, in the next chapter, we discuss the function in the net package:

```
func ResolveIPAddr(net, addr string) (*IPAddr, error)
```

Typical code to manage this is:

```
addr, err := net.ResolveIPAddr("ip", name)
if err != nil {
        ...
}
```

Conclusion

This book assumes a knowledge of the Go programming language. This chapter just highlighted those parts that will be needed for later chapters.

CHAPTER 3

■ ■ ■

Socket-Level Programming

There are many kinds of networks in the world. These range from the very old networks, such as serial links, through to wide area networks made from copper and fiber, to wireless networks of various kinds, both for computers and for telecommunications devices such as phones. These networks obviously differ at the physical link layer, but in many cases they also differ at higher layers of the OSI stack.

Over the years there has been a convergence to the "Internet stack" of IP and TCP/UDP. For example, Bluetooth defines physical layers and protocol layers, but on top of that is an IP stack so that the same Internet programming techniques can be employed on many Bluetooth devices. Similarly, developing Internet of Things (IoT) wireless technologies such as LoRaWAN and 6LoWPAN include an IP stack.

While IP provides the networking layer 3 of the OSI stack, TCP and UDP deal with layer 4. These are not the final word, even in the Internet world: SCTP (Stream Control Transmission Protocol) has come from the telecommunications world to challenge both TCP and UDP, while to provide Internet services in interplanetary space requires new, under development protocols such as DTN (Delay Tolerant Networking). Nevertheless, IP, TCP, and UDP hold sway as principal networking technologies now and at least for a considerable time into the future. Go has full support for this style of programming

This chapter shows how to do TCP and UDP programming using Go, and how to use a raw socket for other protocols.

The TCP/IP Stack

The OSI model was devised using a committee process wherein the standard was set up and then implemented. Some parts of the OSI standard are obscure, some parts cannot easily be implemented, and some parts have not been implemented.

The TCP/IP protocol was devised through a long-running DARPA project. This worked by implementation followed by RFCs (Request for Comments). TCP/IP is the principal UNIX networking protocol. TCP/IP stands for Transmission Control Protocol/Internet Protocol.

The TCP/IP stack is shorter than the OSI one, as shown in Figure 3-1.

© Jan Newmarch 2017
J. Newmarch, *Network Programming with Go*, DOI 10.1007/978-1-4842-2692-6_3

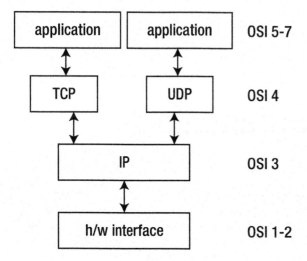

Figure 3-1. *TCP/IP stack versus the OSI*

TCP is a connection-oriented protocol, whereas UDP (User Datagram Protocol) is a connectionless protocol.

IP Datagrams

The IP layer provides a connectionless and unreliable delivery system. It considers each datagram independently of the others. Any association between datagrams must be supplied by the higher layers.

The IP layer supplies a checksum that includes its own header. The header includes the source and destination addresses.

The IP layer handles routing through an internet. It is also responsible for breaking up large datagrams into smaller ones for transmission and reassembling them at the other end.

UDP

UDP is also connectionless and unreliable. What it adds to IP is a checksum for the contents of the datagram and *port numbers*. These are used to give a client-server model, which you'll see later.

TCP

TCP supplies logic to give a reliable connection-oriented protocol above IP. It provides a *virtual circuit* that two processes can use to communicate. It also uses port numbers to identify services on a host.

Internet Addresses

In order to use a service, you must be able to find it. The Internet uses an address scheme for devices such as computers so that they can be located. This addressing scheme was originally devised when there were only a handful of connected computers, and very generously allowed up to 2^32 addresses, using a 32-bit unsigned integer. These are the so-called IPv4 addresses. In recent years, the number of connected (or at least directly addressable) devices has threatened to exceed this number, and there is a progressive transition to IPv6. The transition is patchy, and shown for example in the graph by Google (https://www.google.com/intl/en/ipv6/statistics.html). Sadly—from my viewpoint—few of the Australian IP providers support IPv6.

IPv4 Addresses

The address is a 32-bit integer that gives the IP address. This addresses down to a network interface card on a single device. The address is usually written as four bytes in decimal with a dot . between them, as in 127.0.0.1 or 66.102.11.104.

The IP address of any device is generally composed of two parts: the address of the network in which the device resides, and the address of the device within that network. Once upon a time, the split between network address and internal address was simple and was based on the bytes used in the IP address.

- In a class A network, the first byte identifies the network, while the last three identify the device. There are only 128 class A networks, owned by the very early players in the Internet space such as IBM, the General Electric Company, and MIT[1].

- Class B networks use the first two bytes to identify the network and the last two to identify devices within the subnet. This allows up to 2^{16} (65,536) devices on a subnet.

- Class C networks use the first three bytes to identify the network and the last one to identify devices within that network. This allows up to 2^8 (actually 254, not 256, as the bottom and top addresses are reserved) devices.

This scheme doesn't work well if you want, say, 400 computers on a network. 254 is too small, while 65,536 (-2) is too large. In binary arithmetic terms, you want about 512 (-2). This can be achieved by using a 23-bit network address and 9 bits for the device addresses. Similarly, if you want up to 1024 (-2) devices, you use a 22-bit network address and a 10-bit device address.

Given an IP address of a device and knowing how many bits N are used for the network address gives a relatively straightforward process for extracting the network address and the device address within that network. Form a "network mask" which is a 32-bit binary number with all ones in the first N places and all zeroes in the remaining ones. For example, if 16 bits are used for the network address, the mask is 1111111 1111111110000000000000000. It's a little inconvenient using binary, so decimal bytes are usually used. The netmask for 16-bit network addresses is 255.255.0.0, for 24-bit network addresses it is 255.255.255.0, while for 23-bit addresses it would be 255.255.254.0 and for 22-bit addresses it would be 255.255.252.0.

Then to find the network of a device, bit-wise AND its IP address with the network mask, while the device address within the subnet is found with bit-wise AND of the one's complement of the mask with the IP address. For example, the binary value of the IP address 192.168.1.3 is 1100000010101 0000000000100000011 (using the IP Address Subnet Mask Calculator). If a 16-bit netmask is used, the network is 1100000010101000 0000000000000000 (or 192.168.0.0), while the device address is 0000000000000000 0000000100000011 (or 0.0.1.3).

IPv6 Addresses

The Internet has grown vastly beyond original expectations. The initially generous 32-bit addressing scheme is on the verge of running out. There are unpleasant workarounds such as NAT (Network Address Translation) addressing, but eventually we will have to switch to a wider address space. IPv6 uses 128-bit addresses. Even bytes becomes cumbersome to express such addresses, so hexadecimal digits are used, grouped into four digits and separated by a colon :. A typical address might be FE80:CD00:0000:0CDE:1257:0000:211E:729C.

---

[1]Recently MIT have returned their class A network to the pool. http://www.iana.org/assignments/ipv4-address-space/ipv4-address-space.xml.

These addresses are not easy to remember! DNS will become even more important. There are tricks to reducing some addresses, such as leading zeroes and repeated digits. For example, "localhost" is 0:0:0:0:0:0:0:1, which can be shortened to ::1.

Each address is divided into three components: the first is the network address used for Internet routing and is the first 64 bits of the address. The next part is 16 bits for the netmask. This is used to divide the network into subnets. It can give anything from one subnet only (all zeroes) to 65,535 subnets (all 1s). The last part is the device component, of 48 bits. The above address would be FE80:CD00:0000:0CDE for the network, 1257 for the subnet, and 0000:211E:729C for the device.

IP Address Type

Finally we can start using some of the Go language network packages. The package net defines many types, functions, and methods of use in Go network programming. The type IP is defined as an array of bytes:

```
type IP []byte
```

There are several functions to manipulate a variable of type IP, but you are likely to use only some of them in practice. For example, the function ParseIP(String) will take a dotted IPv4 address or a colon IPv6 address, while the IP method String() will return a string. Note that you may not get back what you started with: the string form of 0:0:0:0:0:0:0:1 is ::1.

A program that illustrates this process is IP.go:

```
/* IP
 */

package main

import (
        "fmt"
        "net"
        "os"
)

func main() {
        if len(os.Args) != 2 {
                fmt.Fprintf(os.Stderr, "Usage: %s ip-addr\n", os.Args[0])
                os.Exit(1)
        }
        name := os.Args[1]

        addr := net.ParseIP(name)
        if addr == nil {
                fmt.Println("Invalid address")
        } else {
                fmt.Println("The address is ", addr.String())
        }
        os.Exit(0)
}
```

This can be run for example as follows:

```
go run IP.go  127.0.0.1
```

Here is the response:

```
The address is 127.0.0.1
```

Or it could be run as:

```
go run IP.go 0:0:0:0:0:0:0:1
```

With this response:

```
The address is ::1
```

The IPMask Type

An IP address is typically divided into the components of a network address, a subnet, and a device portion. The network address and subnet form a *prefix* to the device portion. The mask is an IP address of all binary ones to match the prefix length, followed by all zeroes.

In order to handle masking operations, you use this type:

```
type IPMask []byte
```

The simplest function to create a netmask uses the CIDR notation of ones followed by zeroes up to the number of bits:

```
func CIDRMask(ones, bits int) IPMask
```

A mask can then be used by a method of an IP address to find the network for that IP address:

```
func (ip IP) Mask(mask IPMask) IP
```

An example of the use of this is the following program called Mask.go:

```
/* Mask
 */

package main

import (
        "fmt"
        "net"
        "os"
        "strconv"
)
```

```go
func main() {
        if len(os.Args) != 4 {
                fmt.Fprintf(os.Stderr, "Usage: %s dotted-ip-addr ones bits\n", os.Args[0])
                os.Exit(1)
        }
        dotAddr := os.Args[1]
        ones, _ := strconv.Atoi(os.Args[2])
        bits, _ := strconv.Atoi(os.Args[3])

        addr := net.ParseIP(dotAddr)
        if addr == nil {
                fmt.Println("Invalid address")
                os.Exit(1)
        }
        mask := net.CIDRMask(ones, bits)
        network := addr.Mask(mask)
        fmt.Println("Address is ", addr.String(),
                "\nMask length is ", bits,
                "\nLeading ones count is ", ones,
                "\nMask is (hex) ", mask.String(),
                "\nNetwork is ", network.String())
        os.Exit(0)
}
```

This can be compiled to Mask and run as follows:

```
Mask <ip-address> <ones> <zeroes>
```

Or it can be run directly as follows:

```
go run Mask.go <ip-address> <ones> <zeroes>
```

For an IPv4 address of 103.232.159.187 on a /24 network, we get the following:

```
go run Mask.go 103.232.159.187 24 32
Address is  103.232.159.187
Mask length is  32
Leading ones count is  24
Mask is (hex)  ffffff00
Network is  103.232.159.0
```

For an IPv6 address fda3:97c:1eb:fff0:5444:903a:33f0:3a6b where the network component is fda3:97c:1eb, the subnet is fff0, and the device part is 5444:903a:33f0:3a6b, we get the following:

```
go run Mask.go fda3:97c:1eb:fff0:5444:903a:33f0:3a6b 52 128
Address is  fda3:97c:1eb:fff0:5444:903a:33f0:3a6b
Mask length is  128
Leading ones count is  52
Mask is (hex)  fffffffffffff0000000000000000000
Network is  fda3:97c:1eb:f000::
```

IPv4 netmasks are often given in the 4-byte dotted notation such as 255.255.255.0 for a /24 network. There is a function to create a mask from such a 4-byte IPv4 address:

```
func IPv4Mask(a, b, c, d byte) IPMask
```

Also, there is a method of IP that returns the default mask for IPv4:

```
func (ip IP) DefaultMask() IPMask
```

Note that the string form of a mask is a hex number, such as ffffff00 for a /24 mask.
The following program called IPv4Mask.go illustrates these:

```go
/* IPv4Mask
 */

package main

import (
        "fmt"
        "net"
        "os"
)

func main() {
        if len(os.Args) != 2 {
                fmt.Fprintf(os.Stderr, "Usage: %s dotted-ip-addr\n", os.Args[0])
                os.Exit(1)
        }
        dotAddr := os.Args[1]

        addr := net.ParseIP(dotAddr)
        if addr == nil {
                fmt.Println("Invalid address")
                os.Exit(1)
        }
        mask := addr.DefaultMask()
        network := addr.Mask(mask)
        ones, bits := mask.Size()
        fmt.Println("Address is ", addr.String(),
                "\nDefault mask length is ", bits,
                "\nLeading ones count is ", ones,
                "\nMask is (hex) ", mask.String(),
                "\nNetwork is ", network.String())
        os.Exit(0)
}
```

For example, running this:

```
go run Mask.go 192.168.1.3
```

In my home network gives the following result:

```
Address is  192.168.1.3
Default mask length is  32
Leading ones count is  24
Mask is (hex)  ffffff00
Network is  192.168.1.0
```

The IPAddr Type

Many of the other functions and methods in the net package return a pointer to an IPAddr. This is simply a structure containing an IP (and a zone which may be needed for IPv6 addresses).

```
type IPAddr {
    IP IP
    Zone string
}
```

A primary use of this type is to perform DNS lookups on IP hostnames. The zone may be needed for ambiguous IPv6 addresses with multiple network interfaces.

```
func ResolveIPAddr(net, addr string) (*IPAddr, error)
```

Where net is one of ip, ip4, or ip6. This is shown in the program called ResolveIP.go:

```
/* ResolveIP
 */

package main

import (
        "fmt"
        "net"
        "os"
)

func main() {
        if len(os.Args) != 2 {
                fmt.Fprintf(os.Stderr, "Usage: %s hostname\n", os.Args[0])
                fmt.Println("Usage: ", os.Args[0], "hostname")
                os.Exit(1)
        }
        name := os.Args[1]

        addr, err := net.ResolveIPAddr("ip", name)
        if err != nil {
                fmt.Println("Resolution error", err.Error())
                os.Exit(1)
        }
```

```
        fmt.Println("Resolved address is ", addr.String())
        os.Exit(0)
}
```

Running this:

```
go run ResolveIP.go www.google.com
```

Returns the following:

```
Resolved address is 172.217.25.164
```

If the first parameter to ResolveIPAddr() for the net type is given as ip6 instead of ip, I get this result:

```
Resolved address is  2404:6800:4006:801::2004
```

You may get different results, depending on where Google appears to live from your address's perspective.

Host Lookup

The ResolveIPAddr function will perform a DNS lookup on a hostname and return a single IP address. How it does this depends on the operating system and its configuration. For example, a Linux/UNIX system may use /etc/resolv.conf or /etc/hosts with the order of the search set in /etc/nsswitch.conf.

Some hosts may have multiple IP addresses, usually from multiple network interface cards. They may also have multiple hostnames, acting as aliases. The LookupHost function will return a slice of addresses.

```
func LookupHost(name string) (cname string, addrs []string, err error)
```

One of these addresses will be labeled as the "canonical" hostname. If you want to find the canonical name, use this:

```
func LookupCNAME(name string) (cname string, err error).
```

For www.google.com, it prints both the IPv4 and IPv6 addresses:

```
172.217.25.164
2404:6800:4006:806::2004
```

This is shown in the following program called LookupHost.go:

```
/* LookupHost
 */

package main

import (
        "fmt"
        "net"
        "os"
)
```

```go
func main() {
        if len(os.Args) != 2 {
                fmt.Fprintf(os.Stderr, "Usage: %s hostname\n", os.Args[0])
                os.Exit(1)
        }
        name := os.Args[1]

        addrs, err := net.LookupHost(name)
        if err != nil {
                fmt.Println("Error: ", err.Error())
                os.Exit(2)
        }

        for _, s := range addrs {
                fmt.Println(s)
        }
        os.Exit(0)
}
```

Note that this function returns strings, not IP address values. When it runs:

```
go run LookupHost.go
```

It prints something similar to this:

```
172.217.25.132
2404:6800:4006:807::2004
```

Services

Services run on host machines. They are typically long lived and are designed to wait for requests and respond to them. There are many types of services, and there are many ways in which they can offer their services to clients. The Internet world bases many of these services on two methods of communication—TCP and UDP—although there are other communication protocols such as SCTP waiting in the wings to take over. Many other types of service, such as peer-to-peer, remote procedure calls, communicating agents, and many others, are built on top of TCP and UDP.

Ports

Services live on host machines. We can locate a host using a IP address. But on each computer may be many services, and a simple way is needed to distinguish between them. The method used by TCP, UDP, SCTP, and others is to use a *port number*. This is an unsigned integer between 1 and 65,535 and each service will associate itself with one or more of these port numbers.

There are many "standard" ports. Telnet typically uses port 23 with the TCP protocol. DNS uses port 53, either with TCP or with UDP. FTP uses ports 21 and 20, one for commands, the other for data transfer. HTTP usually uses port 80, but it often uses ports 8000, 8080, and 8088, all with TCP. The X Window System often takes ports 6000-6007, both on TCP and UDP.

On a UNIX system, the commonly used ports are listed in the file /etc/services. Go has a function to look up ports on all systems:

```go
func LookupPort(network, service string) (port int, err error)
```

The network argument is a string such as "tcp" or "udp", while the service is a string such as "telnet" or "domain" (for DNS).

A program using this is LookupPort.go:

```
/* LookupPort
 */

package main

import (
        "fmt"
        "net"
        "os"
)

func main() {
        if len(os.Args) != 3 {
                fmt.Fprintf(os.Stderr,
                        "Usage: %s network-type service\n",
                        os.Args[0])
                os.Exit(1)
        }
        networkType := os.Args[1]
        service := os.Args[2]

        port, err := net.LookupPort(networkType, service)
        if err != nil {
                fmt.Println("Error: ", err.Error())
                os.Exit(2)
        }

        fmt.Println("Service port ", port)
        os.Exit(0)
}
```

For example, running LookupPort tcp telnet prints service port 23.

The TCPAddr Type

The TCPAddr type is a structure containing an IP, a port, and a zone. The zone is required to distinguish between possible ambiguous IPv6 link-local and site-local addresses, as different network interface cards (NICs) may have the same IPv6 address.

```
type TCPAddr struct {
    IP    IP
    Port  int
    Zone  string
}
```

The function to create a TCPAddr is ResolveTCPAddr:

```
func ResolveTCPAddr(net, addr string) (*TCPAddr, error)
```

Where net is one of tcp, tcp4, or tcp6 and the addr is a string composed of a hostname or IP address, followed by the port number after a :, such as www.google.com:80 or 127.0.0.1:22. If the address is an IPv6 address, which already has colons in it, then the host part must be enclosed in square brackets, such as [::1]:23. Another special case is often used for servers, where the host address is zero, so that the TCP address is really just the port name, as in :80 for an HTTP server.

TCP Sockets

When you know how to reach a service via its network and port IDs, what then? If you are a client, you need an API that will allow you to connect to a service and then to send messages to that service and read replies back from the service.

If you are a server, you need to be able to bind to a port and listen at it. When a message comes in, you need to be able to read it and write back to the client.

The net.TCPConn is the Go type that allows full duplex communication between the client and the server. Two major methods of interest are as follows:

```
func (c *TCPConn) Write(b []byte) (n int, err error)
func (c *TCPConn) Read(b []byte) (n int, err error)
```

A TCPConn is used by both a client and a server to read and write messages.

Note that a TCPConn implements the io.Reader and io.Writer interfaces so that any method using a reader or writer can be applied to a TCPConn.

TCP Client

Once a client has established a TCP address for a service, it "dials" the service. If successful, the dial returns a TCPConn for communication. The client and the server exchange messages on this. Typically a client writes a request to the server using the TCPConn and reads a response from the TCPConn. This continues until either (or both) side closes the connection. A TCP connection is established by the client using this function:

```
func DialTCP(net string, laddr, raddr *TCPAddr) (c *TCPConn, err error)
```

Where laddr is the local address, which is usually set to nil, and raddr is the remote address of the service. The net string is one of "tcp4", "tcp6", or "tcp", depending on whether you want a TCPv4 connection, a TCPv6 connection, or don't care.

A simple example can be provided by a client to a web (HTTP) server. We will deal in substantially more detail with HTTP clients and servers in a later chapter, so for now we will keep it simple.

One of the possible messages that a client can send is the HEAD message. This queries a server for information about the server and a document on that server. The server returns information, but does not return the document itself. The request sent to query an HTTP server could be as follows:

```
"HEAD / HTTP/1.0\r\n\r\n"
```

This asks for information about the root document and the server. A typical response might be:

```
HTTP/1.1 200 OK
Server: nginx/1.10.0 (Ubuntu)
Date: Tue, 28 Feb 2017 10:33:01 GMT
Content-Type: text/html
Content-Length: 2152
Last-Modified: Mon, 13 Oct 2008 02:38:03 GMT
Connection: close
ETag: "48f2b48b-868"
Accept-Ranges: bytes
```

We first give the program (GetHeadInfo.go) to establish the connection for a TCP address, send the request string, and then read and print the response. Once compiled, it can be invoked as follows:

```
GetHeadInfo www.google.com:80
```

The program is GetHeadInfo.go:

```go
/* GetHeadInfo
 */
package main

import (
        "fmt"
        "io/ioutil"
        "net"
        "os"
)

func main() {
        if len(os.Args) != 2 {
                fmt.Fprintf(os.Stderr, "Usage: %s host:port ", os.Args[0])
                os.Exit(1)
        }
        service := os.Args[1]

        tcpAddr, err := net.ResolveTCPAddr("tcp4", service)
        checkError(err)

        conn, err := net.DialTCP("tcp", nil, tcpAddr)
        checkError(err)

        _, err = conn.Write([]byte("HEAD / HTTP/1.0\r\n\r\n"))
        checkError(err)

        result, err := ioutil.ReadAll(conn)
        checkError(err)
```

```
        fmt.Println(string(result))

        os.Exit(0)
}

func checkError(err error) {
        if err != nil {
                fmt.Fprintf(os.Stderr, "Fatal error: %s", err.Error())
                os.Exit(1)
        }
}
```

The first point to note is the almost excessive amount of error checking that is going on. This is normal for networking programs: the opportunities for failure are substantially greater than for standalone programs. Hardware may fail on the client, the server, or on any of the routers and switches in the middle; communication may be blocked by a firewall; timeouts may occur due to network load; the server may crash while the client is talking to it. The following checks are performed:

1. There may be syntax errors in the address specified.

2. The attempt to connect to the remote service may fail. For example, the service requested might not be running, or there may be no such host connected to the network.

3. Although a connection has been established, writes to the service might fail if the connection has died suddenly, or if the network times out.

4. Similarly, the reads might fail.

Reading from the server requires a comment. In this case, we read essentially a single response from the server. This will be terminated by end-of-file on the connection. However, it may consist of several TCP packets, so we need to keep reading until the end of file. The io/ioutil function ReadAll will look after these issues and return the complete response. (Thanks to Roger Peppe on the golang-nuts mailing list.)

There are some language issues involved. First, most of the functions return a dual value, with the possible error as second value. If no error occurs, then this will be nil. In C, the same behavior is gained by special values such as NULL, or -1, or zero being returned—if that is possible. In Java, the same error checking is managed by throwing and catching exceptions, which can make the code look very messy.

A Daytime Server

About the simplest service that we can build is the daytime service. This is a standard Internet service, defined by RFC 867, with a default port of 13, on both TCP and UDP. Unfortunately, with the (justified) increase in paranoia over security, hardly any sites run a daytime server any more. Never mind; we can build our own. (For those interested, if you install inetd on your system, you usually get a daytime server thrown in.)

A server registers itself on a port and listens on that port. Then it blocks on an "accept" operation, waiting for clients to connect. When a client connects, the accept call returns, with a connection object. The daytime service is very simple and just writes the current time to the client, closes the connection, and resumes waiting for the next client.

The relevant calls are as follows:

```
func ListenTCP(net string, laddr *TCPAddr) (l *TCPListener, err error)
func (l *TCPListener) Accept() (c Conn, err error)
```

The argument net can be set to one of the strings "tcp", "tcp4", or "tcp6". The IP address should be set to zero if you want to listen on all network interfaces, or to the IP address of a single network interface if you only want to listen on that interface. If the port is set to zero, then the O/S will choose a port for you. Otherwise, you can choose your own. Note that on a UNIX system, you cannot listen on a port below 1024 unless you are the system supervisor, root, and ports below 128 are standardized by the IETF. The example program chooses port 1200 for no particular reason. The TCP address is given as :1200—all interfaces, port 1200.

The program is DaytimeServer.go:

```
/* DaytimeServer
 */
package main

import (
        "fmt"
        "net"
        "os"
        "time"
)

func main() {

        service := ":1200"
        tcpAddr, err := net.ResolveTCPAddr("tcp", service)
        checkError(err)

        listener, err := net.ListenTCP("tcp", tcpAddr)
        checkError(err)

        for {
                conn, err := listener.Accept()
                if err != nil {
                        continue
                }

                daytime := time.Now().String()
                conn.Write([]byte(daytime)) // don't care about return value
                conn.Close()                // we're finished with this client
        }
}

func checkError(err error) {
        if err != nil {
                fmt.Fprintf(os.Stderr, "Fatal error: %s", err.Error())
                os.Exit(1)
        }
}
```

If you run this server, it will just wait there, not doing much. When a client connects to it, it will respond by sending the daytime string to it and then return to waiting for the next client.

Note the changed error handling in the server as compared to a client. The server should run forever, so that if any error occurs with a client, the server just ignores that client and carries on. A client could otherwise try to mess up the connection with the server and bring it down!

We haven't built a client. That is easy, just changing the previous client to omit the initial write. Alternatively, just open a telnet connection to that host:

```
telnet localhost 1200
```

This will produce output such as the following:

```
$telnet localhost 1200
Trying 127.0.0.1...
Connected to localhost.
Escape character is '^]'.
2017-01-02 20:13:21.934698384 +1100 AEDTConnection closed by foreign host.
```

Where 2017-01-02 20:13:21.934698384 +1100 AEDT is the output from the server.

Multi-Threaded Server

echo is another simple IETF service. The SimpleEchoServer.go program just reads what the client types and sends it back:

```go
/* SimpleEchoServer
 */
package main

import (
        "fmt"
        "net"
        "os"
)

func main() {

        service := ":1201"
        tcpAddr, err := net.ResolveTCPAddr("tcp4", service)
        checkError(err)

        listener, err := net.ListenTCP("tcp", tcpAddr)
        checkError(err)

        for {
                conn, err := listener.Accept()
                if err != nil {
                        continue
                }
                handleClient(conn)
                conn.Close() // we're finished
        }
}
```

```go
func handleClient(conn net.Conn) {
        var buf [512]byte
        for {
                n, err := conn.Read(buf[0:])
                if err != nil {
                        return
                }
                fmt.Println(string(buf[0:]))
                _, err2 := conn.Write(buf[0:n])
                if err2 != nil {
                        return
                }
        }
}

func checkError(err error) {
        if err != nil {
                fmt.Fprintf(os.Stderr, "Fatal error: %s", err.Error())
                os.Exit(1)
        }
}
```

While it works, there is a significant issue with this server: it is single-threaded. While a client has a connection open to it, no other client can connect. Other clients are blocked and will probably time out. Fortunately, this is easily fixed by making the client handler a go routine. We have also moved closing the connection into the handler, as it now belongs there. The program is called ThreadedEchoServer.go:

```go
/* ThreadedEchoServer
 */
package main

import (
        "fmt"
        "net"
        "os"
)

func main() {

        service := ":1201"
        tcpAddr, err := net.ResolveTCPAddr("tcp", service)
        checkError(err)

        listener, err := net.ListenTCP("tcp", tcpAddr)
        checkError(err)

        for {
                conn, err := listener.Accept()
                if err != nil {
                        continue
                }
```

```
                // run as a goroutine
                go handleClient(conn)
        }
}

func handleClient(conn net.Conn) {
        // close connection on exit
        defer conn.Close()

        var buf [512]byte
        for {
                // read up to 512 bytes
                n, err := conn.Read(buf[0:])
                if err != nil {
                        return
                }
                fmt.Println(string(buf[0:]))
                // write the n bytes read
                _, err2 := conn.Write(buf[0:n])
                if err2 != nil {
                        return
                }
        }
}

func checkError(err error) {
        if err != nil {
                fmt.Fprintf(os.Stderr, "Fatal error: %s", err.Error())
                os.Exit(1)
        }
}
```

Controlling TCP Connections

Timeout

The server may want to time out a client if it does not respond quickly enough, i.e., does not write a request to the server in time. This should be a long period (several minutes), because the users may be taking their time. Conversely, the client may want to time out the server (after a much shorter time). Both do this as follows:

```
func (c *IPConn) SetDeadline(t time.Time) error
```

This is done before any reads or writes on the socket.

Staying Alive

A client may want to stay connected to a server even if it has nothing to send. It can use this:

```
func (c *TCPConn) SetKeepAlive(keepalive bool) error
```

There are several other connection control methods, which are documented in the net package.

UDP Datagrams

In a connectionless protocol, each message contains information about its origin and destination. There is no "session" established using a long-lived socket. UDP clients and servers make use of datagrams, which are individual messages containing source and destination information. There is no state maintained by these messages, unless the client or server does so. The messages are not guaranteed to arrive, or may arrive out of order.

The most common situation for a client is to send a message and hope that a reply arrives. The most common situation for a server is to receive a message and then send one or more replies back to that client. In a peer-to-peer situation, though, the server may just forward messages to other peers.

The major difference between TCP and UDP handling for Go is how to deal with packets arriving from multiple clients, without the cushion of a TCP session to manage things. The major calls needed are as follows:

```
func ResolveUDPAddr(net, addr string) (*UDPAddr, error)
func DialUDP(net string, laddr, raddr *UDPAddr) (c *UDPConn, err error)
func ListenUDP(net string, laddr *UDPAddr) (c *UDPConn, err error)
func (c *UDPConn) ReadFromUDP(b []byte) (n int, addr *UDPAddr, err error
func (c *UDPConn) WriteToUDP(b []byte, addr *UDPAddr) (n int, err error)
```

The client for a UDP time service doesn't need to make many changes; just change the ...TCP... calls to ...UDP... calls in the program UDPDaytimeClient.go:

```go
/* UDPDaytimeClient
 */
package main

import (
        "fmt"
        "net"
        "os"
)

func main() {
        if len(os.Args) != 2 {
                fmt.Fprintf(os.Stderr, "Usage: %s host:port", os.Args[0])
                os.Exit(1)
        }
        service := os.Args[1]

        udpAddr, err := net.ResolveUDPAddr("udp", service)
        checkError(err)

        conn, err := net.DialUDP("udp", nil, udpAddr)
        checkError(err)

        _, err = conn.Write([]byte("anything"))
        checkError(err)
```

```go
        var buf [512]byte
        n, err := conn.Read(buf[0:])
        checkError(err)

        fmt.Println(string(buf[0:n]))

        os.Exit(0)
}

func checkError(err error) {
        if err != nil {
                fmt.Fprintf(os.Stderr, "Fatal error ", err.Error())
                os.Exit(1)
        }
}
```

While the server has to make a few more changes in the program UDPDaytimeServer.go:

```go
/* UDPDaytimeServer
 */
package main

import (
        "fmt"
        "net"
        "os"
        "time"
)

func main() {

        service := ":1200"
        udpAddr, err := net.ResolveUDPAddr("udp", service)
        checkError(err)

        conn, err := net.ListenUDP("udp", udpAddr)
        checkError(err)

        for {
                handleClient(conn)
        }
}

func handleClient(conn *net.UDPConn) {

        var buf [512]byte

        _, addr, err := conn.ReadFromUDP(buf[0:])
        if err != nil {
                return
        }
```

```
        daytime := time.Now().String()

        conn.WriteToUDP([]byte(daytime), addr)
}

func checkError(err error) {
        if err != nil {
                fmt.Fprintf(os.Stderr, "Fatal error ", err.Error())
                os.Exit(1)
        }
}
```

The server is run as follows:

```
go run UDPDaytimeServer.go
```

A client on the same host is run as follows:

```
go run UDPDaytimeClient.go localhost:1200
```

The output will be something like this:

```
2017-03-01 21:37:03.988603994 +1100 AEDT
```

Server Listening on Multiple Sockets

A server may be attempting to listen to multiple clients not just on one port, but on many. In this case, it has to use some sort of polling mechanism between the ports.

In C, the select() call lets the kernel do this work. The call takes a number of file descriptors. The process is suspended. When I/O is ready on one of these, a wakeup is done, and the process can continue. This is cheaper than busy polling. In Go, you can accomplish the same by using a different go routine for each port. A thread will become runnable when the lower-level select() discovers that I/O is ready for this thread.

The Conn, PacketConn, and Listener Types

So far we have differentiated between the API for TCP and the API for UDP, using for example DialTCP and DialUDP returning a TCPConn and UDPConn, respectively. The Conn type is an interface and both TCPConn and UDPConn implement this interface. To a large extent, you can deal with this interface rather than the two types.

Instead of separate dial functions for TCP and UDP, you can use a single function:

```
func Dial(net, laddr, raddr string) (c Conn, err error)
```

The net can be any of tcp, tcp4 (IPv4-only), tcp6 (IPv6-only), udp, udp4 (IPv4-only), udp6 (IPv6-only), ip, ip4 (IPv4-only), and ip6 IPv6-only) and several UNIX-specific ones such as unix for UNIX sockets. It will return an appropriate implementation of the Conn interface. Note that this function takes a string rather than address as the raddr argument, so that programs using this can avoid working out the address type first.

Using this function makes minor changes to the programs. For example, the earlier program to get HEAD information from a web page can be rewritten as IPGetHeadInfo.go:

```go
/* IPGetHeadInfo
 */
package main

import (
        "bytes"
        "fmt"
        "io"
        "net"
        "os"
)

func main() {
        if len(os.Args) != 2 {
                fmt.Fprintf(os.Stderr, "Usage: %s host:port", os.Args[0])
                os.Exit(1)
        }
        service := os.Args[1]

        conn, err := net.Dial("tcp", service)
        checkError(err)

        _, err = conn.Write([]byte("HEAD / HTTP/1.0\r\n\r\n"))
        checkError(err)

        result, err := readFully(conn)
        checkError(err)

        fmt.Println(string(result))

        os.Exit(0)
}

func checkError(err error) {
        if err != nil {
                fmt.Fprintf(os.Stderr, "Fatal error: %s", err.Error())
                os.Exit(1)
        }
}

func readFully(conn net.Conn) ([]byte, error) {
        defer conn.Close()

        result := bytes.NewBuffer(nil)
        var buf [512]byte
```

```
        for {
                n, err := conn.Read(buf[0:])
                result.Write(buf[0:n])
                if err != nil {
                        if err == io.EOF {
                                break
                        }
                        return nil, err
                }
        }
        return result.Bytes(), nil
}
```

This can be run on my own machine as follows:

```
go run  IPGetHeadInfo.go  localhost:80
```

It prints the following about the server running on port 80:

```
HTTP/1.1 200 OK
Server: nginx/1.10.0 (Ubuntu)
Date: Wed, 01 Mar 2017 10:42:39 GMT
Content-Type: text/html
Content-Length: 2152
Last-Modified: Mon, 13 Oct 2008 02:38:03 GMT
Connection: close
ETag: "48f2b48b-868"
Accept-Ranges: bytes
```

Writing a server can be similarly simplified using this function:

```
func Listen(net, laddr string) (l Listener, err error)
```

This returns an object implementing the Listener interface. This interface has a method:

```
func (l Listener) Accept() (c Conn, err error)
```

This will allow a server to be built. Using this, the multi-threaded Echo server given earlier becomes ThreadedIPEchoServer.go:

```
/* ThreadedIPEchoServer
 */
package main

import (
        "fmt"
        "net"
        "os"
)
```

```go
func main() {

        service := ":1200"
        listener, err := net.Listen("tcp", service)
        checkError(err)

        for {
                conn, err := listener.Accept()
                if err != nil {
                        continue
                }
                go handleClient(conn)
        }
}

func handleClient(conn net.Conn) {
        defer conn.Close()

        var buf [512]byte
        for {
                n, err := conn.Read(buf[0:])
                if err != nil {
                        return
                }
                _, err2 := conn.Write(buf[0:n])
                if err2 != nil {
                        return
                }
        }
}

func checkError(err error) {
        if err != nil {
                fmt.Fprintf(os.Stderr, "Fatal error: %s", err.Error())
                os.Exit(1)
        }
}
```

If you want to write a UDP server, there is an interface called PacketConn and a method to return an implementation of this:

```go
func ListenPacket(net, laddr string) (c PacketConn, err error)
```

This interface has the primary methods ReadFrom and WriteTo that handle packet reads and writes.

The Go net package recommends using these interface types rather than the concrete ones. But by using them, you lose specific methods such as SetKeepAlive of TCPConn and SetReadBuffer of UDPConn, unless you do a type cast. It is your choice.

Raw Sockets and the IPConn Type

This section covers advanced material that most programmers are unlikely to need. it deals with *raw sockets*, which allow programmers to build their own IP protocols, or use protocols other than TCP or UDP.

TCP and UDP are not the only protocols built above the IP layer. The site http://www.iana.org/assignments/protocol-numbers lists about 140 of them (this list is often available on UNIX systems in the file /etc/protocols). TCP and UDP are only numbers 6 and 17, respectively, on this list.

Go allows you to build so-called raw sockets, to enable you to communicate using one of these other protocols, or even to build your own. But it gives minimal support: it will connect hosts and write and read packets between the hosts. In the next chapter, we look at designing and implementing your own protocols above TCP; this section considers the same type of problem, but at the IP layer.

To keep things simple, we use almost the simplest possible example: how to send an IPv4 ping message to a host. Ping uses the echo command from the ICMP protocol. This is a byte-oriented protocol, in which the client sends a stream of bytes to another host, and the host replies. The format of the ICMP packet payload is as follows:

- The first byte is 8, standing for the echo message.

- The second byte is zero.

- The third and fourth bytes are a checksum on the entire message.

- The fifth and sixth bytes are an arbitrary identifier.

- The seventh and eight bytes are an arbitrary sequence number.

- The rest of the packet is user data.

The packet can be sent using the Conn.Write method, which prepares the packet with this payload. The replies received include the IPv4 header, which takes 20 bytes. (See for example, the Wikipedia article on the Internet Control Message Protocol, ICMP.)

The following program called Ping.go will prepare an IP connection, send a ping request to a host, and get a reply. You may need root access in order to run it successfully:

```go
/* Ping
 */
package main

import (
        "bytes"
        "fmt"
        "io"
        "net"
        "os"
)

// change this to my own IP address or set to 0.0.0.0
const myIPAddress = "192.168.1.2"
const ipv4HeaderSize = 20

func main() {
        if len(os.Args) != 2 {
                fmt.Println("Usage: ", os.Args[0], "host")
                os.Exit(1)
        }

        localAddr, err := net.ResolveIPAddr("ip4", myIPAddress)
```

```go
        if err != nil {
                fmt.Println("Resolution error", err.Error())
                os.Exit(1)
        }

        remoteAddr, err := net.ResolveIPAddr("ip4", os.Args[1])
        if err != nil {
                fmt.Println("Resolution error", err.Error())
                os.Exit(1)
        }

        conn, err := net.DialIP("ip4:icmp", localAddr, remoteAddr)
        checkError(err)

        var msg [512]byte
        msg[0] = 8  // echo
        msg[1] = 0  // code 0
        msg[2] = 0  // checksum, fix later
        msg[3] = 0  // checksum, fix later
        msg[4] = 0  // identifier[0]
        msg[5] = 13 // identifier[1] (arbitrary)
        msg[6] = 0  // sequence[0]
        msg[7] = 37 // sequence[1] (arbitrary)
        len := 8

        // now fix checksum bytes
        check := checkSum(msg[0:len])
        msg[2] = byte(check >> 8)
        msg[3] = byte(check & 255)

        // send the message
        _, err = conn.Write(msg[0:len])
        checkError(err)

        fmt.Print("Message sent:    ")
        for n := 0; n < 8; n++ {
                fmt.Print(" ", msg[n])
        }
        fmt.Println()

        // receive a reply
        size, err2 := conn.Read(msg[0:])
        checkError(err2)

        fmt.Print("Message received:")
        for n := ipv4HeaderSize; n < size; n++ {
                fmt.Print(" ", msg[n])
        }
        fmt.Println()
        os.Exit(0)
}
```

```go
func checkSum(msg []byte) uint16 {
        sum := 0

        // assume even for now
        for n := 0; n < len(msg); n += 2 {
                sum += int(msg[n])*256 + int(msg[n+1])
        }
        sum = (sum >> 16) + (sum & 0xffff)
        sum += (sum >> 16)
        var answer uint16 = uint16(^sum)
        return answer
}

func checkError(err error) {
        if err != nil {
                fmt.Fprintf(os.Stderr, "Fatal error: %s", err.Error())
                os.Exit(1)
        }
}

func readFully(conn net.Conn) ([]byte, error) {
        defer conn.Close()

        result := bytes.NewBuffer(nil)
        var buf [512]byte
        for {
                n, err := conn.Read(buf[0:])
                result.Write(buf[0:n])
                if err != nil {
                        if err == io.EOF {
                                break
                        }
                        return nil, err
                }
        }
        return result.Bytes(), nil
}
```

It is run using the destination address as an argument. The received message should differ from the sent message in only the first type byte and the third and fourth checksum bytes, as follows:

```
Message sent:      8 0 247 205 0 13 0 37
Message received: 0 0 255 205 0 13 0 37
```

Conclusion

This chapter considered programming at the IP, TCP, and UDP levels. This is often necessary if you want to implement your own protocol or build a client or server for an existing protocol.

CHAPTER 4

■ ■ ■

Data Serialization

A client and server need to exchange information via messages. TCP and UDP provide the transport mechanisms to do this. The two processes also need to have a protocol in place so that message exchange can take place meaningfully.

Messages are sent across the network as a sequence of bytes, which has no structure except as a linear stream of bytes. We address the various possibilities for messages and the protocols that define them in the next chapter. In this chapter, we concentrate on a component of messages—the data that is transferred.

A program will typically build complex data structures to hold the current program state. In conversing with a remote client or service, the program will be attempting to transfer such data structures across the network—that is, outside of the application's own address space.

Structured Data

Programming languages use structured data such as the following:

- Records/structures

- Variant records

- Array: Fixed size or varying

- String: Fixed size or varying

- Tables: Arrays of records

- Non-linear structures such as

  - Circular linked lists

  - Binary trees

  - Objects with references to other objects

None of the IP, TCP, or UDP packets know the meaning of any of these data types. All that they can contain is a sequence of bytes. Thus an application has to *serialize* any data into a stream of bytes in order to write it, and deserialize the stream of bytes back into suitable data structures on reading it. These two operations are known as *marshalling* and *unmarshalling*, respectively[1].

---

[1]I'm treating serialization and marshalling as synonomous. There are a variety of opinions on this, some more language-specific than others. See, for example, "What is the difference between Serialization and Marshaling?"

© Jan Newmarch 2017
J. Newmarch, *Network Programming with Go*, DOI 10.1007/978-1-4842-2692-6_4

For example, consider sending the following variable length table of two columns of variable length strings:

fred	programmer
liping	analyst
sureerat	manager

This could be done by in various ways. For example, suppose that it is known that the data will be an unknown number of rows in a two-column table. Then a marshalled form could be:

```
3                // 3 rows, 2 columns assumed
4 fred           // 4 char string,col 1
10 programmer    // 10 char string,col 2
6 liping         // 6 char string, col 1
7 analyst        // 7 char string, col 2
8 sureerat       // 8 char string, col 1
7 manager        // 7 char string, col 2
```

Variable length things can alternatively have their length indicated by terminating them with an "illegal" value, such as \0 for strings. The previous table could also be written with the number of rows again, but each string terminated by \0 (the newlines are for readability, not part of the serialization):

```
3
fred\0
programmer\0
liping\0
analyst\0
sureerat\0
manager\0
```

Alternatively, it may be known that the data is a three-row fixed table of two columns of strings of length 8 and 10, respectively. Then a serialization of the table could be (again, the newlines are not part of the serialization):

```
fred\0\0\0\0
programmer
liping\0\0
analyst\0\0\0
sureerat
manager\0\0\0
```

Any of these formats is okay, but the message exchange protocol must specify which one is used or allow it to be determined at runtime.

Mutual Agreement

The previous section gave an overview of the issue of data serialization. In practice, the details can be considerably more complex. For example, consider the first possibility, marshalling a table into the stream:

```
3
4 fred
10 programmer
6 liping
7 analyst
8 sureerat
7 manager
```

Many questions arise. For example, how many rows are possible for the table—that is, how big an integer do we need to describe the row size? If it is 255 or less, then a single byte will do, but if it is more, then a short, integer, or long may be needed. A similar problem occurs for the length of each string. With the characters themselves, to which character set do they belong? 7-bit ASCII? 16-bit Unicode? The question of character sets is discussed at length in a later chapter.

This serialization is *opaque* or *implicit*. If data is marshalled using this format, then there is nothing in the serialized data to say how it should be unmarshalled. The unmarshalling side has to know exactly how the data is serialized in order to unmarshal it correctly. For example, if the number of rows is marshalled as an 8-bit integer, but unmarshalled as a 16-bit integer, then an incorrect result will occur as the receiver tries to unmarshal 3 and 4 as a 16-bit integer, and the receiving program will almost certainly fail later.

An early well-known serialization method is XDR (external data representation) used by Sun's RPC, later known as ONC (Open Network Computing). XDR is defined by RFC 1832 and it is instructive to see how precise this specification is. Even so, XDR is inherently type-unsafe as serialized data contains no type information. The correctness of its use in ONC is ensured primarily by compilers generating code for both marshalling and unmarshalling.

Go contains no explicit support for marshalling or unmarshalling opaque serialized data. The RPC package in Go does not use XDR, but instead uses *Gob* serialization, described later in this chapter.

Self-Describing Data

Self-describing data carries type information along with the data. For example, the previous data might get encoded as follows:

```
table
    uint8 3
    uint 2
string
    uint8 4
    []byte fred
string
    uint8 10
    []byte programmer
string
    uint8 6
    []byte liping
```

```
string
    uint8 7
    []byte analyst
string
    uint8 8
    []byte sureerat
string
    uint8 7
    []byte manager
```

Of course, a real encoding would not normally be as cumbersome and verbose as in the example: small integers would be used as type markers and the whole data would be packed in as small a byte array as possible. (XML provides a counter-example, though.) However, the principle is that the marshaller will generate such type information in the serialized data. The unmarshaller will know the type-generation rules and will be able to use them to reconstruct the correct data structure.

ASN.1

Abstract Syntax Notation One (ASN.1) was originally designed in 1984 for the telecommunications industry. ASN.1 is a complex standard, and a subset of it is supported by Go in the package asn1. It builds self-describing serialized data from complex data structures. Its primary use in current networking systems is as the encoding for X.509 certificates, which are heavily used in authentication systems. The support in Go is based on what is needed to read and write X.509 certificates.

Two functions allow us to marshal and unmarshal data:

```
func Marshal(val interface{}) ([]byte, error)
func Unmarshal(val interface{}, b []byte) (rest []byte, err error)
```

The first marshals a data value into a serialized byte array, and the second unmarshals it. However, the first argument of type interface deserves further examination. Given a variable of a type, we can marshal it by just passing its value. To unmarshal it, we need a variable of a named type that will match the serialized data. The precise details of this are discussed later. But we also need to make sure that the variable is allocated to memory for that type, so that there is actually existing memory for the unmarshalling to write values into.

We illustrate with an almost trivial example in ASN1.go of marshalling and unmarshalling an integer. We can pass an integer value to marshal to return a byte array, and unmarshal the array into an integer variable, as in this program:

```
/* ASN1
 */

package main

import (
        "encoding/asn1"
        "fmt"
        "os"
)
```

```
func main() {
        val := 13
        fmt.Println("Before marshal/unmarshal: ", val)
        mdata, err := asn1.Marshal(val)
        checkError(err)

        var n int
        _, err1 := asn1.Unmarshal(mdata, &n)
        checkError(err1)

        fmt.Println("After marshal/unmarshal: ", n)
}

func checkError(err error) {
        if err != nil {
                fmt.Fprintf(os.Stderr, "Fatal error: %s", err.Error())
                os.Exit(1)
        }
}
```

The program is run as follows:

```
go run ASN1.go
```

The unmarshalled value, is of course, 13.

Once we move beyond this, things get harder. In order to manage more complex data types, we have to look more closely at the data structures supported by ASN.1, and how ASN.1 support is done in Go.

Any serialization method will be able to handle certain data types and not handle some others. So in order to determine the suitability of any serialization such as ASN.1, you have to look at the possible data types supported versus those you want to use in your application. The following ASN.1 types are taken from http://www.obj-sys.com/asn1tutorial/node4.html.

The simple types are as follows:

- BOOLEAN: Two-state variable values

- INTEGER: Models integer variable values

- BIT STRING: Models binary data of arbitrary length

- OCTET STRING: Models binary data whose length is a multiple of eight

- NULL: Indicates effective absence of a sequence element

- OBJECT IDENTIFIER: Names information objects

- REAL: Models real variable values

- ENUMERATED: Models values of variables with at least three states

- CHARACTER STRING: Models values that are strings of characters from a specified character set

Character strings can be from certain character sets:

- NumericString: 0,1,2,3,4,5,6,7,8,9, and space

- PrintableString: Upper- and lowercase letters, digits, space, apostrophe, left/right parenthesis, plus sign, comma, hyphen, full stop, solidus, colon, equal sign, and question mark

- TeletexString (T61String): The Teletex character set in CCITT's T61, space, and delete

- VideotexString: The Videotex character set in CCITT's T.100 and T.101, space, and delete

- VisibleString (ISO646String): Printing character sets of international ASCII, and space

- IA5String: International Alphabet 5 (International ASCII)

- GraphicString 25: All registered G sets, and space GraphicString

- There are additional string types as well as these, notably UTF8String

And finally, there are the structured types:

- SEQUENCE: Models an ordered collection of variables of different types

- SEQUENCE OF: Models an ordered collection of variables of the same type

- SET: Models an unordered collection of variables of different types

- SET OF: Models an unordered collection of variables of the same type

- CHOICE: Specifies a collection of distinct types from which to choose one type

- SELECTION: Selects a component type from a specified CHOICE type

- ANY: Enables an application to specify the type

■ **Note**   ANY is a deprecated ASN.1 Structured Type. It has been replaced with X.680 Open Type.

Not all of these are supported by Go. Not all possible values are supported by Go. The rules, as given in the Go asn1 package documentation, are as follows:

- An ASN.1 INTEGER can be written to an int or int64. If the encoded value does not fit in the Go type, Unmarshal returns a parse error.

- An ASN.1 BIT STRING can be written to a BitString.

- An ASN.1 OCTET STRING can be written to a []byte.

- An ASN.1 OBJECT IDENTIFIER can be written to an ObjectIdentifier.

- An ASN.1 ENUMERATED can be written to an Enumerated.

- An ASN.1 UTCTIME or GENERALIZEDTIME can be written to a *time.Time.

- An ASN.1 PrintableString or IA5String can be written to a string.

- Any of the above ASN.1 values can be written to an interface{}. The value stored in the interface has the corresponding Go type. For integers, that type is int64.

- An ASN.1 SEQUENCE OF x or SET OF x can be written to a slice if an x can be written to the slice's element type.

- An ASN.1 SEQUENCE or SET can be written to a Go struct if each of the elements in the sequence can be written to the corresponding element in the struct.

Go places real restrictions on ASN.1. For example, ASN.1 allows integers of any size, while the Go implementation will only allow up to signed 64-bit integers. On the other hand, Go distinguishes between signed and unsigned types, while ASN.1 doesn't. So for example, transmitting a value of uint64 may fail if it is too large for int64.

In a similar vein, ASN.1 allows several different character sets, while the Go package states that it only supports PrintableString and IA5String (ASCII). ASN.1 now has Unicode UTF8 string type, and this is supported by Go, but not currently documented.

We have seen that a value such as an integer can be easily marshalled and unmarshalled. Other basic types such as Booleans and reals can be similarly dealt with. Strings composed entirely of ASCII characters or UTF8 characters can be marshalled and unmarshalled. This code works as long as the string is composed only of ASCII or UTF8 characters:

```go
s := "hello"
mdata, _ := asn1.Marshal(s)

var newstr string
asn1.Unmarshal(mdata, &newstr)
```

ASN.1 also includes some "useful types" not in this list, such as UTC time. Go supports this UTC time type. This means that you can pass time values in a way that is not possible for other data values. ASN.1 does not support pointers, but Go has special code to manage pointers to time values. The function Now() returns *time.Time. The special code marshals this, and it can be unmarshalled into a pointer variable to a time.Time object. Thus this code works:

```go
t := time.Now()
mdata, err := asn1.Marshal(t)

var newtime = new(time.Time)
_, err1 := asn1.Unmarshal(newtime, mdata)
```

Both LocalTime and new handle pointers to a *time.Time, and Go looks after this special case. The program ASN1basic.go illustrates these:

```go
/* ASN.1 Basic
 */

package main

import (
        "encoding/asn1"
        "fmt"
        "os"
        "time"
)
```

```go
func main() {

        t := time.Now()
        fmt.Println("Before marshalling: ", t.String())

        mdata, err := asn1.Marshal(t)
        checkError(err)
        fmt.Println("Marshalled ok")

        var newtime = new(time.Time)
        _, err1 := asn1.Unmarshal(mdata, newtime)
        checkError(err1)

        fmt.Println("After marshal/unmarshal: ", newtime.String())

        s := "hello \u00bc"
        fmt.Println("Before marshalling: ", s)

        mdata2, err := asn1.Marshal(s)
        checkError(err)
        fmt.Println("Marshalled ok")

        var newstr string
        _, err2 := asn1.Unmarshal(mdata2, &newstr)
        checkError(err2)

        fmt.Println("After marshal/unmarshal: ", newstr)

}

func checkError(err error) {
        if err != nil {
                fmt.Println("Fatal error ", err.Error())
                os.Exit(1)
        }
}
```

When it runs as follows:

```
go run ASN1basic.go
```

It prints something similar to this:

```
Before marshalling:  2017-03-02 22:31:16.878943019 +1100 AEDT
Marshalled ok
After marshal/unmarshal:  2017-03-02 22:31:16 +1100 AEDT
Before marshalling:  hello ¼
Marshalled ok
After marshal/unmarshal:  hello ¼
```

In general, you will probably want to marshal and unmarshal structures. Apart from the special case of time, Go will happily deal with structures, but not with pointers to structures. Operations such as new create pointers, so you have to dereference them before marshalling/unmarshalling them. Go normally dereferences pointers for you when needed, but not in this case, so you have to dereference them explicitly. These both work for a type T:

```
// using variables
var t1 T
t1 = ...
mdata1, _ := asn1.Marshal(t)

var newT1 T
asn1.Unmarshal(&newT1, mdata1)

// using pointers
var t2 = new(T)
*t2 = ...
mdata2, _ := asn1.Marshal(*t2)

var newT2 = new(T)
asn1.Unmarshal(newT2, mdata2)
```

Any suitable mix of pointers and variables will work as well. We don't give a full example here, as it should be straightforward enough to apply the rules.

The fields of a structure must all be exportable, that is, field names must begin with an uppercase letter. Go uses the reflect package to marshal/unmarshal structures, so it must be able to examine all fields. This type cannot be marshalled:

```
type T struct {
    Field1 int
    field2 int // not exportable
}
```

ASN.1 only deals with the data types. It does not consider the names of structure fields. So the following type T1 can be marshalled/unmarshalled into type T2 as the corresponding fields are the same types:

```
type T1 struct {
    F1 int
    F2 string
}

type T2 struct {
    FF1 int
    FF2 string
}
```

Not only must the types of each field match, but the number must match as well. These two types don't work:

```
type T1 struct {
    F1 int
}
```

```
type T2 struct {
    F1 int
    F2 string // too many fields
}
```

We don't give full code examples for these since we won't be using these features.

ASN.1 illustrates many of the choices that can be made by those implementing a serialization method. Pointers could have been given special treatment by using more code, such as the enforcement of name matches. The order and number of strings will depend on the details of the serialization specification, the flexibility it allows, and the coding effort needed to exploit that flexibility. It is worth noting that other serialization formats will make different choices, and implementations in different languages will also enforce different rules.

ASN.1 Daytime Client and Server

Now (finally) let's turn to using ASN.1 to transport data across the network.

We can write a TCP server that delivers the current time as an ASN.1 Time type, using the techniques of the last chapter. A server is ASNDaytimeServer.go:

```
/* ASN1 DaytimeServer
 */
package main

import (
        "encoding/asn1"
        "fmt"
        "net"Calibri
        "os"
        "time"
)

func main() {

        service := ":1200"
        tcpAddr, err := net.ResolveTCPAddr("tcp", service)
        checkError(err)

        listener, err := net.ListenTCP("tcp", tcpAddr)
        checkError(err)

        for {
                conn, err := listener.Accept()
                if err != nil {
                        continue
                }

                daytime := time.Now()
                // Ignore return network errors.
                mdata, _ := asn1.Marshal(daytime)
```

```
                conn.Write(mdata)
                conn.Close() // we're finished
        }
}

func checkError(err error) {
        if err != nil {
                fmt.Fprintf(os.Stderr, "Fatal error: %s", err.Error())
                os.Exit(1)
        }
}
```

This can be compiled to an executable such as ASN1DaytimeServer and run with no arguments. It will wait for connections and then send the time as an ASN.1 string to the client.

A client is ASNDaytimeClient.go:

```
/* ASN.1 DaytimeClient
 */
package main

import (
        "bytes"
        "encoding/asn1"
        "fmt"
        "io"
        "net"
        "os"
        "time"
)

func main() {
        if len(os.Args) != 2 {
                fmt.Fprintf(os.Stderr, "Usage: %s host:port", os.Args[0])
                os.Exit(1)
        }
        service := os.Args[1]

        conn, err := net.Dial("tcp", service)
        checkError(err)

        result, err := readFully(conn)
        checkError(err)

        var newtime time.Time
        _, err1 := asn1.Unmarshal(result, &newtime)
        checkError(err1)

        fmt.Println("After marshal/unmarshal: ", newtime.String())

        os.Exit(0)
}
```

```go
func checkError(err error) {
        if err != nil {
                fmt.Fprintf(os.Stderr, "Fatal error: %s", err.Error())
                os.Exit(1)
        }
}

func readFully(conn net.Conn) ([]byte, error) {
        defer conn.Close()

        result := bytes.NewBuffer(nil)
        var buf [512]byte
        for {
                n, err := conn.Read(buf[0:])
                result.Write(buf[0:n])
                if err != nil {
                        if err == io.EOF {
                                break
                        }
                        return nil, err
                }
        }
        return result.Bytes(), nil
}
```

This connects to the service given in a form such as `localhost:1200`, reads the TCP packet, and decodes the ASN.1 content back into a string, which it prints.

Note that neither of these two—the client or the server—are compatible with the text-based clients and servers of the last chapter. This client and server are exchanging ASN.1 encoded data values, not textual strings.

JSON

JSON stands for JavaScript Object Notation. It was designed to be a lightweight means of passing data between JavaScript systems. It uses a text-based format and is sufficiently general that it has become used as a general-purpose serialization method for many programming languages.

JSON serializes objects, arrays, and basic values. The basic values include string, number, Boolean values, and the null value. Arrays are a comma-separated list of values that can represent arrays, vectors, lists, or sequences of various programming languages. They are delimited by square brackets [...]. Objects are represented by a list of "field: value" pairs enclosed in curly braces { ... }.

For example, the table of employees given earlier could be written as an array of employee objects:

```json
[
    {"Name": "fred", "Occupation": "programmer"},
    {"Name": "liping", "Occupation": "analyst"},
    {"Name": "sureerat", "Occupation": "manager"}
]
```

There is no special support for complex data types such as dates, no distinction between number types, no recursive types, etc. JSON is a very simple language, but nevertheless can be quite useful. Its text-based format makes it easy to use and debug, even though it has the overheads of string handling.

From the Go JSON package specification, marshalling uses the following type-dependent default encodings:

- Boolean values encode as JSON Booleans.

- Floating point and integer values encode as JSON numbers.

- String values encode as JSON strings, with each invalid UTF-8 sequence replaced by the encoding of the Unicode replacement character U+FFFD.

- Array and slice values encode as JSON arrays, except that [ ]byte encodes as a Base64-encoded string.

- Struct values encode as JSON objects. Each struct field becomes a member of the object. By default the object's key name is the struct field name converted to lowercase. If the struct field has a tag, that tag will be used as the name instead.

- Map values encode as JSON objects. The map's key type must be string; the object keys are used directly as map keys.

- Pointer values encode as the value pointed to. (Note: This allows trees but not graphs!). A nil pointer encodes as the null JSON object.

- Interface values encode as the value contained in the interface. A nil interface value encodes as the null JSON object.

- Channel, complex, and function values cannot be encoded in JSON. Attempting to encode such a value causes Marshal to return InvalidTypeError.

- JSON cannot represent cyclic data structures and Marshal does not handle them. Passing cyclic structures to Marshal will result in an infinite recursion.

A program to store JSON serialized data into the file person.json is SaveJSON.go:

```go
/* SaveJSON
 */

package main

import (
        "encoding/json"
        "fmt"
        "os"
)

type Person struct {
        Name   Name
        Email  []Email
}

type Name struct {
        Family   string
        Personal string
}
```

```go
type Email struct {
        Kind    string
        Address string
}

func main() {
        person := Person{
                Name: Name{Family: "Newmarch", Personal: "Jan"},
                Email: []Email{Email{Kind: "home", Address: "jan@newmarch.name"},
                        Email{Kind: "work", Address: "j.newmarch@boxhill.edu.au"}}}

        saveJSON("person.json", person)
}

func saveJSON(fileName string, key interface{}) {
        outFile, err := os.Create(fileName)
        checkError(err)
        encoder := json.NewEncoder(outFile)
        err = encoder.Encode(key)
        checkError(err)
        outFile.Close()
}

func checkError(err error) {
        if err != nil {
                fmt.Println("Fatal error ", err.Error())
                os.Exit(1)
        }
}
```

To load it back into memory, use LoadJSON.go:

```go
/* LoadJSON
 */

package main

import (
        "encoding/json"
        "fmt"
        "os"
)

type Person struct {
        Name  Name
        Email []Email
}
```

```go
type Name struct {
        Family   string
        Personal string
}

type Email struct {
        Kind    string
        Address string
}

func (p Person) String() string {
        s := p.Name.Personal + " " + p.Name.Family
        for _, v := range p.Email {
                s += "\n" + v.Kind + ": " + v.Address
        }
        return s
}
func main() {
        var person Person
        loadJSON("person.json", &person)

        fmt.Println("Person", person.String())
}

func loadJSON(fileName string, key interface{}) {
        inFile, err := os.Open(fileName)
        checkError(err)
        decoder := json.NewDecoder(inFile)
        err = decoder.Decode(key)
        checkError(err)
        inFile.Close()
}

func checkError(err error) {
        if err != nil {
                fmt.Println("Fatal error ", err.Error())
                os.Exit(1)
        }
}
```

The serialized form is (formatted nicely):

```
{"Name":{"Family":"Newmarch",
         "Personal":"Jan"},
 "Email":[{"Kind":"home","Address":"jan@newmarch.name"},
          {"Kind":"work","Address":"j.newmarch@boxhill.edu.au"}
          ]
}
```

A Client and Server

A client to send a person's data and read it back 10 times is `JSONEchoClient.go`:

```
/* JSON EchoClient
 */
package main

import (
        "bytes"
        "encoding/json"
        "fmt"
        "io"
        "net"
        "os"
)

type Person struct {
        Name    Name
        Email   []Email
}

type Name struct {
        Family    string
        Personal  string
}

type Email struct {
        Kind     string
        Address  string
}

func (p Person) String() string {
        s := p.Name.Personal + " " + p.Name.Family
        for _, v := range p.Email {
                s += "\n" + v.Kind + ": " + v.Address
        }
        return s
}

func main() {
        person := Person{
                Name: Name{Family: "Newmarch", Personal: "Jan"},
                Email: []Email{Email{Kind: "home", Address: "jan@newmarch.name"},
                        Email{Kind: "work", Address: "j.newmarch@boxhill.edu.au"}}}

        if len(os.Args) != 2 {
                fmt.Println("Usage: ", os.Args[0], "host:port")
                os.Exit(1)
        }
        service := os.Args[1]
```

```go
        conn, err := net.Dial("tcp", service)
        checkError(err)

        encoder := json.NewEncoder(conn)
        decoder := json.NewDecoder(conn)

        for n := 0; n < 10; n++ {
                encoder.Encode(person)
                var newPerson Person
                decoder.Decode(&newPerson)
                fmt.Println(newPerson.String())
        }

        os.Exit(0)
}

func checkError(err error) {
        if err != nil {
                fmt.Println("Fatal error ", err.Error())
                os.Exit(1)
        }
}

func readFully(conn net.Conn) ([]byte, error) {
        defer conn.Close()

        result := bytes.NewBuffer(nil)
        var buf [512]byte
        for {
                n, err := conn.Read(buf[0:])
                result.Write(buf[0:n])
                if err != nil {
                        if err == io.EOF {
                                break
                        }
                        return nil, err
                }
        }
        return result.Bytes(), nil
}
```

The corresponding server is JSONEchoServer.go:

```go
/* JSON EchoServer
 */
package main
```

```go
import (
        "encoding/json"
        "fmt"
        "net"
        "os"
)

type Person struct {
        Name   Name
        Email  []Email
}

type Name struct {
        Family   string
        Personal string
}

type Email struct {
        Kind    string
        Address string
}

func (p Person) String() string {
        s := p.Name.Personal + " " + p.Name.Family
        for _, v := range p.Email {
                s += "\n" + v.Kind + ": " + v.Address
        }
        return s
}

func main() {

        service := "0.0.0.0:1200"
        tcpAddr, err := net.ResolveTCPAddr("tcp", service)
        checkError(err)

        listener, err := net.ListenTCP("tcp", tcpAddr)
        checkError(err)

        for {
                conn, err := listener.Accept()
                if err != nil {
                        continue
                }

                encoder := json.NewEncoder(conn)
                decoder := json.NewDecoder(conn)

                for n := 0; n < 10; n++ {
                        var person Person
                        decoder.Decode(&person)
```

```
                fmt.Println(person.String())
                encoder.Encode(person)
            }
            conn.Close() // we're finished
        }
    }
}

func checkError(err error) {
    if err != nil {
        fmt.Println("Fatal error ", err.Error())
        os.Exit(1)
    }
}
```

The Gob Package

Gob is a serialization technique specific to Go. It is designed to encode Go data types specifically and does not at present have substantial support for or by any other languages. It supports all Go data types except for channels, functions, and interfaces. It supports integers of all types and sizes, strings and Booleans, structs, arrays, and slices. At present, it has some problems with circular structures such as rings, but that will improve over time.

Gob encodes type information into its serialized forms. This is far more extensive than the type information in say an X.509 serialization, but far more efficient than the type information contained in an XML document. Type information is only included once for each piece of data, but includes, for example, the names of struct fields.

This inclusion of type information makes Gob marshalling and unmarshalling fairly robust to changes or differences between the marshaller and unmarshaller. For example, this struct:

```
struct T {
    a int
    b int
}
```

Can be marshalled and then unmarshalled into a different struct, where the order of fields has changed:

```
struct T {
    b int
    a int
}
```

It can also cope with missing fields (the values are ignored) or extra fields (the fields are left unchanged). It can cope with pointer types, so that the previous struct could be unmarshalled into this one:

```
struct T {
    *a int
    **b int
}
```

To some extent it can cope with type coercions so that an `int` field can be broadened into an `int64`, but not incompatible types such as `int` and `uint`.

To use Gob to marshal a data value, you first need to create an Encoder. This takes a `Writer` as a parameter and marshalling will be done to this write stream. The encoder has a method called `Encode`, which marshals the value to the stream. This method can be called multiple times on multiple pieces of data. Type information for each data type is only written once, though.

You use a Decoder to unmarshal the serialized data stream. This takes a `Reader` and each read returns an unmarshalled data value.

A program to store Gob serialized data into the file `person.go` is `SaveGob.go`:

```
/* SaveGob
 */

package main

import (
        "encoding/gob"
        "fmt"
        "os"
)

type Person struct {
        Name    Name
        Email   []Email
}

type Name struct {
        Family    string
        Personal  string
}

type Email struct {
        Kind       string
        Address    string
}

func main() {
        person := Person{
                Name: Name{Family: "Newmarch", Personal: "Jan"},
                Email: []Email{Email{Kind: "home", Address: "jan@newmarch.name"},
                        Email{Kind: "work", Address: "j.newmarch@boxhill.edu.au"}}}

        saveGob("person.gob", person)
}

func saveGob(fileName string, key interface{}) {
        outFile, err := os.Create(fileName)
        checkError(err)
        encoder := gob.NewEncoder(outFile)
```

```
        err = encoder.Encode(key)
        checkError(err)
        outFile.Close()
}

func checkError(err error) {
        if err != nil {
                fmt.Println("Fatal error ", err.Error())
                os.Exit(1)
        }
}
```

To load it back into memory, use LoadGob.go:

```
/* LoadGob
 */

package main

import (
        "encoding/gob"
        "fmt"
        "os"
)

type Person struct {
        Name   Name
        Email  []Email
}

type Name struct {
        Family   string
        Personal string
}

type Email struct {
        Kind    string
        Address string
}

func (p Person) String() string {
        s := p.Name.Personal + " " + p.Name.Family
        for _, v := range p.Email {
                s += "\n" + v.Kind + ": " + v.Address
        }
        return s
}
```

```go
func main() {
        var person Person
        loadGob("person.gob", &person)

        fmt.Println("Person", person.String())
}

func loadGob(fileName string, key interface{}) {
        inFile, err := os.Open(fileName)
        checkError(err)
        decoder := gob.NewDecoder(inFile)
        err = decoder.Decode(key)
        checkError(err)
        inFile.Close()
}

func checkError(err error) {
        if err != nil {
                fmt.Println("Fatal error ", err.Error())
                os.Exit(1)
        }
}
```

A Client and Server

A client to send a person's data and read it back 10 times is GobEchoClient.go:

```go
/* Gob EchoClient
 */
package main

import (
        "bytes"
        "encoding/gob"
        "fmt"
        "io"
        "net"
        "os"
)

type Person struct {
        Name   Name
        Email  []Email
}

type Name struct {
        Family   string
        Personal string
}
```

```go
type Email struct {
        Kind    string
        Address string
}

func (p Person) String() string {
        s := p.Name.Personal + " " + p.Name.Family
        for _, v := range p.Email {
                s += "\n" + v.Kind + ": " + v.Address
        }
        return s
}

func main() {
        person := Person{
                Name: Name{Family: "Newmarch", Personal: "Jan"},
                Email: []Email{Email{Kind: "home", Address: "jan@newmarch.name"},
                        Email{Kind: "work", Address: "j.newmarch@boxhill.edu.au"}}}

        if len(os.Args) != 2 {
                fmt.Println("Usage: ", os.Args[0], "host:port")
                os.Exit(1)
        }
        service := os.Args[1]

        conn, err := net.Dial("tcp", service)
        checkError(err)

        encoder := gob.NewEncoder(conn)
        decoder := gob.NewDecoder(conn)

        for n := 0; n < 10; n++ {
                encoder.Encode(person)
                var newPerson Person
                decoder.Decode(&newPerson)
                fmt.Println(newPerson.String())
        }

        os.Exit(0)
}

func checkError(err error) {
        if err != nil {
                fmt.Println("Fatal error ", err.Error())
                os.Exit(1)
        }
}
```

```go
func readFully(conn net.Conn) ([]byte, error) {
        defer conn.Close()

        result := bytes.NewBuffer(nil)
        var buf [512]byte
        for {
                n, err := conn.Read(buf[0:])
                result.Write(buf[0:n])
                if err != nil {
                        if err == io.EOF {
                                break
                        }
                        return nil, err
                }
        }
        return result.Bytes(), nil
}
```

The corresponding server is GobEchoServer.go:

```go
/* Gob EchoServer
 */
package main

import (
        "encoding/gob"
        "fmt"
        "net"
        "os"
)

type Person struct {
        Name   Name
        Email []Email
}

type Name struct {
        Family   string
        Personal string
}

type Email struct {
        Kind    string
        Address string
}
```

```go
func (p Person) String() string {
	s := p.Name.Personal + " " + p.Name.Family
	for _, v := range p.Email {
		s += "\n" + v.Kind + ": " + v.Address
	}
	return s
}

func main() {

	service := "0.0.0.0:1200"
	tcpAddr, err := net.ResolveTCPAddr("tcp", service)
	checkError(err)

	listener, err := net.ListenTCP("tcp", tcpAddr)
	checkError(err)

	for {
		conn, err := listener.Accept()
		if err != nil {
			continue
		}

		encoder := gob.NewEncoder(conn)
		decoder := gob.NewDecoder(conn)

		for n := 0; n < 10; n++ {
			var person Person
			decoder.Decode(&person)
			fmt.Println(person.String())
			encoder.Encode(person)
		}
		conn.Close() // we're finished
	}
}

func checkError(err error) {
	if err != nil {
		fmt.Println("Fatal error ", err.Error())
		os.Exit(1)
	}
}
```

Encoding Binary Data as Strings

Once upon a time, transmitting 8-bit data was problematic. It was often transmitted over noisy serial lines and could easily become corrupted. 7-bit data, on the other hand, could be transmitted more reliably because the 8th bit could be used as check digit. For example, in an "even parity" scheme, the check digit would be set to one or zero to make an even number of 1s in a byte. This allows detection of errors of a single bit in each byte.

ASCII is a 7-bit character set. A number of schemes have been developed that are more sophisticated than simple parity checking, but which involve translating 8-bit binary data into 7-bit ASCII format. Essentially, the 8-bit data is stretched out in some way over the 7-bit bytes.

Binary data transmitted in HTTP responses and requests is often translated into an ASCII form. This makes it easy to inspect the HTTP messages with a simple text reader without worrying about what strange 8-bit bytes might do to your display!

One common format is Base64. Go has support for many binary-to-text formats, including Base64. There are two principal functions to use for Base64 encoding and decoding:

```
func NewEncoder(enc *Encoding, w io.Writer) io.WriteCloser
func NewDecoder(enc *Encoding, r io.Reader) io.Reader
```

A simple program just to encode and decode a set of eight binary digits is Base64.go:

```
/**
 * Base64
 */

package main

import (
        "encoding/base64"
        "fmt"
)

func main() {

        eightBitData := []byte{1, 2, 3, 4, 5, 6, 7, 8}

        enc := base64.StdEncoding.EncodeToString(eightBitData)
        dec, _ := base64.StdEncoding.DecodeString(enc)

        fmt.Println("Original data ", eightBitData)
        fmt.Println("Encoded string ", enc)
        fmt.Println("Decoded data ", dec)
}
```

The output is as follows:

```
Original data  [1 2 3 4 5 6 7 8]
Encoded string  AQIDBAUGBwg=
Decoded data  [1 2 3 4 5 6 7 8]
```

Protocol Buffers

The serialization methods considered so far fall into various types:

- ASN.1 encodes the different types using binary tags in the data. In that sense, an ASN.1 encoded data structure is a self-describing structure.

- JSON similarly is a self-describing format, using the rules of JavaScript data structures: lists, dictionaries, etc.

- Gob similarly encodes type information into its encoded form. This is far more detailed than the JSON format.

A separate class of serialization techniques rely on an external specification of the data type to be encoded. There are several major ones, such as the encoding used by ONC RPC.

ONC RPC is an old encoding, targeted toward the C language. A recent one is from Google, known as *protocol buffers*. This is not supported in the Go Standard Libraries, but is supported by the Google Protocol Buffers developer group (`https://developers.google.com/protocol-buffers/`) and is apparently very popular within Google. For that reason, we include a section on protocol buffers, although in the rest of the book we typically deal with the Go Standard Libraries.

Protocol buffers are a binary encoding of data intended to support the data types of a large variety of languages. They rely on an external specification of a data structure, which is used to encode data (in a source language) and also to decode the encoded data back into a target language. (Note: Protocol buffers transitioned to version 3 in July 2016. It is not compatible with version 2. Version 2 will be supported for a long time, but will eventually be obsoleted. See Protocol Buffers v3.0.0 at `https://github.com/google/protobuf/releases/tag/v3.0.0`).

The data structure to be serialized is known as a *message*. The data types supported in each message include:

- Numbers (integers or floats)

- Booleans

- Strings (in UTF-8)

- Raw bytes

- Maps

- Other messages, allowing complex data structures to be built

The fields of a message are all optional (this is a change from `proto2` where fields were required or optional). A field can stand for a list or array by the keyword repeated or a map using the keyword map. Each field has a type, followed by a name, followed by a tag index value. The full language guide is at called the "Protocol Buffers Language Guide" (see `https://developers.google.com/protocol-buffers/docs/proto`).

Messages are defined independent of the possible target language. A version of the `Person` type in the syntax of Protocol Buffers version 3 is `personv3.proto`. Note that the file includes specific tags (1, 2) on each type.

```
syntax = "proto3";
package person;

message Person {
        message Name {
                string family = 1;
                string personal = 2;
        }
```

```
        message Email {
                string kind = 1;
                string address = 2;
        }

        Name   name = 1;
        repeated Email email = 2;
}
```

Installing and Compiling Protocol Buffers

Protocol buffers are compiled using a program called protoc. This is unlikely to be installed on your system. Version 3 was only released in July 2016, so copies in repositories are likely to be version 2.

Install the latest version from the Protocol Buffers v3.0.0 page. For 64-bit Linux for example, download protoc-3.0.0-linux-x86_64.zip from GitHub and unzip it to a suitable place (it includes the binary bin/protoc, which should be placed somewhere in your PATH).

That installs the general binary. You also need the "backend" to generate Go files. To do this, fetch it from GitHub:

```
go get -u github.com/golang/protobuf/protoc-gen-go
```

You are nearly ready to compile a .proto file. The previous example of personv3.proto declares the package person. In your GOPATH, you should have a directory called src. Create a subdirectory called src/person. Then compile the personv3.proto as follows:

```
protoc --go_out=src/person personv3.proto
```

This should create the src/person/personv3.pb.go file.

The Compiled personv3.pb.go File

The compiled file will declare a number of types and methods on these types. The types are as follows:

```
type Person struct {
        Name  *Person_Name   `protobuf:"bytes,1,opt,name=name" json:"name,omitempty"`
        Email []*Person_Email `protobuf:"bytes,2,rep,name=email" json:"email,omitempty"`
}

type Person_Name struct {
        Family   string `protobuf:"bytes,1,opt,name=family" json:"family,omitempty"`
        Personal string `protobuf:"bytes,2,opt,name=personal" json:"personal,omitempty"`
}

type Person_Email struct {
        Kind    string `protobuf:"bytes,1,opt,name=kind" json:"kind,omitempty"`
        Address string `protobuf:"bytes,2,opt,name=address" json:"address,omitempty"`
}
```

They are in the package called person. (Note: Simple types such as strings are encoded directly. In Protocol Buffers v2, a pointer was used. For compound types, a pointer is required, as in v2.)

Using the Compiled Code

There is essentially no difference between the coding used in the JSON example and this one, apart from having to watch pointers for the structs used. A simple program just to marshal and unmarshal a Person is ProtocolBuffer.go:

The output should be a Person before and after marshalling and should be the same:

```
/* ProtocolBuffer
 */

package main

import (
        "fmt"
        "github.com/golang/protobuf/proto"
        "os"
        "person"
)

func main() {
        name := person.Person_Name{
                Family:   "newmarch",
                Personal: "jan"}

        email1 := person.Person_Email{
                Kind:    "home",
                Address: "jan@newmarch.name"}
        email2 := person.Person_Email{
                Kind:    "work",
                Address: "j.newmarch@boxhill.edu.au"}

        emails := []*person.Person_Email{&email1, &email2}
        p := person.Person{
                Name:  &name,
                Email: emails,
        }
        fmt.Println(p)

        data, err := proto.Marshal(&p)
        checkError(err)
        newP := person.Person{}
        err = proto.Unmarshal(data, &newP)
        checkError(err)
        fmt.Println(newP)
}

func checkError(err error) {
        if err != nil {
                fmt.Println("Fatal error ", err.Error())
                os.Exit(1)
        }
}
```

The output should be a Person before and after marshalling and should be the same by running the following:

```
go run ProtocolBuffer.go
```

{family:"newmarch" personal:"jan" [kind:"home" address:"jan@newmarch.name" kind:"work" address:"j.newmarch@boxhill.edu.au"]}
{family:"newmarch" personal:"jan" [kind:"home" address:"jan@newmarch.name" kind:"work" address:"j.newmarch@boxhill.edu.au"]}

We haven't done much with the marshalled object. However, it could be saved to a file or sent across the network and unmarshalled by any of the supported languages: C++, C#, Java, Python, as well as Go.

Conclusion

This chapter discussed the general properties of serializing data types and showed a number of common encodings. There are many more, including XML (included in the Go libraries), CBOR (a binary form of JSON), and YAML (similar to XML), as well as many language-specific ones such as Java Object Serialization and Python's Pickle. Those not in the Go standard packages may often be found on GitHub.

CHAPTER 5

■ ■ ■

Application-Level Protocols

A client and server need to exchange information via messages. TCP and UDP provide the transport mechanisms to do this. The two processes also need to have a protocol in place so that message exchange can take place meaningfully. A protocol defines what type of conversation can take place between two components of a distributed application, by specifying messages, data types, encoding formats, and so on. This chapter looks at some of the issues involved in this process and gives a complete example of a simple client-server application.

Protocol Design

There are many possibilities and issues to be decided on when designing a protocol. Some of the issues include:

Is it to be broadcast or point-to-point? Broadcast can be UDP, local multicast, or the more experimental MBONE. Point-to-point could be either TCP or UDP.

Is it to be stateful or stateless? Is it reasonable for one side to maintain state about the other side? It is often simpler for one side to maintain state about the other, but what happens if something crashes?

Is the transport protocol reliable or unreliable? Reliable is often slower, but then you don't have to worry so much about lost messages.

Are replies needed? If a reply is needed, how do you handle a lost reply? Timeouts may be used.

What data format do you want? Several possibilities were discussed in the last chapter.

Is your communication bursty or steady stream? Ethernet and the Internet are best at bursty traffic. Steady stream is needed for video streams and particularly for voice. If required, how do you manage Quality of Service (QoS)?

Are there multiple streams with synchronization required? Does the data need to be synchronized with anything, such as video and voice?

Are you building a standalone application or a library to be used by others? The standards of documentation required might vary.

© Jan Newmarch 2017
J. Newmarch, *Network Programming with Go*, DOI 10.1007/978-1-4842-2692-6_5

Why Should You Worry?

Jeff Bezos, the CEO of Amazon, reportedly made the following statements in 2002:

- All teams will henceforth expose their data and functionality through service interfaces.

- Teams must communicate with each other through these interfaces.

- There will be no other form of interprocess communication allowed: no direct linking, no direct reads of another team's data store, no shared-memory model, no backdoors whatsoever. The only communication allowed is via service interface calls over the network.

- It doesn't matter what technology they use. HTTP, Corba, Pubsub, custom protocols—it doesn't matter. Bezos doesn't care.

- All service interfaces, without exception, must be designed from the ground up to be externalizable. That is to say, the team must plan and design to be able to expose the interface to developers on the outside world. No exceptions.

- Anyone who doesn't do this will be fired.

(Source: Rip Rowan's blog about Steve Yegge's posting at https://plus.google.com/+RipRowan/posts/eVeouesvaVX.) What Bezos was doing was orienting one of the world's most successful Internet companies around service architectures, and interfaces must be clear enough that *all* communication must be through those interfaces alone—without confusion or errors.

Version Control

A protocol used in a client-server system will evolve over time, changing as the system expands. This raises compatibility problems: a version 2 client will make requests that a version 1 server doesn't understand, whereas a version 2 server will send replies that a version 1 client won't understand.

Each side should ideally be able to understand messages from its own version and all earlier ones. It should be able to write replies to old-style queries in old-style response formats. See Figure 5-1.

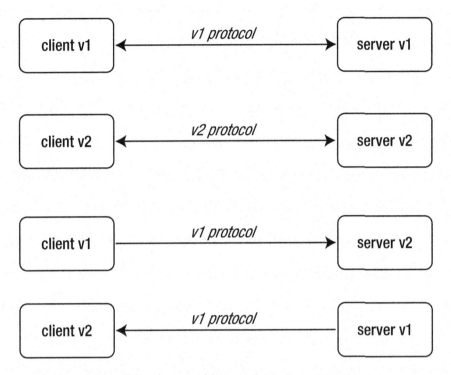

Figure 5-1. *Compatibility versus version control*

The ability to talk earlier version formats may be lost if the protocol changes too much. In this case, you need to be able to ensure that no copies of the earlier version still exist, which is generally impossible.

Part of the protocol setup should involve version information.

The Web

The Web is a good example of a system that has been through multiple different versions. The underlying HTTP protocol manages version control in an excellent manner, even though it has been through four versions. Most servers/browsers support the latest version but also support the earlier versions. The latest version HTTP/2 appears to account for just over 11% of web traffic by January 2017, while HTTP/1.1 accounts for almost all of the rest. The version is given in each request as in the following GET requests:

Request	Version
GET /	Pre 1.0
GET / HTTP/1.0	HTTP 1.0
GET / HTTP/1.1	HTTP 1.1
GET / HTTP/1.1 Connection: Upgrade, HTTP2-Settings Upgrade: h2c	HTTP 2

HTTP/2 is a binary format and is not compatible with earlier versions. Nevertheless, there is a negotiation mechanism of sending an HTTP/1.1 request with upgrade fields to HTTP/2. If the client accepts it, the upgrade can be made. If the client doesn't understand the upgrade parameters, the connection continues with HTTP/1.1.

While originally designed for HTML, HTTP can carry any content. If we just look at HTML, this has been through a large number of versions with, at times, little attempt to ensure compatibility between versions:

- HTML5, which has abandoned any version signaling between dot revisions

- HTML versions 1-4 (all different), with versions in the "browser wars" particularly problematic

- Non-standard tags recognized by different browsers

- Non-HTML documents often require content handlers that may not be present; does your browser have a handler for Flash?

- Inconsistent treatment of document content (e.g., some stylesheet content will crash some browsers)

- Different support for JavaScript (and different versions of JavaScript)

- Different runtime engines for Java

- Many pages do not conform to *any* HTML versions (e.g., with syntax errors)

HTML5 (and indeed many earlier versions) is an excellent example of how *not* to do version control. The latest revision at the time of writing is Revision 5. "In this version, new features are introduced to help Web application authors, new elements are introduced based on research into prevailing authoring practices,..." . Not only are some new features added, but some older ones (which should not be in much use any more) have also been removed and no longer work. There is no means for an HTML5 document to signal which revision it uses.

Message Format

In the last chapter we discussed some possibilities for representing data to be sent across the wire. Now we look one level up, to the messages that may contain such data.

- The client and server will exchange messages with different meanings:

  - Login request

  - Login reply

  - Get record request

  - Record data reply

- The client will prepare a request, which must be understood by the server.

- The server will prepare a reply, which must be understood by the client.

Commonly, the first part of the message will be a message type.

- Client to server:

  ```
  LOGIN <name> <passwd>
  GET <subject> grade
  ```

- Server to client:

  ```
  LOGIN succeeded
  GRADE <subject> <grade>
  ```

The message types can be strings or integers. For example, HTTP uses integers such as 404 to mean "not found" (although these integers are written as strings). The messages from client to server and vice versa are disjoint. The LOGIN message from the client to the server is a different message than the LOGIN message from the server to the client, and they will probably play complementary roles in the protocol.

Data Format

There are two main format choices for messages: byte encoded or character encoded.

Byte Format

In the byte format:

- The first part of the message is typically a byte to distinguish between message types.

- The message handler examines this first byte to distinguish the message type and then performs a switch to select the appropriate handler for that type.

- Further bytes in the message contain message content according to a predefined format (as discussed in the previous chapter).

The advantages are compactness and hence speed. The disadvantages are caused by the opaqueness of the data: it may be harder to spot errors, harder to debug, and require special purpose decoding functions. There are many examples of byte-encoded formats, including major protocols such as DNS and NFS, up to recent ones such as Skype. Of course, if your protocol is not publicly specified, then a byte format can also make it harder for others to reverse-engineer it!

Pseudocode for a byte-format server is as follows:

```
handleClient(conn) {
    while (true) {
        byte b = conn.readByte()
        switch (b) {
            case MSG_1: ...
            case MSG_2: ...
            ...
        }
    }
}
```

Go has basic support for managing byte streams. The interface io.ReaderWriter has these methods:

```
Read(b []byte) (n int, err error)Write(b []byte) (n int, err error)
```

These methods are implemented by TCPConn and UDPConn.

Character Format

In this mode, everything is sent as characters if possible. For example, an integer 234 would be sent as, say, the three characters 2, 3, and 4 instead of as the one byte 234. Data that is inherently binary may be Base64 encoded to change it into a 7-bit format and then sent as ASCII characters, as discussed in the previous chapter.

In character format:

- A message is a sequence of one or more lines. The start of the first line of the message is typically a word that represents the message type.

- String-handling functions may be used to decode the message type and data.

- The rest of the first line and successive lines contain the data.

- Line-oriented functions and line-oriented conventions are used to manage this.

The pseudocode is as follows:

```
handleClient() {
    line = conn.readLine()
    if (line.startsWith(...) {
        ...
    } else if (line.startsWith(...) {
        ...
    }
}
```

Character formats are easier to set up and easier to debug. For example, you can use telnet to connect to a server on any port and send client requests to that server. There isn't a simple tool like telnet to send server responses to a client, but you can use tools like tcpdump or wireshark to snoop on TCP traffic and see immediately what clients are sending to, and receiving from, the servers.

There is not the same level of support in Go for managing character streams. There are significant issues with character sets and character encodings, and we will explore these issues in a later chapter.

If we just pretend everything is ASCII, like it was once upon a time, then character formats are quite straightforward to deal with. The principal complication at this level is the varying status of "newline" across different operating systems. UNIX uses the single character \n. Windows and others (more correctly) use the pair \r\n. On the Internet, the pair \r\n is most common. UNIX systems just need to take care that they don't assume \n.

A Simple Example

This example deals with a directory browsing protocol, which is basically a stripped down version of FTP, but without even the file transfer part. We only consider listing a directory name, listing the contents of a directory, and changing the current directory—all on the server side, of course. This is a complete worked example of creating all components of a client-server application. It is a simple program that includes messages in both directions, as well as a design of messaging protocol.

A Standalone Application

Look at a simple non-client-server program that allows you to list files in a directory and change and print the name of the directory on the server. We omit copying files, as that adds to the length of the program without introducing important concepts. For simplicity, all filenames will be assumed to be in 7-bit ASCII. If we just looked at a standalone application first, it would look like Figure 5-2.

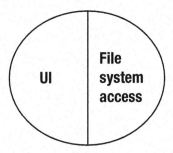

Figure 5-2. *The standalone application*

The pseudocode would be as follows:

```
read line from user
while not eof do
  if line == dir
    list directory // local function call
  else

  if line == cd <directory>
    change directory // local function call
  else

  if line == pwd
    print directory // local function call
  else

  if line == quit
    quit
  else
    complain

  read line from user
```

A non-distributed application would simply link the UI and file access code by local function calls.

93

The Client-Server Application

In a client-server situation, the client would be at the user end, talking to a server somewhere else. Aspects of this program belong solely at the presentation end, such as getting the commands from the user. Some are messages from the client to the server; some are solely at the server end. See Figure 5-3.

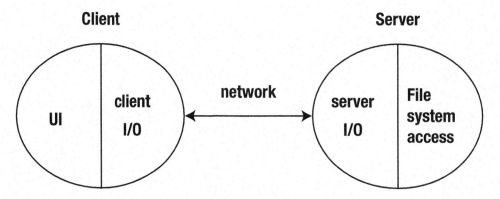

Figure 5-3. *The client-server situation*

The Client Side

For a simple directory browser, assume that all directories and files are at the server end, and we are transferring file information only from the server to the client. The client side (including presentation aspects) will become:

```
read line from user
while not eof do
  if line == dir
    list directory // network call to server
  else

  if line == cd <directory>
    change directory // network call to server
  else

  if line == pwd
    print directory // network call to server
  else

  if line == quit
    quit
  else
    complain

  read line from user
```

Where the calls list directory, change directory, and print directory now all involve network calls to the server. The details are not shown yet and will be discussed later.

Alternative Presentation Aspects

A GUI program would allow directory contents to be displayed as lists, for files to be selected and actions such as change directory to be performed on them. The client would be controlled by actions associated with various events that take place on graphical objects. The pseudocode might look like this:

```
change dir button:
  if there is a selected file
    change directory // remote call to server
  if successful
    update directory label
    list directory // remote call to server
    update directory list
```

The functions called from the different UIs should be the same—changing the presentation should not change the networking code.

The Server Side

The server side is independent of whatever presentation is used by the client. It is the same for all clients:

```
while read command from client
  if command == dir
    send list directory // local call on server
  else

  if command == cd <directory>
    change directory // local call on server
  else

  if command == pwd
    send print directory // local call on server
  else
```

Protocol: Informal

Client Request	Server Response
dir	Send list of files
cd <directory>	Change dir Send an error if failed Send ok if succeed
pwd	Send current directory
quit	Quit

Text Protocol

This is a simple protocol. The most complicated data structure that we need to send is an array of strings for a directory listing. In this case, we don't need the heavy-duty serialization techniques of the last chapter. In this case, we can use a simple text format.

But even if we make the protocol simple, we still have to specify it in detail. We choose the following message format:

- All messages are in 7-bit US-ASCII.

- The messages are case-sensitive.

- Each message consists of a sequence of lines.

- The first word on the first line of each message describes the message type. All other words are message data.

- All words are separated by exactly one space character.

- Each line is terminated by CR-LF.

Some of the choices made above are weaker in real-life protocols. For example:

- Message types could be case-insensitive. This just requires mapping message type strings down to lowercase before decoding.

- An arbitrary amount of whitespace could be left between words. This just adds a little more complication, compressing whitespace.

- Continuation characters such as \ can be used to break long lines over several lines. This starts to make processing more complex.

- Just a \n could be used as line terminator, \r\n can too. This makes recognizing the end of line a bit harder.

All of these variations exist in real protocols. Cumulatively, they make string processing more complex than in this case.

Client Request	Server Response
send "DIR"	Send list of files, one per line, terminated by a blank line
send "CD <directory>"	Change dir Send "ERROR" if failed Send "OK" if succeeded
send "PWD"	Send current working directory

We should also specify the transport:

- All messages are sent over a TCP connection established from the client to the server.

Server Code

The server is FTPServer.go:

```go
/* FTP Server
 */
package main

import (
        "fmt"
        "net"
        "os"
)

const (
        DIR = "DIR"
        CD  = "CD"
        PWD = "PWD"
)

func main() {

        service := "0.0.0.0:1202"
        tcpAddr, err := net.ResolveTCPAddr("tcp", service)
        checkError(err)

        listener, err := net.ListenTCP("tcp", tcpAddr)
        checkError(err)

        for {
                conn, err := listener.Accept()
                if err != nil {
                        continue
                }
                go handleClient(conn)
        }
}

func handleClient(conn net.Conn) {
        defer conn.Close()

        var buf [512]byte
        for {
                n, err := conn.Read(buf[0:])
                if err != nil {
                        conn.Close()
                        return
                }
```

```go
                s := string(buf[0:n])
                // decode request
                if s[0:2] == CD {
                        chdir(conn, s[3:])
                } else if s[0:3] == DIR {
                        dirList(conn)
                } else if s[0:3] == PWD {
                        pwd(conn)
                }


        }
}

func chdir(conn net.Conn, s string) {
        if os.Chdir(s) == nil {
                conn.Write([]byte("OK"))
        } else {
                conn.Write([]byte("ERROR"))
        }
}

func pwd(conn net.Conn) {
        s, err := os.Getwd()
        if err != nil {
                conn.Write([]byte(""))
                return
        }
        conn.Write([]byte(s))
}

func dirList(conn net.Conn) {
        // send a blank line on termination
        defer conn.Write([]byte("\r\n"))

        dir, err := os.Open(".")
        if err != nil {
                return
        }

        names, err := dir.Readdirnames(-1)
        if err != nil {
                return
        }
        for _, nm := range names {
                conn.Write([]byte(nm + "\r\n"))
        }
}

func checkError(err error) {
        if err != nil {
                fmt.Println("Fatal error ", err.Error())
                os.Exit(1)
        }
}
```

Client Code

A command-line client is FTPClient.go:

```go
/* FTPClient
 */
package main

import (
        "bufio"
        "bytes"
        "fmt"
        "net"
        "os"
        "strings"
)

// strings used by the user interface
const (
        uiDir  = "dir"
        uiCd   = "cd"
        uiPwd  = "pwd"
        uiQuit = "quit"
)

// strings used across the network
const (
        DIR = "DIR"
        CD  = "CD"
        PWD = "PWD"
)

func main() {
        if len(os.Args) != 2 {
                fmt.Println("Usage: ", os.Args[0], "host")
                os.Exit(1)
        }

        host := os.Args[1]

        conn, err := net.Dial("tcp", host+":1202")
        checkError(err)

        reader := bufio.NewReader(os.Stdin)
        for {
                line, err := reader.ReadString('\n')
                // lose trailing whitespace
                line = strings.TrimRight(line, " \t\r\n")
                if err != nil {
                        break
                }
```

```go
                    // split into command + arg
                    strs := strings.SplitN(line, " ", 2)
                    // decode user request
                    switch strs[0] {
                    case uiDir:
                            dirRequest(conn)
                    case uiCd:
                            if len(strs) != 2 {
                                    fmt.Println("cd <dir>")
                                    continue
                            }
                            fmt.Println("CD \"", strs[1], "\"")
                            cdRequest(conn, strs[1])
                    case uiPwd:
                            pwdRequest(conn)
                    case uiQuit:
                            conn.Close()
                            os.Exit(0)
                    default:
                            fmt.Println("Unknown command")
                    }
            }
}

func dirRequest(conn net.Conn) {
        conn.Write([]byte(DIR + " "))

        var buf [512]byte
        result := bytes.NewBuffer(nil)
        for {
                // read till we hit a blank line
                n, _ := conn.Read(buf[0:])
                result.Write(buf[0:n])
                length := result.Len()
                contents := result.Bytes()
                if string(contents[length-4:]) == "\r\n\r\n" {
                        fmt.Println(string(contents[0 : length-4]))
                        return
                }
        }
}

func cdRequest(conn net.Conn, dir string) {
        conn.Write([]byte(CD + " " + dir))
        var response [512]byte
        n, _ := conn.Read(response[0:])
        s := string(response[0:n])
        if s != "OK" {
                fmt.Println("Failed to change dir")
        }
}
```

```
func pwdRequest(conn net.Conn) {
        conn.Write([]byte(PWD))
        var response [512]byte
        n, _ := conn.Read(response[0:])
        s := string(response[0:n])
        fmt.Println("Current dir \"" + s + "\"")
}

func checkError(err error) {
        if err != nil {
                fmt.Println("Fatal error ", err.Error())
                os.Exit(1)
        }
}
```

Textproto Package

The textproto package contains functions designed to simplify management of text protocols similar to HTTP and SNMP.

These formats have some little-known rules with regard to a single logical line continued over multiple lines such as: "HTTP/1.1 header field values can be folded onto multiple lines if the continuation line begins with a space or horizontal tab" (HTTP1.1 specification). Formats allowing lines like these can be read using the ReadContinuedLine() function, in addition to simpler functions like ReadLine().

These protocols also signal status values with lines beginning with three-digit codes such as 404. These can be read using ReadCodeLine(). They also have key: value lines such as Content-Type: image/gif. Such lines can be read into a map by ReadMIMEHeader().

State Information

Applications often use state information to simplify what is going on. For example:

- Keeping file pointers to a current file location.

- Keeping the current mouse position.

- Keeping the current customer value.

In a distributed system, such state information may be kept in the client, in the server, or in both.

The important point is to whether one process is keeping state information about *itself* or about the *other* process. One process may keep as much state information about itself as it wants, without causing any problems. If it needs to keep information about the state of the other process, then problems arise. The process' actual knowledge of the state of the other may become incorrect. This can be caused by loss of messages (in UDP), by failure to update, or by software errors.

An example is reading a file. In single process applications, the file-handling code runs as part of the application. It maintains a table of open files and the location in each of them. Each time a read or write is done, this file location is updated. In distributed systems, this simple model does not hold. See Figure 5-4.

DCE File System

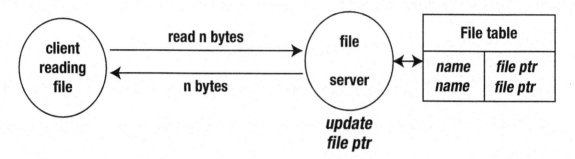

Figure 5-4. *The DCE file system*

In the DCE file system shown in Figure 5-4, the file server keeps track of a client's open files and where the client's file pointer is. If a message could get lost (but DCE uses TCP), these could get out of synch. If the client crashes, the server must eventually time out on the client's file tables and remove them.

NFS File System

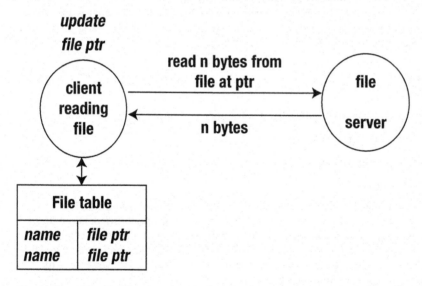

Figure 5-5. *The NFS file system*

In NFS, the server does not maintain this state. The client does. Each file access from the client that reaches the server must open the file at the appropriate point, as given by the client, in order to perform the action. See Figure 5-5.

If the server maintains information about the client, it must be able to recover if the client crashes. If information is not saved, then on each transaction, the client must transfer sufficient information for the server to function.

If the connection is unreliable, additional handling must be in place to ensure that the two do not get out of synch. The classic example is of bank account transactions where the messages get lost. A transaction server may need to be part of the client-server system.

Application State Transition Diagram

A state transition diagram keeps track of the current state of an application and the changes that move it to new states.

The previous example basically only had one state: file transfer. If we add a login mechanism, that would add an extra state called *login*, and the application would need to change states between login and file transfer, as shown in Figure 5-6.

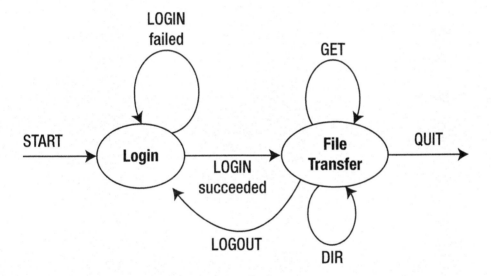

Figure 5-6. *The state-transition diagram*

This state change can also be expressed as a table:

Current State	Transition	Next State
login	login failed	login
	login succeeded	file transfer
file transfer	dir	file transfer
	get	file transfer
	logout	login
	quit	-

Client State Transition Diagrams

The client state diagram must follow the application diagram. It has more detail though: it *writes* and then *reads*:

Current State	Write	Read	Next State
login	LOGIN name password	FAILED	login
		OK	file transfer
file transfer	CD dir	OK	file transfer
		FAILED	file transfer
	GET filename	#lines + contents	file transfer
		FAILED	file transfer
	DIR	File names + blank line	file transfer
		blank line (Error)	file transfer
	quit	none	quit

Server State Transition Diagrams

The server state diagram must also follow the application diagram. It also has more detail: it *reads* and then *writes*:

Current State	Read	Write	Next State
login	LOGIN name password	FAILED	login
		OK	file transfer
file transfer	CD dir	SUCCEEDED	file transfer
		FAILED	file transfer
	GET filename	#lines + contents	file transfer
		FAILED	file transfer
	DIR	filenames + blank line	file transfer
		blank line (failed)	file transfer
	quit	none	login

Server Pseudocode

Here is the server pseudocode:

```
state = login
while true
    read line
    switch (state)
        case login:
            get NAME from line
            get PASSWORD from line
            if NAME and PASSWORD verified
                write SUCCEEDED
                state = file_transfer
            else
                write FAILED
                state = login
        case file_transfer:
            if line.startsWith CD
                get DIR from line
                if chdir DIR okay
                    write SUCCEEDED
                    state = file_transfer
                else
                    write FAILED
                    state = file_transfer
        ...
```

We don't give the actual code for this server or client since it is pretty straightforward.

Conclusion

Building any application requires design decisions before you start writing code. With distributed applications, you have a wider range of decisions to make compared to standalone systems. This chapter considered some of those aspects and demonstrated what the resultant code might look like. We only touched on the elements of protocol design. There are many formal and informal models. The IETF (Internet Engineering Task Force) created a standard format for its protocol specifications in its RFCs (Requests for Comments), and sooner or later, every network engineer will need to work with RFCs.

CHAPTER 6

▪ ▪ ▪

Managing Character Sets and Encodings

Once upon a time, there was EBCDIC and ASCII. Actually, it was never that simple and has just become more complex over time. There is light on the horizon, but some estimates are that it may be 50 years before we all live in the daylight on this!

Early computers were developed in the English-speaking countries of the United States, the UK, and Australia. As a result of this, assumptions were made about the language and character sets in use. Basically, the Latin alphabet was used, plus numerals, punctuation characters, and a few others. These were then encoded into bytes using ASCII or EBCDIC.

The character-handling mechanisms were based on this: text files and I/O consisted of a sequence of bytes, with each byte representing a single character. String comparison could be done by matching corresponding bytes; conversions from upper- to lowercase could be done by mapping individual bytes, and so on.

There are about 6,500 spoken languages in the world (850 of them in Papua New Guinea!). A few languages use the "English" characters, but most do not. The Romanic languages such as French have adornments on various characters, so that you can write "j'ai arrêté" with two differently accented vowels. Similarly, the Germanic languages have extra characters such as "ß". Even UK English has characters not in the standard ASCII set: the pound symbol "£" and recently the euro "€".

But the world is not restricted to variations on the Latin alphabet. Thailand has its own alphabet, with words looking like this: "ภาษาไทย". There are many other alphabets, and Japan even has two, Hiragana and Katagana.

There are also the hierographic languages such as Chinese where you can write "百度一下，你就知道".

It would be nice from a technical viewpoint if the world just used ASCII. However, the trend is in the opposite direction, with more and more users demanding that software use the language that they are familiar with. If you build an application that can be run in different countries then users will demand that it uses their own language. In a distributed system, different components of the system may be used by users expecting different languages and characters.

Internationalization (i18n) is how you write your applications so that they can handle the variety of languages and cultures. *Localization* (l10n) is the process of customizing your internationalized application to a particular cultural group.

i18n and l10n are big topics in themselves. For example, they cover issues such as colors: while white means "purity" in Western cultures, it means "death" to the Chinese, and "joy" to Egyptians. In this chapter, we just look at issues of character handling.

© Jan Newmarch 2017
J. Newmarch, *Network Programming with Go*, DOI 10.1007/978-1-4842-2692-6_6

Definitions

It is important to be careful about exactly what part of a text-handling system you are talking about. Here is a set of definitions that have proven useful.

Character

A *character* is a "unit of information that roughly corresponds to a grapheme (written symbol) of a natural language, such as a letter, numeral, or punctuation mark" (Wikipedia). A character is "the smallest component of written language that has a semantic value" (Unicode). This includes letters such as 'a' and 'À' (or letters in any other language), digits such as "2", punctuation characters such as "," and various symbols such as the English pound currency symbol "£".

A character is some sort of abstraction of any actual symbol: the character "a" is to any written "a" as a Platonic circle is to any actual circle. The concept of character also includes control characters, which do not correspond to natural language symbols but to other bits of information used to process texts of the language.

A character does not have any particular appearance, although we use the appearance to help recognize the character. However, even the appearance may have to be understood in a context: in mathematics, if you see the symbol π (pi) it is the character for the ratio of circumference to radius of a circle, while if you are reading Greek text, it is the sixteenth letter of the alphabet: "προσ" is the Greek word for "with" and has nothing to do with 3.14159.

Character Repertoire/Character Set

A character repertoire is a set of distinct characters, such as the Latin alphabet. No particular ordering is assumed. In English, although we say that "a" is earlier in the alphabet than "z," we wouldn't say that "a" is less than "z". The "phone book" ordering which puts "McPhee" before "MacRea" shows that "alphabetic ordering" isn't critical to the characters.

A repertoire specifies the names of the characters and often a sample of how the characters might look. For example, the letter "a" might look like "a", "*a*" or "**a**". But it doesn't force them to look like that—they are just samples. The repertoire may make distinctions such as upper- and lowercase, so that "a" and "A" are different. But it may regard them as the same, just with different sample appearances. (Just like some programming languages treat upper- and lowercase as different—Go—but some don't—Basic.). On the other hand, a repertoire might contain different characters with the same sample appearance: the repertoire for a Greek mathematician would have two different characters with appearance π. This is also called a noncoded character set.

Character Code

A character code is a mapping from characters to integers. The mapping for a character set is also called a coded character set or code set. The value of each character in this mapping is often called a code point. ASCII is a code set. The code point for "a" is 97 and for "A" is 65 (decimal).

The character code is still an abstraction. It isn't yet what we will see in text files, or in TCP packets. However, it is getting close, as it supplies the mapping from human-oriented concepts into numerical ones.

Character Encoding

To communicate or store a character, you need to encode it in some way. To transmit a string, you need to encode all characters in the string. There are many possible encodings for any code set.

For example, 7-bit ASCII code points can be encoded as themselves into 8-bit bytes (an octet). So ASCII "A" (with code point 65) is encoded as the 8-bit octet 01000001. However, a different encoding would be to use the top bit for parity checking. For example, with odd parity ASCII "A" would be the octet 11000001. Some protocols such as Sun's XDR use 32-bit word-length encoding. ASCII "A" would be encoded as 00000000 00000000 0000000 01000001.

The character encoding is where we function at the programming level. Our programs deal with encoded characters. It obviously makes a difference whether we are dealing with 8-bit characters with or without parity checking, or with 32-bit characters.

The encoding extends to strings of characters. A word-length even parity encoding of "ABC" might be 10000000 (parity bit in high byte) 0100000011 (C) 01000010 (B) 01000001 (A in low byte). The comments about the importance of an encoding apply equally strongly to strings, where the rules may be different.

Transport Encoding

A character encoding will suffice for handling characters within a single application. However, once you start sending text *between* applications, then there is the further issue of how the bytes, shorts, or words are put on the wire. An encoding can be based on space- and hence bandwidth-saving techniques such as zipping the text. Or it could be reduced to a 7-bit format to allow a parity checking bit, such as base64.

If we do know the character and transport encoding, then it is a matter of programming to manage characters and strings. If we don't know the character or transport encoding then it is a matter of guesswork as to what to do with any particular string. There is no convention for files to signal the character encoding.

There *is* however a convention for signaling encoding in text transmitted across the Internet. It is simple: the header of a text message contains information about the encoding. For example, an HTTP header can contain lines such as the following:

```
Content-Type: text/html; charset=ISO-8859-4
Content-Encoding: gzip
```

This says that the character set is ISO 8859-4 (corresponding to certain countries in Europe) with the default encoding, but then gziped. The second part—the content encoding—is what we are referring to as "transfer encoding" (IETF RFC 2130).

But how do you read this information? Isn't it encoded? Don't we have a chicken and egg situation? Well, no. The convention is that such information is given in ASCII (to be precise, US ASCII) so that a program can read the headers and then adjust its encoding for the rest of the document.

ASCII

ASCII has the repertoire of the English characters plus digits, punctuation, and some control characters. The code points for ASCII are given by this familiar table:

Oct	Dec	Hex	Char	Oct	Dec	Hex	Char
000	0	00	NUL '¥0'	100	64	40	@
001	1	01	SOH	101	65	41	A
002	2	02	STX	102	66	42	B
003	3	03	ETX	103	67	43	C
004	4	04	EOT	104	68	44	D
005	5	05	ENQ	105	69	45	E
006	6	06	ACK	106	70	46	F
007	7	07	BEL '\a'	107	71	47	G

010	8	08	BS	'\b'	110	72	48	H
011	9	09	HT	'\t'	111	73	49	I
012	10	0A	LF	'\n'	112	74	4A	J
013	11	0B	VT	'\v'	113	75	4B	K
014	12	0C	FF	'\f'	114	76	4C	L
015	13	0D	CR	'\r'	115	77	4D	M
016	14	0E	SO		116	78	4E	N
017	15	0F	SI		117	79	4F	O
020	16	10	DLE		120	80	50	P
021	17	11	DC1		121	81	51	Q
022	18	12	DC2		122	82	52	R
023	19	13	DC3		123	83	53	S
024	20	14	DC4		124	84	54	T
025	21	15	NAK		125	85	55	U
026	22	16	SYN		126	86	56	V
027	23	17	ETB		127	87	57	W
030	24	18	CAN		130	88	58	X
031	25	19	EM		131	89	59	Y
032	26	1A	SUB		132	90	5A	Z
033	27	1B	ESC		133	91	5B	[
034	28	1C	FS		134	92	5C	\
035	29	1D	GS		135	93	5D	]
036	30	1E	RS		136	94	5E	^
037	31	1F	US		137	95	5F	_
040	32	20	SPACE		140	96	60	`
041	33	21	!		141	97	61	a
042	34	22	"		142	98	62	b
043	35	23	#		143	99	63	c
044	36	24	$		144	100	64	d
045	37	25	%		145	101	65	e
046	38	26	&		146	102	66	f
047	39	27	'		147	103	67	g
050	40	28	(		150	104	68	h
051	41	29	)		151	105	69	i
052	42	2A	*		152	106	6A	j
053	43	2B	+		153	107	6B	k
054	44	2C	,		154	108	6C	l
055	45	2D	-		155	109	6D	m
056	46	2E	.		156	110	6E	n
057	47	2F	/		157	111	6F	o
060	48	30	0		160	112	70	p
061	49	31	1		161	113	71	q
062	50	32	2		162	114	72	r
063	51	33	3		163	115	73	s
064	52	34	4		164	116	74	t
065	53	35	5		165	117	75	u
066	54	36	6		166	118	76	v
067	55	37	7		167	119	77	w
070	56	38	8		170	120	78	x
071	57	39	9		171	121	79	y
072	58	3A	:		172	122	7A	z

073	59	3B	;		173	123	7B	{
074	60	3C	<		174	124	7C		
075	61	3D	=		175	125	7D	}
076	62	3E	>		176	126	7E	~
077	63	3F	?		177	127	7F	DEL

(An interesting four-column version is at Robbie's Garbage, Four Column ASCII at https://garbagecollected.org/2017/01/31/four-column-ascii/.)

The most common encoding for ASCII uses the code points as 7-bit bytes, so that the encoding of "A" for example is 65.

This set is actually *US ASCII*. Due to European desires for accented characters, some punctuation characters are omitted to form a minimal set, ISO 646, while there are "national variants" with suitable European characters. The web site http://www.cs.tut.fi/~jkorpela/chars.html by Jukka Korpela has more information for those interested. You don't need these variants for the work in this book, though.

ISO 8859

Octets are now the standard size for bytes. This allows 128 extra code points for extensions to ASCII. A number of different code sets to capture the repertoires of various subsets of European languages are the ISO 8859 series. ISO 8859-1 is also known as Latin-1 and covers many languages in western Europe, while others in this series cover the rest of Europe and even Hebrew, Arabic, and Thai. For example, ISO 8859-5 includes the Cyrillic characters of countries such as Russia, while ISO 8859-8 includes the Hebrew alphabet.

The standard encoding for these character sets is to use their code point as an 8-bit value. For example, the character "Á" in ISO 8859-1 has the code point 193 and is encoded as 193. All of the ISO 8859 series have the bottom 128 values identical to ASCII, so that the ASCII characters are the same in all of these sets.

The HTML specifications used to recommend the ISO 8859-1 character set. HTML 3.2 was the last one to do so, and after that HTML 4.0 recommended Unicode. In 2008 Google made an estimate that of the pages it sees, about 20% were still in ISO 8859 format while 20% were still in ASCII (See "Unicode nearing 50% of the web" at http://googleblog.blogspot.com/2010/01/unicode-nearing-50-of-web.html). See also http://pinyin.info/news/2015/utf-8-unicode-vs-other-encodings-over-time/ and https://w3techs.com/technologies/history_overview/character_encoding for more background information.

Unicode

Neither ASCII nor ISO 8859 cover the languages based on hieroglyphs. Chinese is estimated to have about 20,000 separate characters, with about 5,000 in common use. These need more than a byte, and typically two bytes has been used. There have been many of these two-byte character sets: Big5, EUC-TW, GB2312, and GBK/GBX for Chinese, JIS X 0208 for Japanese, and so on. These encodings are generally not mutually compatible.

Unicode is an embracing standard character set intended to cover all major character sets in use. It includes European, Asian, Indian, and many more. It is now up to version 9.0 and has 128,172 characters. The number of code points now exceeds 65,536. That is more than 2^{16}. This has implications for character encodings.

The first 256 code points correspond to ISO 8859-1, with US ASCII as the first 128. There is thus a backward compatibility with these major character sets, as the code points for ISO 8859-1 and ASCII are exactly the same in Unicode. The same is not true for other character sets: for example, while most of the Big5 characters are also in Unicode, the code points are not the same. The web site http://moztw.org/docs/big5/table/unicode1.1-obsolete.txt contains one example of a (large) table mapping from Big5 to Unicode.

To represent Unicode characters in a computer system, an encoding must be used. The encoding UCS is a two-byte encoding using the code point values of the Unicode characters. However, since there are now too many characters in Unicode to fit them all into 2 bytes, this encoding is obsolete and no longer used. Instead there are:

- UTF-32 is a 4-byte encoding, but is not commonly used, and HTML 5 warns explicitly against using it.

- UTF-16 encodes the most common characters into 2 bytes with a further 2 bytes for the "overflow," with ASCII and ISO 8859-1 having the usual values.

- UTF-8 uses between 1 and 4 bytes per character, with ASCII having the usual values (but not ISO 8859-1).

- UTF-7 is used sometimes, but is not common.

UTF-8, Go, and Runes

UTF-8 is the most commonly used encoding. Google estimated that in 2008 that 50% of the pages that it sees are encoded in UTF-8 and that proportion is increasing. The ASCII set has the same encoding values in UTF-8, so a UTF-8 reader can read text consisting of just ASCII characters as well as text from the full Unicode set.

Go uses UTF-8 encoded characters in its strings. Each character is of type rune. This is an alias for int32. A Unicode character can be up to 4 bytes in UTF-8 encoding so that 4 bytes are needed to represent all characters. In terms of characters, a string is an array of runes using 1, 2, or 4 bytes per rune.

A string is also an array of bytes, but you have to be careful: only for the ASCII subset is a byte equal to a character. All other characters occupy 2, 3, or 4 bytes. This means that the length of a string in characters (runes) is generally not the same as the length of its byte array. They are equal only when the string consists of ASCII characters only.

The following program fragment illustrates this. If you take a UTF-8 string and test its length, you get the length of the underlying byte array. But if you cast the string to an array of runes [ ]rune then you get an array of the Unicode code points, which is generally the number of characters:

```
str := "百度一下，你就知道"

println("String length", len([]rune(str)))
println("Byte length", len(str))

prints
String length 9
Byte length 27
```

A more detailed explanation of strings and runes is given by The Go Blog (see https://blog.golang.org/strings).

UTF-8 Client and Server

Possibly surprisingly, you need do nothing special to handle UTF-8 text in either the client or the server. The underlying data type for a UTF-8 string in Go is a byte array, and as we just saw, Go looks after encoding the string into 1, 2, 3, or 4 bytes as needed. The length of the string is the length of the byte array, so you write any UTF-8 string by writing the byte array.

Similarly to read a string, you just read into a byte array and then cast the array to a string using `string([]byte)`. If Go cannot properly decode bytes into Unicode characters, then it gives the Unicode Replacement Character `\uFFFD`. The length of the resulting byte array is the length of the legal portion of the string.

So the clients and servers given in earlier chapters work perfectly well with UTF-8 encoded text.

ASCII Client and Server

The ASCII characters have the same encoding in ASCII and in UTF-8. So ordinary UTF-8 character handling works fine for ASCII characters. No special handling needs to be done.

UTF-16 and Go

UTF-16 deals with arrays of short 16-bit unsigned integers. The package utf16 is designed to manage such arrays. To convert a normal Go string, that is a UTF-8 string, into UTF-16, you first extract the code points by coercing it into a `[]rune` and then use `utf16.Encode` to produce an array of type uint16.

Similarly, to decode an array of unsigned short UTF-16 values into a Go string, you use `utf16.Decode` to convert it into code points as type `[]rune` and then to a string. The following code fragment illustrates this:

```
str := "百度一下，你就知道"

runes := utf16.Encode([]rune(str))
ints := utf16.Decode(runes)

str = string(ints)
```

These type conversions need to be applied by clients or servers as appropriate, to read and write 16-bit short integers, as shown next.

Little-Endian and Big-Endian

Unfortunately, there is a little devil lurking behind UTF-16. It is basically an encoding of characters into 16-bit short integers. The big question is: for each short, how is it written as two bytes? The top one first, or the top one second? Either way is fine, as long as the receiver uses the same convention as the sender.

Unicode has addressed this with a special character known as the *BOM* (byte order marker). This is a zero-width non-printing character, so you never see it in text. But its value `0xfffe` is chosen so that you can tell the byte order:

- In a big-endian system, it is FF FE
- In a little-endian system, it is FE FF

Text will sometimes place the BOM as the first character in the text. The reader can then examine these two bytes to determine what endian-ness has been used.

UTF-16 Client and Server

Using the BOM convention, you can write a server that prepends a BOM and writes a string in UTF-16 as UTF16Server.go:

```go
/* UTF16 Server
 */
package main

import (
        "fmt"
        "net"
        "os"
        "unicode/utf16"
)

const BOM = '\ufffe'

func main() {

        service := "0.0.0.0:1210"
        tcpAddr, err := net.ResolveTCPAddr("tcp", service)
        checkError(err)

        listener, err := net.ListenTCP("tcp", tcpAddr)
        checkError(err)

        for {
                conn, err := listener.Accept()
                if err != nil {
                        continue
                }

                str := "j'ai arrÃªtÃ©"
                shorts := utf16.Encode([]rune(str))
                writeShorts(conn, shorts)

                conn.Close() // we're finished
        }
}

func writeShorts(conn net.Conn, shorts []uint16) {
        var bytes [2]byte

        // send the BOM as first two bytes
        bytes[0] = BOM >> 8
        bytes[1] = BOM & 255
        _, err := conn.Write(bytes[0:])
        if err != nil {
                return
        }
```

```
        for _, v := range shorts {
                bytes[0] = byte(v >> 8)
                bytes[1] = byte(v & 255)

                _, err = conn.Write(bytes[0:])
                if err != nil {
                        return
                }
        }
}

func checkError(err error) {
        if err != nil {
                fmt.Println("Fatal error ", err.Error())
                os.Exit(1)
        }
}
```

While a client that reads a byte stream, extracts and examines the BOM, and then decodes the rest of the stream is UTF16Client.go:

```
/* UTF16 Client
 */
package main

import (
        "fmt"
        "net"
        "os"
        "unicode/utf16"
)

const BOM = '\ufffe'

func main() {
        if len(os.Args) != 2 {
                fmt.Println("Usage: ", os.Args[0], "host:port")
                os.Exit(1)
        }
        service := os.Args[1]

        conn, err := net.Dial("tcp", service)
        checkError(err)

        shorts := readShorts(conn)
        ints := utf16.Decode(shorts)
        str := string(ints)

        fmt.Println(str)

        os.Exit(0)
}
```

```go
func readShorts(conn net.Conn) []uint16 {
        var buf [512]byte

        // read everything into the buffer
        n, err := conn.Read(buf[0:2])
        for true {
                m, err := conn.Read(buf[n:])
                if m == 0 || err != nil {
                        break
                }
                n += m
        }

        checkError(err)
        var shorts []uint16
        shorts = make([]uint16, n/2)

        if buf[0] == 0xff && buf[1] == 0xfe {
                // big endian
                for i := 2; i < n; i += 2 {
                        shorts[i/2] = uint16(buf[i])<<8 + uint16(buf[i+1])
                }
        } else if buf[1] == 0xff && buf[0] == 0xfe {
                // little endian
                for i := 2; i < n; i += 2 {
                        shorts[i/2] = uint16(buf[i+1])<<8 + uint16(buf[i])
                }
        } else {
                // unknown byte order
                fmt.Println("Unknown order")
        }
        return shorts

}

func checkError(err error) {
        if err != nil {
                fmt.Println("Fatal error ", err.Error())
                os.Exit(1)
        }
}
```

The client prints "j'ai arrÃªtÃ©" as sent by the server.

Unicode Gotchas

This book is not about i18n issues. In particular, we don't want to delve into the arcane areas of Unicode. But you should know that Unicode is not a simple encoding and there are many complexities. For example, some earlier character sets used *non-spacing* characters, particularly for accents. This was brought into Unicode, so you can produce accented characters in two ways: as a single Unicode character, or as a pair of non-spacing accent plus non-accented character. For example, U+04D6, "Cyrillic capital letter ie with breve" is a single character, Ӗ. It is equivalent to U+0415, "Cyrillic capital letter ie" combined with the breve accent U+0306 "combining breve". This makes string comparison difficult on occasions. This could potentially be the cause of some very obscure errors.

There is a package called golang.org/x/text/unicode/norm in the Go experimental tree that can normalize Unicode strings. It can be installed into your Go package tree:

```
go get golang.org/x/text/unicode/norm
```

Note that it is a package in the "sub-repositories" Go Project tree and may not be stable.

There are actually four standard Unicode forms. The most common is NFC. A string can be converted to NFC form by norm.NFC.String(str). The following program called norm.go forms strings of Ӗ in two ways as a single character and as a composed character and prints the strings, their bytes, and then the normalized form and its bytes.

```go
package main

import (
        "fmt"
        "golang.org/x/text/unicode/norm"
)

func main() {
        str1 := "\u04d6"
        str2 := "\u0415\u0306"
        norm_str2 := norm.NFC.String(str2)
        bytes1 := []byte(str1)
        bytes2 := []byte(str2)
        norm_bytes2 := []byte(norm_str2)

        fmt.Println("Single char ", str1, " bytes ", bytes1)
        fmt.Println("Composed char ", str2, " bytes ", bytes2)
        fmt.Println("Normalized char", norm_str2, " bytes ", norm_bytes2)
}
```

Here is the output:

```
Single char  Ӗ bytes  [211 150]
Composed char  Ӗ bytes  [208 149 204 134]
Normalized char Ӗ bytes  [211 150]
```

ISO 8859 and Go

The ISO 8859 series are 8-bit character sets for different parts of Europe and some other areas. They all have the ASCII set common in the low part, but differ in the top part. According to Google, ISO 8859 codes accounted for about 20% of the web pages it saw, but that has now dropped.

The first code, ISO 8859-1 or Latin-1, has the first 256 characters in common with Unicode. The encoded value of the Latin-1 characters is the same in UTF-16 and in the default ISO 8859-1 encoding. But this doesn't really help much, as UTF-16 is a 16-bit encoding and ISO 8859-1 is an 8-bit encoding. UTF-8 is a 8-bit encoding, but it uses the top bit to signal extra bytes, so only the ASCII subset overlaps for UTF-8 and ISO 8859-1. So UTF-8 doesn't help much either.

But the ISO 8859 series don't have any complex issues. Each character in each set corresponds to a unique Unicode character. For example, in ISO 8859-2, the character "Latin capital letter I with ogonek" has ISO 8859-2 code point 0xc7 (in hexadecimal) and corresponding Unicode code point of U+012E. Transforming either way between an ISO 8859 set and the corresponding Unicode characters is essentially just a table lookup.

The table from ISO 8859 code points to the Unicode code points and could be done as an array of 256 integers. But many of these will have the same value as the index. So we just use a map of the different ones, and those not in the map take the index value.

For ISO 8859-2 a portion of the map is as follows:

```
var unicodeToISOMap = map[int] uint8 {
    0x12e: 0xc7,
    0x10c: 0xc8,
    0x118: 0xca,
    // plus more
}
```

A function to convert UTF-8 strings to an array of ISO 8859-2 bytes is as follows:

```
/* Turn a UTF-8 string into an ISO 8859 encoded byte array
*/
func unicodeStrToISO(str string) []byte {
        // get the unicode code points
        codePoints := []int(str)

        // create a byte array of the same length
        bytes := make([]byte, len(codePoints))

        for n, v := range(codePoints) {
                // see if the point is in the exception map
                iso, ok := unicodeToISOMap[v]
                if !ok {
                        // just use the value
                        iso = uint8(v)
                }
                bytes[n] = iso
        }
        return bytes
}
```

In a similar way, you can change an array of ISO 8859-2 bytes into a UTF-8 string:

```
var isoToUnicodeMap = map[uint8] int {
    0xc7: 0x12e,
    0xc8: 0x10c,
    0xca: 0x118,
    // and more
}
```

```
func isoBytesToUnicode(bytes []byte) string {
        codePoints := make([]int, len(bytes))
        for n, v := range(bytes) {
                unicode, ok :=isoToUnicodeMap[v]
                if !ok {
                        unicode = int(v)
                }
                codePoints[n] = unicode
        }
        return string(codePoints)
}
```

These functions can be used to read and write UTF-8 strings as ISO 8859-2 bytes. By changing the mapping table, you can cover the other ISO 8859 codes. Latin-1, or ISO 8859-1, is a special case—the exception map is empty as the code points for Latin-1 are the same in Unicode. You could also use the same technique for other character sets based on a table mapping, such as Windows 1252.

Other Character Sets and Go

There are very, very many character set encodings. According to Google, these generally only have a small use in Web documents, which will hopefully decrease even further with time. But if your software wants to capture all markets, then you may need to handle them.

In the simplest cases, a lookup table will suffice. But that doesn't always work. The character coding ISO 2022 minimized character set sizes by using a finite state machine to swap code pages in and out. This was borrowed by some of the Japanese encodings and makes things very complex.

Go presently only gives package support for any of these other character sets in the "sub-repositories" package tree. For example, the package golang.org/x/text/encoding/japanese handles EUC-JP and Shift JIS.

Conclusion

There hasn't been much code in this chapter. Instead, there have been some of the concepts of a very complex area. It's up to you: if you want to assume everyone speaks U.S. English then the world is simple. But if you want your applications to be usable by the rest of the world, you need to pay attention to these complexities.

CHAPTER 7

Security

Although the Internet was originally designed as a system to withstand attacks by hostile agents, it developed into a cooperative environment of relatively trusted entities. Alas, those days are long gone. Spam mail, denial of service (DoS) attacks, phishing attempts, and so on are indicative that anyone using the Internet does so at their own risk.

Applications have to be built to work correctly in hostile situations. "Correctly" no longer means just getting the functional aspects of the program correct, but also means ensuring privacy and integrity of data transferred, access only to legitimate users, and other security issues.

This of course makes your programs much more complex. There are *difficult* and *subtle* computing problems involved in making applications secure. Attempts to do it yourself (such as making up your own encryption libraries) are usually doomed to failure. Instead, you need to use the libraries designed by security professionals.

Why should you bother, if it makes things harder? Almost every day there are reports of leaked credit card details, of private servers being run by government officials and being hacked, and reports of systems being brought down by denial of service attacks. Many of these attacks are possible by coding errors in network-facing applications, such as buffer overflows, cross-site scripting, and SQL injection. But a large number of errors can be traced to poor network handling: passwords passed in plain text, security credentials requested and then not checked, and just trusting the environment you are in. For example, a colleague recently purchased a home IoT (Internet of Things) device. He used wireshark to see what it was doing on his network and discovered it was sending RTMP messages with authentication token `admin`. `admin`. An easy attack vector, without even having to crack passwords! Drones made by one well-known company use encryption with known flaws and can be "stolen" by other drones. An increasingly common method of stealing data is to act as a "rogue" wireless access point, pretending to be a legitimate access point in a local coffee shop, but monitoring everything that passes through, including your bank account details. These are "low hanging fruit". The scope of data breaches is shown by "World's Biggest Data Breaches" at `http://www.informationisbeautiful.net/visualizations/worlds-biggest-data-breaches-hacks/`.

This chapter addresses the basic cryptographic tools given by Go that you can build into your applications. If you don't and your company loses a million dollars—or worse, your customers lose a million dollars—then the blame comes back to you.

ISO Security Architecture

The ISO OSI (open systems interconnect) seven-layer model of distributed systems is well known and is repeated in Figure 7-1.

© Jan Newmarch 2017
J. Newmarch, *Network Programming with Go*, DOI 10.1007/978-1-4842-2692-6_7

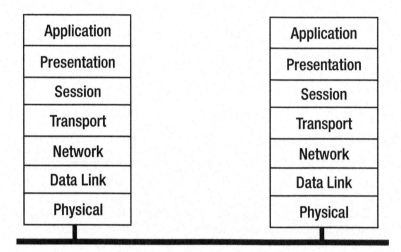

Figure 7-1. *The OSI seven-layer model of distributed systems*

What is less well known is that ISO built a whole series of documents upon this architecture. For our purposes here, the most important is the ISO Security Architecture model, ISO 7498-2. This requires purchase, but the ITU has produced a document technically aligned with this, X.800, which is available from ITU at `https://www.itu.int/rec/dologin_pub.asp?lang=e&id=T-REC-X.800-199103-I!!PDF-E&type=items`.

Functions and Levels

The principal functions required of a security system are as follows:

- Authentication: Proof of identity

- Data integrity: Data is not tampered with

- Confidentiality: Data is not exposed to others

- Notarization/signature

- Access control

- Assurance/availability

These are required at the following levels of the OSI stack:

- Peer entity authentication (3, 4, 7)

- Data origin authentication (3, 4, 7)

- Access control service (3, 4, 7)

- Connection confidentiality (1, 2, 3, 4, 6, 7)

- Connectionless confidentiality (1, 2, 3, 4, 6, 7)

- Selective field confidentiality (6, 7)

- Traffic flow confidentiality (1, 3, 7)

- Connection integrity with recovery (4, 7)

- Connection integrity without recovery (4, 7)

- Connection integrity selective field (7)

- Connectionless integrity selective field (7)

- Non-repudiation at origin (7)

- Non-repudiation of receipt (7)

Mechanisms

The mechanisms to achieve this level of security are as follows:

- Peer entity authentication

  - Encryption

  - Digital signature

  - Authentication exchange

- Data origin authentication

  - Encryption

  - Digital signature

- Access control service

  - Access control lists

  - Passwords

  - Capabilities lists

  - Labels

- Connection confidentiality

  - Encryption

  - Routing control

- Connectionless confidentiality

  - Encryption

  - Routing control

- Selective field confidentiality

  - Encryption

- Traffic flow confidentiality

  - Encryption

  - Traffic padding

  - routing control

- Connection integrity with recovery

    - Encryption

    - Data integrity

- Connection integrity without recovery

    - Encryption

    - Data integrity

- Connection integrity selective field

    - encryption

    - data integrity

- Connectionless integrity

    - Encryption

    - Digital signature

    - Data integrity

- Connectionless integrity selective field

    - Encryption

    - Digital signature

    - Data integrity

- Non-repudiation at origin

    - Digital signature

    - Data integrity

    - Notarization

- Non-repudiation of receipt

    - Digital signature

    - Data integrity

    - Notarization

Data Integrity

Ensuring data integrity means supplying a means of testing that the data has not been tampered with. Usually this is done by forming a simple number out of the bytes in the data. This process is called *hashing* and the resulting number is called a *hash* or *hash value*.

A naive hashing algorithm is just to sum up all the bytes in the data. However, this still allows almost any amount of changing the data around and still preserving the hash values. For example, an attacker could just swap two bytes. This preserves the hash value, but could end up with you owing someone $65,536 instead of $256.

Hashing algorithms used for security purposes have to be "strong," so that it is very difficult for an attacker to find a different sequence of bytes with the same hash value. This makes it hard to modify the data to the attacker's purposes. Security researchers are constantly testing hash algorithms to see if they can break them— that is, find a simple way of coming up with byte sequences to match a hash value. They have devised a series of *cryptographic* hashing algorithms that are believed to be strong.

Go has support for several hashing algorithms, including MD4, MD5, RIPEMD-160, SHA1, SHA224, SHA256, SHA384, and SHA512. They all follow the same pattern as far as the Go programmer is concerned: a function New (or similar) in the appropriate package returns a Hash object from the hash package.

A hash has an io.Writer, and you write the data to be hashed to this writer. You can query the number of bytes in the hash value by Size and the hash value by Sum.

A typical case is MD5 hashing. This uses the md5 package. The hash value is a 16-byte array. This is typically printed out in ASCII form as four hexadecimal numbers, each made of four bytes. A simple program is MD5Hash.go:

```
/* MD5Hash
 */

package main

import (
        "crypto/md5"
        "fmt"
)

func main() {
        hash := md5.New()
        bytes := []byte("hello\n")
        hash.Write(bytes)
        hashValue := hash.Sum(nil)
        hashSize := hash.Size()
        for n := 0; n < hashSize; n += 4 {
                var val uint32
                val = uint32(hashValue[n])<<24 +
                        uint32(hashValue[n+1])<<16 +
                        uint32(hashValue[n+2])<<8 +
                        uint32(hashValue[n+3])
                fmt.Printf("%x ", val)
        }
        fmt.Println()
}
```

This program prints "b1946ac9 2492d234 7c6235b4 d2611184".

A variation on this is HMAC (Keyed-Hash Message Authentication Code), which adds a key to the hash algorithm. There is little change in using this. To use MD5 hashing along with a key, replace the call to hash := md5.New() with this:

```
hash := hmac.New(md5.New, []byte("secret"))
```

Symmetric Key Encryption

There are two major mechanisms used for encrypting data. Symmetric key encryption uses a single key that is the same for both encryption and decryption. This key needs to be known to both the encrypting and the decrypting agents. How this key is transmitted between the agents is not discussed.

As with hashing, there are many encryption algorithms. Many are now known to have weaknesses, and in general algorithms become weaker over time as computers get faster. Go has support for several symmetric key algorithms such as AES and DES.

The algorithms are *block* algorithms. That is, they work on blocks of data. If your data is not aligned to the block size, you will have to pad it with extra blanks at the end.

Each algorithm is represented by a Cipher object. This is created by NewCipher in the appropriate package and takes the symmetric key as parameter.

Once you have a cipher, you can use it to encrypt and decrypt blocks of data. We use AES-128, which has a key size of 128 bits (16 bytes) and a block size of 128 bits. The size of the key determines which version of AES is used. A program to illustrate this is Aes.go:

```go
/* Aes
 */

package main

import (
        "bytes"
        "crypto/aes"
        "fmt"
)

func main() {
        key := []byte("my key, len 16 b")
        cipher, err := aes.NewCipher(key)
        if err != nil {
                fmt.Println(err.Error())
        }
        src := []byte("hello 16 b block")

        var enc [16]byte
        cipher.Encrypt(enc[0:], src)

        var decrypt [16]byte
        cipher.Decrypt(decrypt[0:], enc[0:])
        result := bytes.NewBuffer(nil)
        result.Write(decrypt[0:])
        fmt.Println(string(result.Bytes()))
}
```

This encrypts and decrypts the 16-byte block "hello 16 b block" using the shared 16-byte key "my key, len 16 b".

Public Key Encryption

The other major type of encryption is public key encryption. Public key encryption and decryption requires *two* keys: one to encrypt and a second one to decrypt. The encryption key is usually made public in some way so that anyone can encrypt messages to you. The decryption key must stay private; otherwise, everyone would be able to decrypt those messages! Public key systems are asymmetric, with different keys for different uses.

There are many public key encryption systems supported by Go. A typical one is the RSA scheme.

A program generating RSA private and public keys from a random number is GenRSAKeys.go:

```go
/* GenRSAKeys
 */

package main

import (
        "crypto/rand"
        "crypto/rsa"
        "crypto/x509"
        "encoding/gob"
        "encoding/pem"
        "fmt"
        "os"
)

func main() {
        reader := rand.Reader
        bitSize := 512
        key, err := rsa.GenerateKey(reader, bitSize)
        checkError(err)

        fmt.Println("Private key primes", key.Primes[0].String(), key.Primes[1].String())
        fmt.Println("Private key exponent", key.D.String())

        publicKey := key.PublicKey
        fmt.Println("Public key modulus", publicKey.N.String())
        fmt.Println("Public key exponent", publicKey.E)

        saveGobKey("private.key", key)
        saveGobKey("public.key", publicKey)

        savePEMKey("private.pem", key)
}

func saveGobKey(fileName string, key interface{}) {
        outFile, err := os.Create(fileName)
        checkError(err)
        encoder := gob.NewEncoder(outFile)
        err = encoder.Encode(key)
```

```
            checkError(err)
            outFile.Close()
}

func savePEMKey(fileName string, key *rsa.PrivateKey) {

            outFile, err := os.Create(fileName)
            checkError(err)

            var privateKey = &pem.Block{Type: "RSA PRIVATE KEY",
                    Bytes: x509.MarshalPKCS1PrivateKey(key)}

            pem.Encode(outFile, privateKey)

            outFile.Close()
}

func checkError(err error) {
        if err != nil {
                fmt.Println("Fatal error ", err.Error())
                os.Exit(1)
        }
}
```

The program also saves the certificates using gob serialization. They can be read back by the LoadRSAKeys.go program:

```
/* LoadRSAKeys
 */

package main

import (
        "crypto/rsa"
        "encoding/gob"
        "fmt"
        "os"
)

func main() {
        var key rsa.PrivateKey
        loadKey("private.key", &key)

        fmt.Println("Private key primes", key.Primes[0].String(), key.Primes[1].String())
        fmt.Println("Private key exponent", key.D.String())

        var publicKey rsa.PublicKey
        loadKey("public.key", &publicKey)
```

```
        fmt.Println("Public key modulus", publicKey.N.String())
        fmt.Println("Public key exponent", publicKey.E)
}

func loadKey(fileName string, key interface{}) {
        inFile, err := os.Open(fileName)
        checkError(err)
        decoder := gob.NewDecoder(inFile)
        err = decoder.Decode(key)
        checkError(err)
        inFile.Close()
}

func checkError(err error) {
        if err != nil {
                fmt.Println("Fatal error ", err.Error())
                os.Exit(1)
        }
}
```

X.509 Certificates

A Public Key Infrastructure (PKI) is a framework for a collection of public keys, along with additional information such as owner name and location, and links between them giving some sort of approval mechanism.

The principal PKI in use today is based on X.509 certificates. For example, web browsers use them to verify the identity of web sites.

An example program to generate a self-signed X.509 certificate for my web site and store it in a .cer file is GenX509Cert.go:

```
/* GenX509Cert
 */

package main

import (
        "crypto/rand"
        "crypto/rsa"
        "crypto/x509"
        "crypto/x509/pkix"
        "encoding/gob"
        "encoding/pem"
        "fmt"
        "math/big"
        "os"
        "time"
)
```

```go
func main() {
        random := rand.Reader

        var key rsa.PrivateKey
        loadKey("private.key", &key)

        now := time.Now()
        then := now.Add(60 * 60 * 24 * 365 * 1000 * 1000 * 1000) // one year
        template := x509.Certificate{
                SerialNumber: big.NewInt(1),
                Subject: pkix.Name{
                        CommonName:   "jan.newmarch.name",
                        Organization: []string{"Jan Newmarch"},
                },
                NotBefore: now,
                NotAfter:  then,

                SubjectKeyId: []byte{1, 2, 3, 4},
                KeyUsage:     x509.KeyUsageCertSign | x509.KeyUsageKeyEncipherment | x509.
KeyUsageDigitalSignature,

                BasicConstraintsValid: true,
                IsCA:        true,
                DNSNames: []string{"jan.newmarch.name", "localhost"},
        }
        derBytes, err := x509.CreateCertificate(random, &template,
                &template, &key.PublicKey, &key)
        checkError(err)

        certCerFile, err := os.Create("jan.newmarch.name.cer")
        checkError(err)
        certCerFile.Write(derBytes)
        certCerFile.Close()

        certPEMFile, err := os.Create("jan.newmarch.name.pem")
        checkError(err)
        pem.Encode(certPEMFile, &pem.Block{Type: "CERTIFICATE", Bytes: derBytes})
        certPEMFile.Close()

        keyPEMFile, err := os.Create("private.pem")
        checkError(err)
        pem.Encode(keyPEMFile, &pem.Block{Type: "RSA PRIVATE KEY",
                Bytes: x509.MarshalPKCS1PrivateKey(&key)})
        keyPEMFile.Close()
}

func loadKey(fileName string, key interface{}) {
        inFile, err := os.Open(fileName)
        checkError(err)
```

```
          decoder := gob.NewDecoder(inFile)
          err = decoder.Decode(key)
          checkError(err)
          inFile.Close()
}

func checkError(err error) {
          if err != nil {
                    fmt.Println("Fatal error ", err.Error())
                    os.Exit(1)
          }
}
```

This can then be read back in by LoadX509Cert.go:

```
/* LoadX509Cert
 */

package main

import (
          "crypto/x509"
          "fmt"
          "os"
)

func main() {
          certCerFile, err := os.Open("jan.newmarch.name.cer")
          checkError(err)
          derBytes := make([]byte, 1000) // bigger than the file
          count, err := certCerFile.Read(derBytes)
          checkError(err)
          certCerFile.Close()

          // trim the bytes to actual length in call
          cert, err := x509.ParseCertificate(derBytes[0:count])
          checkError(err)

          fmt.Printf("Name %s\n", cert.Subject.CommonName)
          fmt.Printf("Not before %s\n", cert.NotBefore.String())
          fmt.Printf("Not after %s\n", cert.NotAfter.String())

}

func checkError(err error) {
          if err != nil {
                    fmt.Println("Fatal error ", err.Error())
                    os.Exit(1)
          }
}
```

TLS

Encryption/decryption schemes are of limited use if you have to do all the heavy lifting yourself. The most popular mechanism on the Internet to give support for encrypted message passing is currently TLS (Transport Layer Security), which was formerly SSL (Secure Sockets Layer).

In TLS, a client and a server negotiate identity using X.509 certificates. Once this is complete, a secret key is invented between them, and all encryption/decryption is done using this key. The negotiation is relatively slow, but once it's complete, the faster secret key mechanism is used. The server is *required* to have a certificate; the client *may* have one if needed.

A Basic Client

We first illustrate connecting to a server that has a certificate signed by a "well known" certificate authority (CA) such as RSA. The program to get head information from a web server can be adapted to get head information from a TLS web server. The program is TLSGetHead.go. (We are illustrating TLS.Dial here, and will discuss HTTPS in a later chapter.)

```
/* TLSGetHead
 */
package main

import (
        "crypto/tls"
        "fmt"
        "io/ioutil"
        "os"
)

func main() {
        if len(os.Args) != 2 {
                fmt.Println("Usage: ", os.Args[0], "host:port")
                os.Exit(1)
        }
        service := os.Args[1]

        conn, err := tls.Dial("tcp", service, nil)
        checkError(err)

        _, err = conn.Write([]byte("HEAD / HTTP/1.0\r\n\r\n"))
        checkError(err)

        result, err := ioutil.ReadAll(conn)
        checkError(err)

        fmt.Println(string(result))

        conn.Close()
        os.Exit(0)
}
```

```
func checkError(err error) {
        if err != nil {
                fmt.Println("Fatal error ", err.Error())
                os.Exit(1)
        }
}
```

When run against an appropriate site such as `www.google.com:443`:

```
go run TLSGetHead.go www.google.com:443
```

It produces output such as this:

```
HTTP/1.0 302 Found
Cache-Control: private
Content-Type: text/html; charset=UTF-8
Location: https://www.google.com.au/?gfe_rd=cr&ei=L3lvWKSXMdPr8AfvhqKIBg
Content-Length: 263
Date: Fri, 06 Jan 2017 11:02:07 GMT
Alt-Svc: quic=":443"; ma=2592000; v="35,34"
```

Other sites may produce other responses, but this client is still happy to have set up the TLS session with a properly authenticating server.

It's interesting to run this against the site `www.gooogle.com` (note the extra *o*!):

```
go run TLSGetHead.go www.gooogle.com:443
```

This site actually belongs to Google, as they have probably bought it to reduce fraud risk. The program throws a fatal error, as the site certificate is not for *gooogle* with three os:

```
Fatal error  x509: certificate is valid for google.com, *.2mdn.net, *.android.com,
*.appengine.google.com, *.au.doubleclick.net, *.cc-dt.com, *.cloud.google.com, ...
```

A browser such as Firefox pointed to the same triple-o site will also give a security alert.

Server Using a Self-Signed Certificate

If the server uses a self-signed certificate, as might be used internally in an organization or when experimenting, the Go package when will generate an error: `"x509: certificate signed by unknown authority"`. Either the certificate must be installed into the client's operating system (which will be O/S dependent), or the client must install the certificate as a root CA. We will show this second way.

An echo server using TLS with *any* certificate is `TLSEchoServer.go`:

```
/* TLSEchoServer
 */
package main

import (
        "crypto/rand"
        "crypto/tls"
```

```go
        "fmt"
        "net"
        "os"
        "time"
)

func main() {

        cert, err := tls.LoadX509KeyPair("jan.newmarch.name.pem", "private.pem")
        checkError(err)
        config := tls.Config{Certificates: []tls.Certificate{cert}}

        now := time.Now()
        config.Time = func() time.Time { return now }
        config.Rand = rand.Reader

        service := "0.0.0.0:1200"

        listener, err := tls.Listen("tcp", service, &config)
        checkError(err)
        fmt.Println("Listening")
        for {
                conn, err := listener.Accept()
                if err != nil {
                        fmt.Println(err.Error())
                        continue
                }
                fmt.Println("Accepted")
                go handleClient(conn)
        }
}

func handleClient(conn net.Conn) {
        defer conn.Close()

        var buf [512]byte
        for {
                fmt.Println("Trying to read")
                n, err := conn.Read(buf[0:])
                if err != nil {
                        fmt.Println(err)
                        return
                }
                _, err = conn.Write(buf[0:n])
                if err != nil {
                        return
                }
        }
}
```

```
func checkError(err error) {
        if err != nil {
                fmt.Println("Fatal error ", err.Error())
                os.Exit(1)
        }
}
```

A simple TLS client won't work with this server if the certificate is self-signed, which it is here. We need to set a configuration as the third parameter to TLS.Dial, which has our certificate installed as a root certificate. Thanks to Josh Bleecher Snyder in "Getting x509: Certificate Signed by Unknown Authority" (https://groups.google.com/forum/#!topic/golang-nuts/v5ShM8R7Tdc), for showing how to do this. The server then works with the TLSEchoClient.go client.

```
/* TLSEchoClient
 */
package main

import (
        "crypto/tls"
        "crypto/x509"
        "fmt"
        "os"
)

func main() {
        if len(os.Args) != 2 {
                fmt.Println("Usage: ", os.Args[0], "host:port")
                os.Exit(1)
        }
        service := os.Args[1]

        // Load the PEM self-signed certificate
        certPemFile, err := os.Open("jan.newmarch.name.pem")
        checkError(err)
        pemBytes := make([]byte, 1000) // bigger than the file
        _, err = certPemFile.Read(pemBytes)
        checkError(err)
        certPemFile.Close()

        // Create a new certificate pool
        certPool := x509.NewCertPool()
        // and add our certificate
        ok := certPool.AppendCertsFromPEM(pemBytes)
        if !ok {
                fmt.Println("PEM read failed")
        } else {
                fmt.Println("PEM read ok")
        }
```

```
        // Dial, using a config with root cert set to ours
        conn, err := tls.Dial("tcp", service, &tls.Config{RootCAs: certPool})
        checkError(err)

        // Now write and read lots
        for n := 0; n < 10; n++ {
                fmt.Println("Writing...")
                conn.Write([]byte("Hello " + string(n+48)))

                var buf [512]byte
                n, err := conn.Read(buf[0:])
                checkError(err)

                fmt.Println(string(buf[0:n]))
        }
        conn.Close()
        os.Exit(0)
}

func checkError(err error) {
        if err != nil {
                fmt.Println("Fatal error ", err.Error())
                os.Exit(1)
        }
}
```

Conclusion

Security is a huge area in itself, and this chapter barely touches on it. However, the major concepts have been covered. What has not been stressed is how much security needs to be built into the design phase: security as an afterthought is nearly always a failure.

CHAPTER 8

HTTP

The World Wide Web is a major distributed system, with millions of users. A site may become a web host by running an HTTP server. While web clients are typically users with a browser, there are many other "user agents" such as web spiders, web application clients, and so on.

The Web is built on top of the HTTP (Hypertext Transport Protocol), which is layered on top of TCP. HTTP has been through four publically available versions. Version 1.1 (the third version) is the most commonly used, but there is expected to be a rapid transition to HTTP/2 and this is now at over 10% of the current traffic.

This chapter is an overview of HTTP, followed by the Go APIs to manage HTTP connections.

URLs and Resources

URLs specify the location of a *resource*. A resource is often a static file, such as an HTML document, an image, or a sound file. But increasingly, it may be a dynamically generated object, perhaps based on information stored in a database.

When a user agent requests a resource, what is returned is not the resource itself, but some *representation* of that resource. For example, if the resource is a static file, then what is sent to the user agent is a copy of the file.

Multiple URLs may point to the same resource, and an HTTP server will return appropriate representations of the resource for each URL. For example, an company might make product information available both internally and externally using different URLs for the same product. The internal representation of the product might include information such as internal contact officers for the product, while the external representation might include the location of stores selling the product.

This view of resources means that the HTTP protocol can be fairly simple and straightforward, while an HTTP server can be arbitrarily complex. HTTP has to deliver requests from user agents to servers and return a byte stream, while a server might have to do any amount of processing of the request.

I18n

There are complications arising from the increasing internationalization (i18n) of the Internet. Hostnames may be given in an internationalized form known as IDN (Internationalized Domain Name). In order to preserve compatibility with legacy implementations that do not understand Unicode (such as older e-mail servers), non-ASCII domain names are mapped into an ASCII representation known as *punycode*. For example, the domain name 日本語.jp has the punycode value xn--wgv71a119e.jp. The translation from a non-ASCII domain to a punycode value is not performed automatically by the Go net libraries (as of Go 1.7), but there is an extension package called golang.org/x/net/idna that will convert between Unicode and its punycode value. There is an ongoing discussion at "Figure Out IDNA Punycode Story" (https://github.com/golang/go/issues/13835) about this topic.

© Jan Newmarch 2017
J. Newmarch, *Network Programming with Go*, DOI 10.1007/978-1-4842-2692-6_8

Internationalized domain names open up the possibility of what are called *homograph* attacks. Many Unicode characters have a similar appearance, such as the Russian o (U+043E), the Greek o (U+03BF), and the English o (U+006F). A domain name using a homograph such as `google.com` (with two Russian o's could cause havoc. A variety of defenses are known, such as always displaying the punycode (here `xn—ggle-55da.com`, using the Punycode converter).

The path in a URI/URL is more complex to handle, as it refers to a path relative to an HTTP server that may be running in a particular localized environment, The encoding may not be UTF-8, or even Unicode. The IRI (internationalized Resource Identifier) manages this by first converting any localized string to UTF-8 and then percent-escaping any non-ASCII bytes. The W3C page entitled "An Introduction to Multilingual Web Addresses" (`https://www.w3.org/International/articles/idn-and-iri/`) has more information. Converting from other encodings to UTF-8 was covered in Chapter 6, while Go has the functions in net/url of `Queryescape/Queryunescape` and in Go 1.8 of `PathEscape/PathUnescape` to do the percent conversions.

HTTP Characteristics

HTTP is a stateless, connectionless, reliable protocol. In the simplest form, each request from a user agent is handled reliably and then the connection is broken.

In the earliest version of HTTP, each request involved a separate TCP connection, so if many resources were required (such as images embedded in an HTML page), then many TCP connections had to be set up and torn down in a short space of time.

HTTP 1.1 added many optimizations in HTTP, which added complexity to the simple structure, but created a more efficient and reliable protocol. HTTP/2 has adopted a binary form for further efficient gains.

Versions

There are four versions of HTTP:

- Version 0.9 (1991): Totally obsolete

- Version 1.0 (1996): Almost obsolete

- Version 1.1 (1999): Most popular version at present

- Version 2 (2015): The latest version

Each version must understand the requests and responses of earlier versions.

HTTP 0.9

Request format:

```
Request = Simple-Request

Simple-Request = "GET" SP Request-URI CRLF
```

Response Format

A response is of the form:

```
Response = Simple-Response

Simple-Response = [Entity-Body]
```

HTTP 1.0

This version added much more information to the requests and responses. Rather than "grow" the 0.9 format, it was just left alongside the new version.

Request Format

The format of requests from client to server is:

```
Request = Simple-Request | Full-Request

Simple-Request = "GET" SP Request-URI CRLF

Full-Request = Request-Line
                    *(General-Header
                        | Request-Header
                        | Entity-Header)
                 CRLF
                 [Entity-Body]
```

A Simple-Request is an HTTP/0.9 request and must be replied to by a Simple-Response. A Request-Line has this format:

```
Request-Line = Method SP Request-URI SP HTTP-Version CRLF
```

Where

```
Method = "GET" | "HEAD" | POST |
         extension-method
```

Here's an example:

```
GET http://jan.newmarch.name/index.html HTTP/1.0
```

Response Format

A response is of the form:

```
Response = Simple-Response | Full-Response

Simple-Response = [Entity-Body]

Full-Response = Status-Line
                   *(General-Header
                       | Response-Header
                       | Entity-Header)
                CRLF
                [Entity-Body]
```

The Status-Line gives information about the fate of the request:

```
Status-Line = HTTP-Version SP Status-Code SP Reason-Phrase CRLF
```

Here's an example:

```
HTTP/1.0 200 OK
```

The status codes in the status line are as follows:

```
Status-Code =    "200" ; OK
               | "201" ; Created
               | "202" ; Accepted
               | "204" ; No Content
               | "301" ; Moved permanently
               | "302" ; Moved temporarily
               | "304" ; Not modified
               | "400" ; Bad request
               | "401" ; Unauthorized
               | "403" ; Forbidden
               | "404" ; Not found
               | "500" ; Internal server error
               | "501" ; Not implemented
               | "502" ; Bad gateway
               | "503" | Service unavailable
               | extension-code
```

The General-Header is typically the date, whereas the Response-Header is the location, the server, or an authentication field.

The Entity-Header contains useful information about the Entity-Body to follow:

```
Entity-Header = Allow
               | Content-Encoding
               | Content-Length
               | Content-Type
               | Expires
               | Last-Modified
               | extension-header
```

For example, (where the types of field are given after a //):

```
HTTP/1.1 200 OK                            // status line
Date: Fri, 29 Aug 2003 00:59:56 GMT        // general header
Server: Apache/2.0.40 (Unix)               // response header
Content-Length: 1595                       // entity header

Content-Type: text/html; charset=ISO-8859-1 // entity header
```

HTTP 1.1

HTTP 1.1 fixes many problems with HTTP 1.0, but is more complex because of it. This version is done by extending or refining the options available to HTTP 1.0. For example:

- There are more commands such as TRACE and CONNECT

- HTTP 1.1 tightened up the rules for the request URLs to allow proxy handling. If the request is directed through a proxy, the URL should be an absolute URL, as in:

```
GET http://www.w3.org/index.html HTTP/1.1
```

Otherwise an absolute path should be used and should include a Host header field, as in:

```
GET /index.html HTTP/1.1
Host: www.w3.org
```

- There are more attributes such as If-Modified-Since, also for use by proxies

The changes include

- Hostname identification (allows virtual hosts)

- Content negotiation (multiple languages)

- Persistent connections (reduces TCP overheads; this is very complex)

- Chunked transfers

- Byte ranges (request parts of documents)

- Proxy support

HTTP/2

All the earlier versions of HTTP are text-based. The most significant departure for HTTP/2 is that it is a binary format. In order to ensure backward compatibility, this can't be managed by sending a binary message to an older server to see what it does. Instead an HTTP 1.1 message is sent with extra attributes, essentially asking if the server wants to switch to HTTP/2. If it doesn't understand the extra fields it replies with a normal HTTP 1.1 response and the session continues with HTTP 1.1.

Otherwise the server can respond that it is willing to change, and the session can continue with HTTP/2.

The 0.9 protocol took one page. The 1.0 protocol was described in about 20 pages and includes the 0.9 protocol. The 1.1 protocol takes 120 pages and is a substantial extension to 1.0, whereas HTTP/2 takes about 96 pages. The HTTP/2 specification just adds to the HTTP 1.1 specification.

Simple User Agents

User agents such as browsers make requests and get responses. This involves Go types and associated method calls.

The Response Type

The response type is as follows:

```
type Response struct {
    Status     string // e.g. "200 OK"
    StatusCode int    // e.g. 200
    Proto      string // e.g. "HTTP/1.0"
```

```
ProtoMajor int     // e.g. 1
ProtoMinor int     // e.g. 0

Header map[string][]string

Body io.ReadCloser

ContentLength int64

TransferEncoding []string

Close bool

Trailer map[string][]string

Request *Request // the original request

TLS *tls.ConnectionState // info about the TLS connection or nil
}
```

The HEAD Method

We examine this data structure through examples. Each HTTP request type has its own Go function in the net/http package The simplest request is from a user agent called HEAD, which asks for information about a resource and its HTTP server. This function can be used to make the query:

```
func Head(url string) (r *Response, err error)
```

The status of the response is in the response field Status, while the field Header is a map of the header fields in the HTTP response. A program called Head.go to make this request and display the results is as follows:

```
/* Head
 */

package main

import (
        "fmt"
        "net/http"
        "os"
)

func main() {
        if len(os.Args) != 2 {
                fmt.Println("Usage: ", os.Args[0], "host:port")
                os.Exit(1)
        }
        url := os.Args[1]
```

```
response, err := http.Head(url)
if err != nil {
        fmt.Println(err.Error())
        os.Exit(2)
}

fmt.Println(response.Status)
for k, v := range response.Header {
        fmt.Println(k+":", v)
}

os.Exit(0)
}
```

When run against a resource, as in this:

```
go run Head.go http://www.golang.com/
```

It prints something like this:

```
200 OK
Date: [Fri, 06 Jan 2017 11:20:37 GMT]
Server: [Google Frontend]
Content-Length: [7902]
Alt-Svc: [quic=":443"; ma=2592000; v="35,34"]
Strict-Transport-Security: [max-age=31536000; preload]
Content-Type: [text/html; charset=utf-8]
X-Cloud-Trace-Context: [6e28ebc86bb1026ae7b784c891d0117c]
```

The response comes from a server out of our control, and it may pass through other servers on the way. The fields displayed may be different, and certainly the values of the fields will differ.

The GET Method

Usually, we want to retrieve a representation of a resource rather than just get information about it. The GET request will do this and can be done using the following:

```
func Get(url string) (r *Response, finalURL string, err error)
```

The content of the response is in the response field Body, which is of type io.ReadCloser. We can print the content to the screen with the program Get.go:

```
/* Get
 */

package main
```

```
import (
        "fmt"
        "net/http"
        "net/http/httputil"
        "os"
        "strings"
)

func main() {
        if len(os.Args) != 2 {
                fmt.Println("Usage: ", os.Args[0], "host:port")
                os.Exit(1)
        }
        url := os.Args[1]

        response, err := http.Get(url)
        if err != nil {
                fmt.Println(err.Error())
                os.Exit(2)
        }

        if response.Status != "200 OK" {
                fmt.Println(response.Status)
                os.Exit(2)
        }

        fmt.Println("The response header is")
        b, _ := httputil.DumpResponse(response, false)
        fmt.Print(string(b))

        contentTypes := response.Header["Content-Type"]
        if !acceptableCharset(contentTypes) {Arial
                fmt.Println("Cannot handle", contentTypes)
                os.Exit(4)
        }

        fmt.Println("The response body is")
        var buf [512]byte
        reader := response.Body
        for {
                n, err := reader.Read(buf[0:])
                if err != nil {
                        os.Exit(0)
                }
                fmt.Print(string(buf[0:n]))
        }
        os.Exit(0)
}

func acceptableCharset(contentTypes []string) bool {
        // each type is like [text/html; charset=utf-8]
        // we want the UTF-8 only
```

144

```
        for _, cType := range contentTypes {
                if strings.Index(cType, "utf-8") != -1 {
                        return true
                }
        }
        return false
}
```

When it runs against http://www.golang.com as follows:

```
go run Get.go   http://www.golang.com
```

The response header is:

```
HTTP/2.0 200 OK
Content-Length: 7902
Alt-Svc: quic=":443"; ma=2592000; v="35,34"
Content-Type: text/html; charset=utf-8
Date: Fri, 06 Jan 2017 11:29:12 GMT
Server: Google Frontend
Strict-Transport-Security: max-age=31536000; preload
X-Cloud-Trace-Context: ea9b41b4796f379af487388b1474ed4e
```

The response body is:

```
<!DOCTYPE html>
<html>
<head>
<meta http-equiv="Content-Type" content="text/html; charset=utf-8">
<meta name="viewport" content="width=device-width, initial-scale=1">
<meta name="theme-color" content="#375EAB">

  <title>The Go Programming Language</title>
...
```

(Note that this been sent with HTTP/2. The Go library has performed the version negotiation for you.)

Note that there are important character set issues of the type discussed in the previous chapter. The server will deliver the content using some character set encoding, and possibly some transfer encoding. Usually this is a matter of negotiation between user agent and server, but the simple GET command that we used does not include the user agent component of the negotiation. So the server can send whatever character encoding it wants.

At the time of first writing, I was in China (and Google could be accessed). When I tried this program on www.google.com, Google's server tried to be helpful by guessing my location and sending me the text in the Chinese character set Big5! How to tell the server what character encoding is okay for me is discussed later.

Configuring HTTP Requests

Go also supplies a lower-level interface for user agents to communicate with HTTP servers. As you might expect, not only does it give you more control over the client requests, but it also requires you to spend more effort in building the requests. However, there is only a small increase in complexity.

The data type used to build requests is the type Request. This is a complex type, and we only show the principal fields for now. Several fields, and the full Go doc, are omitted.

```
type Request struct {
    Method     string      // GET, POST, PUT, etc.
    URL        *url.URL    // Parsed URL.
    Proto      string // "HTTP/1.0"
    ProtoMajor int    // 1
    ProtoMinor int    // 0

    // A header maps request lines to their values.
    Header Header  // map[string][]string

    // The message body.
    Body io.ReadCloser

    // ContentLength records the length of the associated content.
    // The value -1 indicates that the length is unknown.
    // Values >= 0 indicate that the given number of bytes may be read from Body.
    ContentLength int64

    // TransferEncoding lists the transfer encodings from outermost to innermost.
    // An empty list denotes the "identity" encoding.
    TransferEncoding []string

    // The host on which the URL is sought.
    // Per RFC 2616, this is either the value of the Host: header
    // or the host name given in the URL itself.
    Host string
}
```

There is a lot of information that can be stored in a request. You do not need to fill in all the fields, only those of interest. The simplest way to create a request with default values is using this, for example:

```
request, err := http.NewRequest("GET", url.String(), nil)
```

Once a request has been created, you can modify the fields. For example, to specify that you want to receive only UTF-8, add an Accept-Charset field to a request as follows:

```
request.Header.Add("Accept-Charset", "UTF-8;q=1, ISO-8859-1;q=0")
```

(Note that the default set ISO-8859-1 always gets a value of 1 unless mentioned explicitly in the list. The HTTP 1.1 specification dates back to 1999!)

A client setting a charset request is simple. But there is some confusion about what happens with the server's return value of a charset. The returned resource *should* have a Content-Type that will specify the media type of the content such as text/html. If appropriate, the media type should state the charset, such as text/html; charset=UTF-8. If there is no charset specification, then according to the HTTP specification it should be treated as the default ISO8859-1 charset. But the HTML4 specification states that since many servers don't conform to this, you can't make any assumptions.

If there is a charset specified in the server's Content-Type, then assume it is correct. If there is none specified, since more than 50% of pages are in UTF-8 and some are in ASCII, it is safe to assume UTF-8. Fewer than 10% of pages may be wrong :-(.

The Client Object

To send a request to a server and get a reply, the convenience object Client is the easiest way. This object can manage multiple requests and will look after issues such as whether the server keeps the TCP connection alive, and so on.

This is illustrated in the following program, ClientGet.go.

The program shows how to add HTTP headers, as we add the header Accept-Charset to only accept UTF-8. There is a little hiccup here, caused by a bug in Go which has only been fixed in Go 1.8. The Client. Do function will automatically do a redirect if it gets a 301, 302, 303, or 307 response. Prior to Go 1.8, it didn't copy across the HTTP headers in this redirect.

If you try against a site such as http://www.google.com, then it will redirect to a site such as http://www.google.com.au but will lose the Accept-Charset header and return ISO8859-1 (as it should do according to the 1999 HTTP 1.1 specification!). With that proviso—that the program may not give correct results on versions prior to Go 1.8—the program is as follows:

```
/* ClientGet
 */

package main

import (
        "fmt"
        "net/http"
        "net/http/httputil"
        "net/url"
        "os"
        "strings"
)

func main() {
        if len(os.Args) != 2 {
                fmt.Println("Usage: ", os.Args[0], "http://host:port/page")
                os.Exit(1)
        }
        url, err := url.Parse(os.Args[1])
        checkError(err)

        client := &http.Client{}

        request, err := http.NewRequest("HEAD", url.String(), nil)

        // only accept UTF-8
        request.Header.Add("Accept-Charset", "utf-8;q=1, ISO-8859-1;q=0")
        checkError(err)

        response, err := client.Do(request)
        checkError(err)
        if response.Status != "200 OK" {
                fmt.Println(response.Status)
                os.Exit(2)
        }
```

```
            fmt.Println("The response header is")
            b, _ := httputil.DumpResponse(response, false)
            fmt.Print(string(b))

            chSet := getCharset(response)
            if chSet != "utf-8" {
                    fmt.Println("Cannot handle", chSet)
                    os.Exit(4)
            }

            var buf [512]byte
            reader := response.Body
            fmt.Println("got body")
            for {
                    n, err := reader.Read(buf[0:])
                    if err != nil {
                            os.Exit(0)
                    }
                    fmt.Print(string(buf[0:n]))
            }

            os.Exit(0)
}

func getCharset(response *http.Response) string {
        contentType := response.Header.Get("Content-Type")
        if contentType == "" {
                // guess
                return "utf-8"
        }
        idx := strings.Index(contentType, "charset=")
        if idx == -1 {
                // guess
                return "utf-8"
        }
        chSet := strings.Trim(contentType[idx+8:], " ")
        return strings.ToLower(chSet)
}

func checkError(err error) {
        if err != nil {
                fmt.Println("Fatal error ", err.Error())
                os.Exit(1)
        }
}
```

The program is run as follows, for example:

```
go run ClientGet.go  http://www.golang.com
```

Proxy Handling

It is very common now for HTTP requests to pass through specific HTTP proxies. This is in addition to the servers that form the TCP connection and act at the application layer. Companies use proxies to limit what their own staff can see, while many organizations use proxy services such as Cloudflare to act as caches, reducing the load on the organization's own servers. Accessing web sites through proxies requires additional handling by the client.

Simple Proxy

HTTP 1.1 laid out how HTTP should work through a proxy. A GET request should be made to a proxy. However, the URL requested should be the full URL of the destination. In addition, the HTTP header should contain a Host field, set to the proxy. As long as the proxy is configured to pass such requests through, then that is all that needs to be done.

Go considers this to be part of the HTTP transport layer. To manage this, it has a class Transport. This contains a field that can be set to a *function* that returns an URL for a proxy. If we have an URL as a string for the proxy, the appropriate transport object is created and then given to a client object as follows:

```
proxyURL, err := url.Parse(proxyString)
transport := &http.Transport{Proxy: http.ProxyURL(proxyURL)}
client := &http.Client{Transport: transport}
```

The client can then continue as before.
The following program ProxyGet.go illustrates this

```
/* ProxyGet
 */

package main

import (
        "fmt"
        "io"
        "net/http"
        "net/http/httputil"
        "net/url"
        "os"
)

func main() {
        if len(os.Args) != 3 {
                fmt.Println("Usage: ", os.Args[0], "http://proxy-host:port
                http://host:port/page")
                os.Exit(1)
        }
        proxyString := os.Args[1]
        proxyURL, err := url.Parse(proxyString)
        checkError(err)
        rawURL := os.Args[2]
```

```
        url,err := url.Parse(rawURL)
        checkError(err)

        transport := &http.Transport{Proxy: http.ProxyURL(proxyURL)}
        client := &http.Client{Transport: transport}

        request, err := http.NewRequest("GET", url.String(), nil)

        urlp, _ := transport.Proxy(request)
        fmt.Println("Proxy ", urlp)
        dump, _ := httputil.DumpRequest(request, false)
        fmt.Println(string(dump))

        response, err := client.Do(request)

        checkError(err)
        fmt.Println("Read ok")

        if response.Status != "200 OK" {
                fmt.Println(response.Status)
                os.Exit(2)
        }
        fmt.Println("Response ok")

        var buf [512]byte
        reader := response.Body
        for {
                n, err := reader.Read(buf[0:])
                if err != nil {
                        os.Exit(0)
                }
                fmt.Print(string(buf[0:n]))
        }

        os.Exit(0)
}

func checkError(err error) {
        if err != nil {
                if err == io.EOF {
                        return
                }
                fmt.Println("Fatal error ", err.Error())
                os.Exit(1)
        }
}
```

If you have a proxy at, say XYZ.com on port 8080, you can test this as follows:

```
go run ProxyGet.go http://XYZ.com:8080/ http://www.google.com
```

If you don't have a suitable proxy to test this, then download and install the Squid proxy (`http://www.squid-cache.org/`) to your own computer.

This program used a known proxy passed as an argument to the program. There are many ways that proxies can be made known to applications. Most browsers have a configuration menu in which you can enter proxy information: such information is not available to a Go application. Some applications may get proxy information using the Web Proxy Autodiscovery Protocol (`https://en.wikipedia.org/wiki/Web_Proxy_Autodiscovery_Protocol`) from a file often known as `autoproxy.pac` somewhere in your network. Go does not (yet) know how to parse these JavaScript files and so cannot use them. Particular operating systems may have system-specific means of specifying proxies. Go cannot access these. But it can find proxy information if it is set in operating system environment variables such as `HTTP_PROXY` or `http_proxy` using this function:

```
func ProxyFromEnvironment(req *Request) (*url.URL, error)
```

If your programs are running in such an environment, you can use this function instead of having to explicitly know the proxy parameters.

Authenticating Proxy

Some proxies will require authentication, by a username and password in order to pass requests. A common scheme is "basic authentication" in which the username and password are concatenated into a string `"user:password"` and then Base64 encoded. This is then given to the proxy by the HTTP request header `"Proxy-Authorization"` with the flag that it is the basic authentication

The following program `ProxyAuthGet.go` illustrates this, adding the `Proxy-Authentication` header to the previous proxy program:

```
/* ProxyAuthGet
 */

package main

import (
        "encoding/base64"
        "fmt"
        "io"
        "net/http"
        "net/http/httputil"
        "net/url"
        "os"
)

const auth = "jannewmarch:mypassword"

func main() {
        if len(os.Args) != 3 {
                fmt.Println("Usage: ", os.Args[0], "http://proxy-host:port
                http://host:port/page")
                os.Exit(1)
        }
        proxy := os.Args[1]
```

```go
        proxyURL, err := url.Parse(proxy)
        checkError(err)
        rawURL := os.Args[2]
        url, err := url.Parse(rawURL)
        checkError(err)

        // encode the auth
        basic := "Basic " + base64.StdEncoding.EncodeToString([]byte(auth))

        transport := &http.Transport{Proxy: http.ProxyURL(proxyURL)}
        client := &http.Client{Transport: transport}

        request, err := http.NewRequest("GET", url.String(), nil)

        request.Header.Add("Proxy-Authorization", basic)
        dump, _ := httputil.DumpRequest(request, false)
        fmt.Println(string(dump))

        // send the request
        response, err := client.Do(request)

        checkError(err)
        fmt.Println("Read ok")

        if response.Status != "200 OK" {
                fmt.Println(response.Status)
                os.Exit(2)
        }
        fmt.Println("Response ok")

        var buf [512]byte
        reader := response.Body
        for {
                n, err := reader.Read(buf[0:])
                if err != nil {
                        os.Exit(0)
                }
                fmt.Print(string(buf[0:n]))
        }

        os.Exit(0)
}

func checkError(err error) {
        if err != nil {
                if err == io.EOF {
                        return
                }
                fmt.Println("Fatal error ", err.Error())
                os.Exit(1)
        }
}
```

There don't seem to be publically available test sites for this program. I tested it at work where an authenticating proxy is used. Setting up such a proxy is beyond the scope of this book. There is a discussion on how to do this called "How to Set Up a Squid Proxy with Basic Username and Password Authentication" (see http://stackoverflow.com/questions/3297196/how-to-set-up-a-squid-proxy-with-basic-username-and-password-authentication).

HTTPS Connections by Clients

For secure, encrypted connections, HTTP uses TLS, which is described in Chapter 7. The protocol of HTTP+TLS is called HTTPS and uses https:// URLs instead of http:// URLs.

Servers are required to return valid X.509 certificates before a client will accept data from them. If the certificate is valid, then Go handles everything under the hood and the clients given previously run okay with https URLs. That is, programs such as the earlier ClientGet.go run unchanged—you just give them an HTTPS URL.

Many sites have invalid certificates. They may have expired, they may be self-signed instead of by a recognized certificate authority, or they may just have errors (such as having an incorrect server name). Browsers such as Firefox put a big warning notice with a "Get me out of here!" button, but you can carry on at your risk, which many people do.

Go presently bails out when it encounters certificate errors. However, you can configure a client to ignore certificate errors. This is, of course, not advisable—sites with misconfigured certificates may have other problems.

In Chapter 7, we generated self-signed X.509 certificates. Later in this chapter, we will give an HTTPS server using X.509 certificates, and if the self-signed certificates are used, then ClientGet.go will generate this error:

```
x509: certificate signed by unknown authority
```

A client that removes these errors and continues does so by turning on the Transport configuration flag InsecureSkipVerify. The unsafe program is TLSUnsafeClientGet.go:

```
/* TLSUnsafeClientGet
 */

package main

import (
        "fmt"
        "net/http"
        "net/url"
        "os"
        "strings"
        "crypto/tls"
)

func main() {
        if len(os.Args) != 2 {
                fmt.Println("Usage: ", os.Args[0], "https://host:port/page")
                os.Exit(1)
        }
```

153

```go
    url, err := url.Parse(os.Args[1])
    checkError(err)
    if url.Scheme != "https" {
        fmt.Println("Not https scheme ", url.Scheme)
        os.Exit(1)
    }

    transport := &http.Transport{}
    transport.TLSClientConfig = &tls.Config{InsecureSkipVerify: true}
    client := &http.Client{Transport: transport}

    request, err := http.NewRequest("GET", url.String(), nil)
    // only accept UTF-8
    checkError(err)

    response, err := client.Do(request)
    checkError(err)

    if response.Status != "200 OK" {
        fmt.Println(response.Status)
        os.Exit(2)
    }
    fmt.Println("get a response")

    chSet := getCharset(response)
    fmt.Printf("got charset %s\n", chSet)
    if chSet != "UTF-8" {
        fmt.Println("Cannot handle", chSet)
        os.Exit(4)
    }

    var buf [512]byte
    reader := response.Body
    fmt.Println("got body")
    for {
        n, err := reader.Read(buf[0:])
        if err != nil {
            os.Exit(0)
        }
        fmt.Print(string(buf[0:n]))
    }

    os.Exit(0)
}

func getCharset(response *http.Response) string {
    contentType := response.Header.Get("Content-Type")
    if contentType == "" {
        // guess
        return "UTF-8"
    }
```

```
        idx := strings.Index(contentType, "charset:")
        if idx == -1 {
                // guess
                return "UTF-8"
        }
        return strings.Trim(contentType[idx:], " ")
}

func checkError(err error) {
        if err != nil {
                fmt.Println("Fatal error ", err.Error())
                os.Exit(1)
        }
}
```

Servers

The other side to building a client is a web server handling HTTP requests. The simplest—and earliest—servers just returned copies of files. However, any URL can now trigger an arbitrary computation in current servers.

File Server

We start with a basic file server. Go supplies a *multiplexer*, that is, an object that will read and interpret requests. It hands out requests to handlers, which run in their own thread. Thus much of the work of reading HTTP requests, decoding them, and branching to suitable functions in their own thread is done for us.

For a file server, Go also gives a FileServer object, which knows how to deliver files from the local file system. It takes a "root" directory, which is the top of a file tree in the local system, and a pattern to match URLs against. The simplest pattern is /, which is the top of any URL. This will match all URLs.

An HTTP server delivering files from the local file system is almost embarrassingly trivial given these objects. It is FileServer.go:

```
/* File Server
 */

package main

import (
        "fmt"
        "net/http"
        "os"
)

func main() {
        // deliver files from the directory /var/www
        fileServer := http.FileServer(http.Dir("/var/www"))

        // register the handler and deliver requests to it
        err := http.ListenAndServe(":8000", fileServer)
```

```
        checkError(err)
        // That's it!
}

func checkError(err error) {
        if err != nil {
                fmt.Println("Fatal error ", err.Error())
                os.Exit(1)
        }
}
```

The server is run as follows:

```
go run FileServer.go
```

This server even delivers "404 not found" messages for requests for file resources that don't exist! If the file requested is a directory, it returns a list wrapped in <pre> ... </pre> tags with no other HTML headers or markup. If Wireshark or a simple telnet client is used, directories are sent as text/html, HTML files as text/html, Perl files as text/x-perl, Java files as text/x-java, and so on. The FileServer employs some type recognition and includes that in the HTTP request, but it does not give the control over markup that a server such as Apache does.

Handler Functions

In this last program, the handler was given in the second argument to ListenAndServe. Any number of handlers can be registered first by calls to Handle or HandleFunc, with these signatures:

```
func Handle(pattern string, handler Handler)
func HandleFunc(pattern string, handler func(ResponseWriter, *Request))
```

The second argument to ListenAndServe could be nil, and then calls are dispatched to all registered handlers. Each handler should have a different URL pattern. For example, the file handler might have URL pattern /, while a function handler might have URL pattern /cgi-bin. A more specific pattern takes precedence over a more general pattern.

Common CGI programs are test-cgi (written in the shell) and printenv (written in Perl), which print the values of the environment variables. A handler can be written to work in a similar manner as PrintEnv.go.

```
/* Print Env
 */

package main

import (
        "fmt"
        "net/http"
        "os"
)
Arial
func main() {
        // file handler for most files
        fileServer := http.FileServer(http.Dir("/var/www"))
        http.Handle("/", fileServer)
```

```
        // function handler for /cgi-bin/printenv
        http.HandleFunc("/cgi-bin/printenv", printEnv)

        // deliver requests to the handlers
        err := http.ListenAndServe(":8000", nil)
        checkError(err)
        // That's it!
}

func printEnv(writer http.ResponseWriter, req *http.Request) {
        env := os.Environ()
        writer.Write([]byte("<h1>Environment</h1>\n<pre>"))
        for _, v := range env {
                writer.Write([]byte(v + "\n"))
        }
        writer.Write([]byte("</pre>"))
}

func checkError(err error) {
        if err != nil {
                fmt.Println("Fatal error ", err.Error())
                os.Exit(1)
        }
}
```

■ **Note** *For simplicity, this program does not deliver well-formed HTML. It is missing html, head, and body tags.* Running the program on the localhost and pointing a browser to `http://localhost/cgi-bin/printenv` produces output like this on my computer:

```
Environment

XDG_VTNR=7
XDG_SESSION_ID=c2
CLUTTER_IM_MODULE=xim
XDG_GREETER_DATA_DIR=/var/lib/lightdm-data/newmarch
SESSION=gnome-flashback-compiz
GPG_AGENT_INFO=/home/newmarch/.gnupg/S.gpg-agent:0:1
TERM=xterm-256color
SHELL=/bin/bash
...
```

Using the `cgi-bin` directory in this program is a bit cheeky: it doesn't call an external program like CGI scripts do. It just calls the Go function `printEnv`. Go does have the ability to call external programs using `os.ForkExec`, but does not yet have support for dynamically linkable modules like Apache's `mod_perl`.

Bypassing the Default Multiplexer

HTTP requests received by a Go server are usually handled by a multiplexer, which examines the path in the HTTP request and calls the appropriate file handler, etc. You can define your own handlers. These can be registered with the default multiplexer by calling http.HandleFunc, which takes a pattern and a function. The functions such as ListenAndServe then take a nil handler function. This was done in the last example.

However, if you want to take over the multiplexer role then you can give a non-nil function as the handler function to ListenAndServe. This function will then be responsible for managing the requests and responses.

The following example is trivial, but illustrates the use of this. The multiplexer function simply returns a "204 No content" for *all* requests to ServerHandler.go:

```
/* ServerHandler
 */

package main

import (
        "net/http"
)

func main() {

        myHandler := http.HandlerFunc(func(rw http.ResponseWriter, request *http.Request) {
                // Just return no content - arbitrary headers can be set, arbitrary body
                rw.WriteHeader(http.StatusNoContent)
        })

        http.ListenAndServe(":8080", myHandler)
}
```

The server may be tested by running telnet against it to give output such as this:

```
$telnet localhost 8080
Trying 127.0.0.1...
Connected to localhost.
Escape character is '^]'.
GET / HTTP/1.0

HTTP/1.0 204 No Content
Date: Tue, 10 Jan 2017 05:32:53 GMT
```

Or by using this:

```
curl -v localhost:8080
```

To give this output:

```
* Rebuilt URL to: localhost:8080/
*   Trying 127.0.0.1...
* Connected to localhost (127.0.0.1) port 8080 (#0)
```

```
> GET / HTTP/1.1
> Host: localhost:8080
> User-Agent: curl/7.47.0
> Accept: */*
>
< HTTP/1.1 204 No Content
< Date: Wed, 08 Mar 2017 08:46:35 GMT
<
* Connection #0 to host localhost left intact
```

Arbitrarily complex behavior can be built instead.

HTTPS

For secure, encrypted connections, HTTP uses TLS, which is described in Chapter 7. The protocol of HTTP+TLS is called HTTPS and uses `https://` URLs instead of `http://` URLs.

For a server to use HTTPS, it needs an X.509 certificate and a private key file for that certificate. Go at present requires that these be PEM-encoded as used in Chapter 7. Then the HTTP function `ListenAndServe` is replaced with the HTTPS (HTTP+TLS) function `ListenAndServeTLS`.

The file server program given earlier can be written as an HTTPS server as `HTTPSFileServer.go`:

```go
/* HTTPSFileServer
 */

package main

import (
        "fmt"
        "net/http"
        "os"
)

func main() {
        // deliver files from the directory /var/www
        fileServer := http.FileServer(http.Dir("/var/www"))

        // register the handler and deliver requests to it
        err := http.ListenAndServeTLS(":8000", "jan.newmarch.name.pem",
                "private.pem", fileServer)
        checkError(err)
        // That's it!
}

func checkError(err error) {
        if err != nil {
                fmt.Println("Fatal error ", err.Error())
                os.Exit(1)
        }
}
```

This server is accessed by `https://localhost:8000/index.html`, for example. If the certificate is a self-signed certificate, an unsafe client will be needed to access the server contents. For example:

```
curl -kv https://localhost:8000
```

If you want a server that supports both HTTP and HTTPs, run each listener in its own go routine.

Conclusion

Go has extensive support for HTTP. This is not surprising, since Go was partly invented to fill a need by Google for their own servers. This chapter discussed the various levels of support given by Go for HTTP and HTTPS.

CHAPTER 9

Templates

Most server-side languages have a mechanism for taking predominantly static pages and inserting a dynamically generated component, such as a list of items. Typical examples are scripts in Java Server Pages, PHP scripting, and many others. Go has adopted a relatively simple scripting language in the template package.

The package is designed to take text as input and output different text, based on transforming the original text using the values of an object. Unlike JSP or similar, it is not restricted to HTML files but it is likely to find greatest use there. We first describe the text/template package and later the html/template package.

The original source is called a *template* and will consist of text that is transmitted unchanged, and embedded commands that can act on and change text. The commands are delimited by {{ ... }}, similar to the JSP commands <%= ... =%> and PHP's <?php ... ?>.

Inserting Object Values

A template is applied to a Go object. Fields from that Go object can be inserted into the template, and you can "dig" into the object to find subfields, etc. The current object is represented as the *cursor* ., so that to insert the value of the current object as a string, you use {{.}}. The package uses the fmt package by default to work out the string used as inserted values.

To insert the value of a field of the current cursor object, you use the field name prefixed by .. For example, if the current cursor object is of type

```
type Person struct {
        Name        string
        Age         int
        Emails      []string
        Jobs        []*Job
}
```

You insert the values of Name and Age as follows:

```
The name is {{.Name}}.
The age is {{.Age}}.
```

You can loop over the elements of an array or other lists using the range command. So to access the contents of the Emails array, you use this:

```
{{range .Emails}}
        The email is {{.}}
{{end}}
```

During the loop over e-mails, the cursor . is set to each e-mail in turn. On conclusion of the loop, the cursor reverts to the person. If Job is defined as follows:

```
type Job struct {
    Employer string
    Role     string
}
```

And we want to access the fields of a person's jobs, we can do it as above with a {{range .Jobs}}. An alternative is to switch the current object to the Jobs field. This is done using the {{with ...}} ... {{end}} construction, where now {{.}} is the Jobs field, which is an array:

```
{{with .Jobs}}
    {{range .}}
        An employer is {{.Employer}}
        and the role is {{.Role}}
    {{end}}
{{end}}
```

You can use this with any field, not just an array.

Using Templates

Once you have a template, you can apply it to an object to generate a new string, using the object to fill in the template values. This is a two-step process that involves parsing the template and then applying it to an object. The result is output to a Writer, as in:

```
t := template.New("Person template")
t, err := t.Parse(templ)
if err == nil {
        buff := bytes.NewBufferString("")
        t.Execute(buff, person)
}
```

An example program to apply a template to an object and print to standard output is PrintPerson.go:

```
/**
 * PrintPerson
 */

package main
```

```go
import (
        "fmt"
        "text/template"
        "os"
)

type Person struct {
        Name    string
        Age     int
        Emails  []string
        Jobs    []*Job
}

type Job struct {
        Employer string
        Role     string
}

const templ = `The name is {{.Name}}.
The age is {{.Age}}.
{{range .Emails}}
        An email is {{.}}
{{end}}

{{with .Jobs}}
    {{range .}}
        An employer is {{.Employer}}
        and the role is {{.Role}}
    {{end}}
{{end}}
`

func main() {
        job1 := Job{Employer: "Box Hill Institute", Role: "Director, Commerce and ICT"}
        job2 := Job{Employer: "Canberra University", Role: "Adjunct Professor"}

        person := Person{
                Name:   "jan",
                Age:    66,
                Emails: []string{"jan@newmarch.name", "jan.newmarch@gmail.com"},
                Jobs:   []*Job{&job1, &job2},
        }

        t := template.New("Person template")
        t, err := t.Parse(templ)
        checkError(err)

        err = t.Execute(os.Stdout, person)
        checkError(err)
}
```

```
func checkError(err error) {
        if err != nil {
                fmt.Println("Fatal error ", err.Error())
                os.Exit(1)
        }
}
```

The output from this is as follows:

```
The name is jan.
The age is 66.

        An email is jan@newmarch.name

        An email is jan.newmarch@gmail.com

        An employer is Canberra University
        and the role is Adjunct Professor

        An employer is Box Hill Institute
        and the role is Director, Commerce and ICT
```

Note that there is plenty of whitespace as newlines in this printout. This is due to the whitespace we have in our template. If you want to reduce this whitespace, eliminate the newlines in the template as follows:

```
{{range .Emails}} An email is {{.}} {{end}}
```

An alternative is to use the command delimiters "{{- " and " -}}" to eliminate all trailing whitespace from the immediately preceding text, and all leading whitespace from the immediately following text, respectively.

In the example, we used a string in the program as the template. You can also load templates from a file using the `template.ParseFiles()` function. For some reason that I don't understand (and which wasn't required in earlier versions), the name assigned to the template must be the same as the basename of the first file in the list of files. Is this a bug?

Pipelines

The above transformations insert pieces of text into a template. Those pieces of text are essentially arbitrary, whatever the string values of the fields are. If we want them to appear as part of an HTML document (or other specialized form), we will have to escape particular sequences of characters. For example, to display arbitrary text in an HTML document, we have to change < to <. The Go templates have a number of built-in functions, and one of these is `html()`. These functions act in a similar manner to UNIX pipelines, reading from standard input and writing to standard output.

To take the value of the current object . and apply HTML escapes to it, you write a "pipeline" in the template:

```
{{. | html}}
```

And do similarly for other functions.

Defining Functions

The templates use the string representation of an object to insert values, using the fmt package to convert the object to a string. Sometimes this isn't what is needed. For example, to avoid spammers getting hold of e-mail addresses, it is quite common to see the symbol @ replaced by the word "at," as in "jan at newmarch. name". If we want to use a template to display e-mail addresses in that form, we have to build a custom function to do this transformation.

Each template function has a name that is used in the templates themselves and an associated Go function. These are linked by this type:

```
type FuncMap map[string]interface{}
```

For example, if we want our template function to be emailExpand, which is linked to the Go function EmailExpander, we add this to the functions in a template as follows:

```
t = t.Funcs(template.FuncMap{"emailExpand": EmailExpander})
```

The signature for EmailExpander is typically this:

```
func EmailExpander(args ...interface{}) string
```

For the use we are interested in, there should be only one argument to the function, which will be a string. Existing functions in the Go template library have some initial code to handle non-conforming cases, so we just copy that. Then it is just simple string manipulation to change the format of the e-mail address. A program is PrintEmails.go:

```go
/**
 * PrintEmails
 */

package main

import (
        "fmt"
        "os"
        "strings"
        "text/template"
)

type Person struct {
        Name    string
        Emails  []string
}

const templ = `The name is {{.Name}}.
{{range .Emails}}
        An email is "{{. | emailExpand}}"
{{end}}
`
```

```go
func EmailExpander(args ...interface{}) string {
        ok := false
        var s string
        if len(args) == 1 {
                s, ok = args[0].(string)
        }
        if !ok {
                s = fmt.Sprint(args...)
        }

        // find the @ symbol
        substrs := strings.Split(s, "@")
        if len(substrs) != 2 {
                return s
        }
        // replace the @ by " at "
        return (substrs[0] + " at " + substrs[1])
}

func main() {
        person := Person{
                Name:   "jan",
                Emails: []string{"jan@newmarch.name", "jan.newmarch@gmail.com"},
        }

        t := template.New("Person template")

        // add our function
        t = t.Funcs(template.FuncMap{"emailExpand": EmailExpander})

        t, err := t.Parse(templ)

        checkError(err)

        err = t.Execute(os.Stdout, person)
        checkError(err)
}

func checkError(err error) {
        if err != nil {
                fmt.Println("Fatal error ", err.Error())
                os.Exit(1)
        }
}
```

The output is as follows:

```
The name is jan.

        An email is "jan at newmarch.name"

        An email is "jan.newmarch at gmail.com"
```

Variables

The template package allows you to define and use variables. As motivation for this, consider how we might print each person's e-mail address *prefixed* by their name. The type we use is again this one:

```
type Person struct {
        Name        string
        Emails      []string
}
```

To access the e-mail strings, we use a range statement such as this:

```
{{range .Emails}}
    {{.}}
{{end}}
```

But at that point we cannot access the Name field, as . is now traversing the array elements and Name is outside of this scope. The solution is to save the value of the Name field in a variable that can be accessed anywhere in its scope. Variables in templates are prefixed by $. So we write this:

```
{{$name := .Name}}
{{range .Emails}}
    Name is {{$name}}, email is {{.}}
{{end}}
```

The program is PrintNameEmails.go:

```
/**
 * PrintNameEmails
 */

package main

import (
        "text/template"
        "os"
        "fmt"
)

type Person struct {
        Name    string
        Emails  []string
}

const templ = `{{$name := .Name}}
{{range .Emails}}
    Name is {{$name}}, email is {{.}}
{{end}}
`
```

```
func main() {
        person := Person{
                Name:   "jan",
                Emails: []string{"jan@newmarch.name", "jan.newmarch@gmail.com"},
        }

        t := template.New("Person template")
        t, err := t.Parse(templ)
        checkError(err)

        err = t.Execute(os.Stdout, person)
        checkError(err)
}

func checkError(err error) {
        if err != nil {
                fmt.Println("Fatal error ", err.Error())
                os.Exit(1)
        }
}
```

Here is the output:

```
Name is jan, email is jan@newmarch.name

Name is jan, email is jan.newmarch@gmail.com
```

Conditional Statements

Continuing with the Person example, suppose you just want to print out the list of e-mails, without digging into it. You can do that with a template:

```
Name is {{.Name}}
Emails are {{.Emails}}
```

This will print the following:

```
Name is jan
Emails are [jan@newmarch.name jan.newmarch@gmail.com]
```

Because this is how the fmt package will display a list.

In many circumstances that may be fine, if that is what you want. Let's consider a case where it is *almost* right, but not quite. There is a JSON package to serialize objects, which we looked at in Chapter 4. This would produce the following:

```
{"Name": "jan",
 "Emails": ["jan@newmarch.name", "jan.newmarch@gmail.com"]
}
```

The JSON package is the one you use in practice, but let's see if we can produce JSON output using templates. We can do something similar just by the templates we have. This is *almost* right as a JSON serializer:

```
{"Name": "{{.Name}}",
 "Emails": {{.Emails}}
}
```

It will produce this:

```
{"Name": "jan",
 "Emails": [jan@newmarch.name jan.newmarch@gmail.com]
}
```

This has two problems: the addresses aren't in quotes and the list elements should be , separated. How about this—look at the array elements, put them in quotes, and add commas?

```
{"Name": {{.Name}},
  "Emails": [
  {{range .Emails}}
      "{{.}}",
  {{end}}
  ]
}
```

This will produce:

```
{"Name": "jan",
 "Emails": ["jan@newmarch.name", "jan.newmarch@gmail.com",]
}
```

(Plus some whitespace.)

Again, it's almost correct, but if you look carefully, you will see a trailing , after the last list element. According to the JSON syntax (see http://www.json.org/), this trailing , is not allowed. Implementations may vary in how they deal with this.

What we want is to print every element followed by a , except for the last one. This is actually a bit hard to do, so a better way is to print every element *preceded* by a , except for the *first* one. (I got this tip from "brianb" at Stack Overflow—http://stackoverflow.com/questions/201782/can-you-use-a-trailing-comma-in-a-json-object). This is easier, because the first element has index zero and many programming languages, including the Go template language, treat zero as a Boolean false.

One form of the conditional statement is {{if pipeline}} T1 {{else}} T0 {{end}}. We need the pipeline to be the index into the array of e-mails. Fortunately, a variation on the range statement gives us this. There are two forms that introduce variables:

```
{{range $elmt := array}}
{{range $index, $elmt := array}}
```

So we set up a loop through the array, and if the index is false (0), we just print the element. Otherwise, we print it preceded by a ,. The template is as follows:

```
{"Name": "{{.Name}}",
 "Emails": [
 {{range $index, $elmt := .Emails}}
     {{if $index}}
          , "{{$elmt}}"
     {{else}}
          "{{$elmt}}"
     {{end}}
 {{end}}
 ]
}
```

The full program is PrintJSONEmails.go:

```
/**
 * PrintJSONEmails
 */

package main

import (
        "text/template"
        "os"
        "fmt"
)

type Person struct {
        Name    string
        Emails []string
}

const templ = `{"Name": "{{.Name}}",
 "Emails": [
{{range $index, $elmt := .Emails}}
    {{if $index}}
         , "{{$elmt}}"
    {{else}}
         "{{$elmt}}"
    {{end}}
{{end}}
 ]
}
`

func main() {
        person := Person{
                Name:   "jan",
                Emails: []string{"jan@newmarch.name", "jan.newmarch@gmail.com"},
        }
```

```
        t := template.New("Person template")
        t, err := t.Parse(templ)
        checkError(err)

        err = t.Execute(os.Stdout, person)
        checkError(err)
}

func checkError(err error) {
        if err != nil {
                fmt.Println("Fatal error ", err.Error())
                os.Exit(1)
        }
}
```

This gives the correct JSON output.

Before leaving this section, note that the problem of formatting a list with comma separators can be approached by defining suitable functions in Go that are made available as template functions. To reuse a well known saying from another programming language, "There's more than one way to do it!". The following program was sent to me by Roger Peppe as Sequence.go:

```
/**
 * Sequence.go
 * Copyright Roger Peppe
 */

package main

import (
        "errors"
        "fmt"
        "os"
        "text/template"
)

var tmpl = `{{$comma := sequence "" ", "}}
{{range $}}{{$comma.Next}}{{.}}{{end}}
{{$comma := sequence "" ", "}}
{{$colour := cycle "black" "white" "red"}}
{{range $}}{{$comma.Next}}{{.}} in {{$colour.Next}}{{end}}
`

var fmap = template.FuncMap{
        "sequence": sequenceFunc,
        "cycle":    cycleFunc,
}

func main() {
        t, err := template.New("").Funcs(fmap).Parse(tmpl)
        if err != nil {
                fmt.Printf("parse error: %v\n", err)
                return
        }
```

```
        err = t.Execute(os.Stdout, []string{"a", "b", "c", "d", "e", "f"})
        if err != nil {
                fmt.Printf("exec error: %v\n", err)
        }
}

type generator struct {
        ss []string
        i  int
        f  func(s []string, i int) string
}

func (seq *generator) Next() string {
        s := seq.f(seq.ss, seq.i)
        seq.i++
        return s
}

func sequenceGen(ss []string, i int) string {
        if i >= len(ss) {
                return ss[len(ss)-1]
        }
        return ss[i]
}

func cycleGen(ss []string, i int) string {
        return ss[i%len(ss)]
}

func sequenceFunc(ss ...string) (*generator, error) {
        if len(ss) == 0 {
                return nil, errors.New("sequence must have at least one element")
        }
        return &generator{ss, 0, sequenceGen}, nil
}

func cycleFunc(ss ...string) (*generator, error) {
        if len(ss) == 0 {
                return nil, errors.New("cycle must have at least one element")
        }
        return &generator{ss, 0, cycleGen}, nil
}
```

Here is the output:

```
a, b, c, d, e, f

a in black, b in white, c in red, d in black, e in white, f in red
```

The HTML/Template Package

The preceding programs all dealt with the `text/template` package. This applies transformations without regard to any context in which the text might be used. For example, if the text in `PrintPerson.go` changes to:

```
job1 := Job{Employer: "<script>alert('Could be nasty!')</script>", Role: "Director, Commerce
and ICT"}
```

The program will generate this text:

```
An employer is <script>alert('Could be nasty!')</script>
```

This will cause an unexpected effect if downloaded to a browser.

The use of the `html` command in a pipeline can reduce this, as in {{. | html}}, and will produce the following:

```
An employer is &lt;script&gt;alert(&#39;Could be nasty!&#39;)&lt;/script&gt
```

Applying this filter to all expressions will become tedious. In addition, it may not catch potentially dangerous JavaScript, CSS, or URI expressions.

The `html/template` package is designed to overcome these issues. By the simple step of replacing `text/template` with `html/template`, the appropriate transformations will be applied to the resultant text, sanitizing it so that it is suitable for web contexts.

Conclusion

The Go template package is useful for certain kinds of text transformations involving inserting values of objects. It does not have the power of regular expressions for example, but it is faster and in many cases will be easier to use than regular expressions.

CHAPTER 10

■ ■ ■

A Complete Web Server

This chapter is principally an illustration of the HTTP chapter, building a complete Web server in Go. It also shows how to use templates in order to use expressions in text files to insert variable values and to generate repeated sections. It deals with serialized data and Unicode character sets. The programs in this chapter are sufficiently long and complex so they are not always given in their entirety, but can be downloaded from the book's web site, which is `http://www.apress.com/9781484226919`.

I am learning Chinese. Rather, after many years of trying, I am still *attempting* to learn Chinese. Of course, rather than buckling down and getting on with it, I have tried all sorts of technical aids. I tried text books, videos, and many other teaching aids. Eventually I realized that the reason for my poor progress was that there *wasn't a good computer program for Chinese flashcards*, and so in the interests of learning, I needed to build one.

I found a program in Python to do some of the task. But sad to say it wasn't well written and after a few attempts at turning it upside down and inside out, I came to the conclusion that it was better to start from scratch. Of course, a web solution would be far better than a standalone one, because then all the other people in my Chinese class could share it, as well as any other learners out there. And of course, the server would be written in Go.

I used the vocabulary from the lessons in the book *Intensive Spoken Chinese* by Zhang Pengpeng (Sinolingua, 2007, ISBN 978-7-80052577-3) but the program is applicable to any vocabulary sets.

Browser Site Diagram

The resultant program as viewed in the browser has three types of pages, illustrated in Figure 10-1.

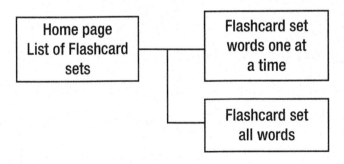

Figure 10-1. *Browser pages*

The home page shows a list of flashcard sets (see Figure 10-2). It consists of a list of flashcard sets currently available, how you want a set displayed (random card order, Chinese or English shown first, or random), and whether to display a set of cards or just the words in a set.

Flashcards

Flashcard Sets		Card order
All	○	Random ● Sequential ○
Common Words	○	
Lesson 04: Surname, First Name	○	Half card display
Lesson 05: Country, Nationality	○	Random ● English ○ Chinese ○
Lesson 06: City, Native Place	○	
Lesson 07: Year, Month, Date, Day	○	
Lesson 08: Birthdays, Age	○	
Lesson 09: Time, Daily Schedule	○	
Lesson 10: Public Places	○	
Lesson 11: Daily Necessities, Fruits	○	
Lesson 12: Buying Things, Prices	○	
Lesson 13: Wines, Drinks	○	
Lesson 14: Coffee Bar, Tea House	○	
Lesson 15: Menu, Foods	○	
Lesson 16: In the Restaurant	○	
Lesson 17: Eating Habits	○	
Lesson 18: Family, Profession	○	
Lesson 19: Languages, Learning	○	
Show cards in set	List words in set	

Figure 10-2. *The home page of the web site*

The flashcard set shows a flashcard, one at a time. One looks like Figure 10-3.

Flashcards for Common Words

hello

hello
hi
how are you?

nǐ hǎo

你好   你好

Press <Space> or Tap to continue
Return to Flash Cards list

Figure 10-3. *Typical flashcard showing all the components*

The set of words for a flashcard set looks like Figure 10-4.

Words for Common Words

English	Pinyin	Traditional	Simplified
hello	nǐ hǎo	你好	你好
hello (interj., esp. on telephone)	wèi	喂	喂
good	hǎo	好	好
goodbye	zài jiàn	再見	再见
How are you?	nǐ hǎo ma	你好嗎	你好吗
toilet	cè suǒ	廁所	厕所
thanks	xiè xie	謝謝	谢谢

Return to Flash Cards list

Figure 10-4. *The list of words in a flashcard set*

Browser Files

The browser side has HTML, CSS, and JavaScript files. These are as follows:

- Home page (flashcards.html):
  - html/ListFlashcardsStylesheet.css
- Flashcard set (ShowFlashcards.html):
  - css/CardStyleSheet.css
  - jscript/jquery.js
  - jscript/slideviewer.js
- Flashcard set words (ListWords.html): None extra

Basic Server

The server is an HTTP server as discussed in the previous chapter. It has a number of functions to handle different URLs. The functions are outlined here:

Path	Function	HTML Delivered
/	listFlashCards	html/ListFlashcards.html
/flashcards.html	listFlashCards	html/ListFlashcards.html
/flashcardSets	manageFlashCards	html/showFlashcards.html
/flashcardSets	manageFlashCards	html/ListWords.html
/jscript/*	fileServer	Files from directory /jscript
/html/*	fileServer	Files from directory /html

Omitting the functions themselves for now, the server is Server.go under Ch10 of http://www.apress.com/9781484226919.

```go
/* Server
 */

package main

import (
        "fmt"
        "net/http"
        "os"
        "html/template"
)

import (
        "dictionary"
        "flashcards"
        "templatefuncs"
)

func main() {
        if len(os.Args) != 2 {
                fmt.Fprint(os.Stderr, "Usage: ", os.Args[0], ":port\n")
                os.Exit(1)
        }
        port := os.Args[1]

        http.HandleFunc("/", listFlashCards)
        fileServer := http.StripPrefix("/jscript/", http.FileServer(http.Dir("jscript")))
        http.Handle("/jscript/", fileServer)
        fileServer = http.StripPrefix("/html/", http.FileServer(http.Dir("html")))
        http.Handle("/html/", fileServer)

        http.HandleFunc("/flashcards.html", listFlashCards)
        http.HandleFunc("/flashcardSets", manageFlashCards)

        // deliver requests to the handlers
        err := http.ListenAndServe(port, nil)
        checkError(err)
        // That's it!
}

func listFlashCards(rw http.ResponseWriter, req *http.Request) {
        ...
}

/*
 * Called from ListFlashcards.html on form submission
 */
```

```go
func manageFlashCards(rw http.ResponseWriter, req *http.Request) {
        ...
}

func showFlashCards(rw http.ResponseWriter, cardname, order, half string) {
        ...
}

func listWords(rw http.ResponseWriter, cardname string) {
        ...
}

func checkError(err error) {
        if err != nil {
                fmt.Println("Fatal error ", err.Error())
                os.Exit(1)
        }
}
```

We now turn to discussion of the individual functions.

The listFlashCards Function

The listFlashCards function is called to create HTML for the top-level page. The list of flashcard names is extensible and is the set of file entries in the directory flashcardSets. This list is used to create the table in the top-level page and is best done using the template package:

```html
<table>
  {{range .}}
  <tr>
    <td>
      {{.}}
    </td>
  </tr>
</table>
```

Where the range is over the list of names. The file html/ListFlashcards.html contains this template as well as the HTML for the side lists of card order, half card display, and the form buttons at the bottom. Omitting the side lists and the submit buttons, the HTML is as follows:

```html
<html>
  <head>
    <title>
      Flashcards
    </title>
    <link type="text/css" rel="stylesheet"
          href="/html/ListFlashcardsStylesheet.css">
    </link>
  </head>
  <body>
```

```
  <h1>
    Flashcards
  </h1>
  <p>

    <div id="choose">
      <form method="GET" action="http:flashcardSets">

        <table border="1" id="sets">
          <tr>
            <th  colspan="2">
              Flashcard Sets
            </th>
          </tr>
          {{range .}}
          <tr>
            <td>
              {{.}}
            </td>
            <td>
              <input type="radio" name="flashcardSets" value="{{.}}" />
            </td>
          </tr>
          {{end}}
        </table>
    </div>
  </p>
  </body>
</html>
```

The function listFlashCards, which applies the template to this, is as follows:

```go
func listFlashCards(rw http.ResponseWriter, req *http.Request) {

        flashCardsNames := flashcards.ListFlashCardsNames()
        t, err := template.ParseFiles("html/ListFlashcards.html")
        if err != nil {
                http.Error(rw, err.Error(), http.StatusInternalServerError)
                return
        }
        t.Execute(rw, flashCardsNames)
}
```

The function flashcards.ListFlashCardsNames() just iterates through the flashcards directory, returning an array of strings (the filenames of each flashcard set):

```go
func ListFlashCardsNames() []string {
      flashcardsDir, err := os.Open("flashcardSets")
      if err != nil {
            return nil
      }
      files, err := flashcardsDir.Readdir(-1)
```

```
        fileNames := make([]string, len(files))
        for n, f := range files {
                fileNames[n] = f.Name()
        }
        sort.Strings(fileNames)
        return fileNames
}
```

The manageFlashCards Function

The manageFlashCards function is called to manage the form submission on pressing the "Show Cards in Set" button or the "List Words in Set" button. It extracts values from the form request and then chooses between showFlashCards and listWords:

```
func manageFlashCards(rw http.ResponseWriter, req *http.Request) {

        set := req.FormValue("flashcardSets")
        order := req.FormValue("order")
        action := req.FormValue("submit")
        half := req.FormValue("half")
        cardname := "flashcardSets/" + set

        fmt.Println("cardname", cardname, "action", action)
        if action == "Show cards in set" {
                showFlashCards(rw, cardname, order, half)
        } else if action == "List words in set" {
                listWords(rw, cardname)
        }
}
```

The Chinese Dictionary

The previous code was fairly generic: it delivers static files using a FileServer, creates HTML tables using templates based on a listing of files in a directory, and processes information from an HTML form. To proceed further by looking at what is displayed in each card, we have to get into the application-specific detail and that means looking at the source of words (a dictionary), how to represent it and the cards, and how to send flashcard data to the browser. First, the dictionary.

Chinese is a complex language—aren't they all :-(. The written form is hieroglyphic, that is "pictograms," instead of using an alphabet. But this written form has evolved over time, and even recently split into two forms: "traditional" Chinese as used in Taiwan and Hong Kong, and "simplified" Chinese as used in mainland China. While most of the characters are the same, about 1,000 are different. Thus a Chinese dictionary will often have two written forms of the same character.

Most Westerners like me can't understand these characters. So there is a "Latinized" form called Pinyin, which writes the characters in a phonetic alphabet based on the Latin alphabet. It isn't quite the Latin alphabet, because Chinese is a tonal language, and the Pinyin form has to show the tones (much like accents in French and other European languages). So a typical dictionary has to show four things: the traditional form, the simplified form, the Pinyin, and the English. In addition (just like in English), a word may have multiple meanings. For example, there is a free Chinese/English dictionary at http://www.mandarintools.com/worddict.html, and even better, you can download it as a UTF-8 file. In it, the word 好 has this entry:

Traditional	Simplified	Pinyin	English	Meanings
好	好	hǎo	good	/good/well/proper/good to/easy to/very/so/(suffix indicating completion or readiness)/

There is a little complication in this dictionary. Most keyboards are not good at representing accents such as the caron in ǎ. So while the Chinese characters are written in Unicode, the Pinyin characters are not. Although there are Unicode characters for letters such as ǎ, many dictionaries including this one use the Latin a and place the tone at the end of the word. Here it is the third tone, so hǎo is written as hao3. This makes it easier for those who only have U.S. keyboards and no Unicode editor to still communicate in Pinyin. A copy of the dictionary as used by the web server is cedict_ts_u8.

This data format mismatch is not a big deal. Just that somewhere along the line, between the original text dictionary and the display in the browser, a data massage has to be performed. Go templates allow this to be done by defining a custom template, so I chose that route. Alternative approaches include doing this as the dictionary is read in, or in the JavaScript to display the final characters.

The Dictionary Type

We use an Entry to hold the basic information about one word:

```
type Entry struct {
    Traditional string
    Simplified string
    Pinyin     string
    Translations []string
}
```

The word above would be represented by the following:

```
Entry{Traditional: 好,
      Simplified: 好,
      Pinyin: `hao3`
      Translations: []string{`good`, `well`,`proper`,
                              `good to`, `easy to`, `very`, `so`,
                              `(suffix indicating completion or readiness)`}
}
```

The dictionary itself is just an array of these entries:

```
type Dictionary struct {
    Entries []*Entry
}
```

Flashcard Sets

A single flashcard is meant to represent a Chinese word and the English translation of that word. We have already seen that a single Chinese word can have many possible English meanings. But this dictionary also sometimes has multiple occurrences of a Chinese word. For example, 好 occurs at least twice, once with the meaning we have already seen, but also with another meaning, "to be fond of". It turned out to be overkill, but to allow for this, each flashcard is given a full dictionary of words. Typically there is only one entry in the dictionary! The rest of a flashcard is just the simplified and English words to act as possible keys:

```
type FlashCard struct {
        Simplified string
        English    string
        Dictionary *dictionary.Dictionary
}
```

The *set* of flashcards is an array of these, plus the name of the set, and information that will be sent to the browser for presentation of the set: random or fixed order, showing the top or bottom of each card first, or random.

```
type FlashCards struct {
        Name      string
        CardOrder string
        ShowHalf  string
        Cards     []*FlashCard
}
```

We have shown one function for this type already, ListFlashCardsNames(). There is one other function of interest for this type to load a JSON file for a flashcard set. This uses the techniques of Chapter 4, *serialization*.

```
func LoadJSON(fileName string, key interface{}) {
        inFile, err := os.Open(fileName)
        checkError(err)
        decoder := json.NewDecoder(inFile)
        err = decoder.Decode(key)
        checkError(err)
        inFile.Close()
}
```

A typical flashcard set is of common words. When the JSON file is pretty printed by Python (print json.dump(string, indent=4, separators=(',', ':'))), part of it looks like this:

```
{
    "ShowHalf":"",
    "Cards":[
        {
            "Simplified":"\u4f60\u597d",
            "Dictionary":{
                "Entries":[
                    {
                        "Traditional":"\u4f60\u597d",
```

```
                            "Pinyin":"ni3 hao3",
                            "Translations":[
                                "hello",
                                "hi",
                                "how are you?"
                            ],
                            "Simplified":"\u4f60\u597d"
                        }
                    ]
                },
                "English":"hello"
            },
            {
                "Simplified":"\u5582",
                "Dictionary":{
                    "Entries":[
                        {
                            "Traditional":"\u5582",
                            "Pinyin":"wei4",
                            "Translations":[
                                "hello (interj., esp. on telephone)",
                                "hey",
                                "to feed (sb or some animal)"
                            ],
                            "Simplified":"\u5582"
                        }
                    ]
                },
                "English":"hello (interj., esp. on telephone)"
            },
        ],
        "CardOrder":"",
        "Name":"Common Words"
}
```

Fixing Accents

There is one last major task before we can complete the code for the server. The accents as given in the dictionaries place the accent at the end of the Pinyin word, as in hao3 for hǎo. The translation to Unicode can be performed by a custom template, as discussed in Chapter 9.

The code for the Pinyin formatter is given here. Don't bother reading it unless you are *really* interested in knowing the rules for Pinyin formatting. The program is PinyinFormatter.go:

```
package templatefuncs

import (
        "fmt"
        "strings"
)
```

```go
func PinyinFormatter(args ...interface{}) string {
        ok := false
        var s string
        if len(args) == 1 {
                s, ok = args[0].(string)
        }
        if !ok {
                s = fmt.Sprint(args...)
        }
        fmt.Println("Formatting func " + s)
        // the string may consist of several pinyin words
        // each one needs to be changed separately and then
        // added back together
        words := strings.Fields(s)

        for n, word := range words {
                // convert "u:" to "ü" if present
                uColon := strings.Index(word, "u:")
                if uColon != -1 {
                        parts := strings.SplitN(word, "u:", 2)
                        word = parts[0] + "ü" + parts[1]
                }
                println(word)
                // get last character, will be the tone if present
                chars := []rune(word)
                tone := chars[len(chars)-1]
                if tone == '5' {
                        // there is no accent for tone 5
                        words[n] = string(chars[0 : len(chars)-1])
                        println("lost accent on", words[n])
                        continue
                }
                if tone < '1' || tone > '4' {
                        // not a tone value
                        continue
                }
                words[n] = addAccent(word, int(tone))
        }
        s = strings.Join(words, ` `)
        return s
}

var (
        // maps 'a1' to '\u0101' etc
        aAccent = map[int]rune{
                '1': '\u0101',
                '2': '\u00e1',
                '3': '\u01ce',
                '4': '\u00e0'}
        eAccent = map[int]rune{
                '1': '\u0113',
```

```go
                    '2': '\u00e9',
                    '3': '\u011b',
                    '4': '\u00e8'}
        iAccent = map[int]rune{
                    '1': '\u012b',
                    '2': '\u00ed',
                    '3': '\u01d0',
                    '4': '\u00ec'}
        oAccent = map[int]rune{
                    '1': '\u014d',
                    '2': '\u00f3',
                    '3': '\u01d2',
                    '4': '\u00f2'}
        uAccent = map[int]rune{
                    '1': '\u016b',
                    '2': '\u00fa',
                    '3': '\u01d4',
                    '4': '\u00f9'}
        üAccent = map[int]rune{
                    '1': 'ǖ',
                    '2': 'ǘ',
                    '3': 'ǚ',
                    '4': 'ǜ'}
)

func addAccent(word string, tone int) string {
        /*
         * Based on "Where do the tone marks go?"
         * at http://www.pinyin.info/rules/where.html
         */

        n := strings.Index(word, "a")
        if n != -1 {
                aAcc := aAccent[tone]
                // replace 'a' with its tone version
                word = word[0:n] + string(aAcc) + word[(n+1):len(word)-1]
        } else {
                n := strings.Index(word, "e")
                if n != -1 {
                        eAcc := eAccent[tone]
                        word = word[0:n] + string(eAcc) +
                                word[(n+1):len(word)-1]
                } else {
                        n = strings.Index(word, "ou")
                        if n != -1 {
                                oAcc := oAccent[tone]
                                word = word[0:n] + string(oAcc) + "u" +
                                        word[(n+2):len(word)-1]
                        } else {
                                chars := []rune(word)
                                length := len(chars)
```

```
                                 // put tone on the last vowel
                          L:
                                 for n, _ := range chars {
                                         m := length - n - 1
                                         switch chars[m] {
                                         case 'i':
                                                 chars[m] = iAccent[tone]
                                                 break L
                                         case 'o':
                                                 chars[m] = oAccent[tone]
                                                 break L
                                         case 'u':
                                                 chars[m] = uAccent[tone]
                                                 break L
                                         case 'ü':
                                                 chars[m] = üAccent[tone]
                                                 break L
                                         default:
                                         }
                                 }
                                 word = string(chars[0 : len(chars)-1])
                         }
                 }
         }
         return word
}
```

The ListWords Function

We can now return to the outstanding functions of the server. One was to list the words in a flashcards set. This populates an HTML table using a template for a flashcards set. The HTML for this uses the template package to walk over a FlashCards struct and insert the fields from that struct:

```
<html>
  <head>
    <title>
      Words for {{.Name}}
    </title>

  </head>
  <body>
    <h1>
      Words for {{.Name}}
    </h1>
    <p>
      <table border="1" class="sortable">
        <tr>
          <th> English </th>
          <th> Pinyin </th>
```

```
            <th> Traditional </th>
            <th> Simplified </th>
          </tr>
        {{range .Cards}}
          <div class="card">
            <tr>
            <div class="english">
              <div class="vcenter">
                <td>
                  {{.English}}
                </td>
              </div>
            </div>

            {{with .Dictionary}}
              {{range .Entries}}
                <div class="pinyin">
                  <div class="vcenter">
                    <td>
                      {{.Pinyin|pinyin}}
                    </td>
                  </div>
                </div>

                <div class="traditional">
                  <div class="vcenter">
                    <td>
                      {{.Traditional}}
                    </td>
                  </div>
                </div>

                <div class="simplified">
                  <div class="vcenter">
                    <td>
                      {{.Simplified}}
                    </td>
                  </div>
                </div>

              {{end}}
            {{end}}
            </tr>
          </div>
        {{end}}
        </table>
    </p>
    <p class ="return">
      <a href="http:/flashcards.html"> Return to Flash Cards list</a>
    </p>
  </body>
</html>
```

The Go function in Server.go to do this uses the PinyinFormatter discussed in the last section:

```
func listWords(rw http.ResponseWriter, cardname string) {
        cards := new(flashcards.FlashCards)
        flashcards.LoadJSON(cardname, cards)
        fmt.Println("Card name", cards.Name)

        t := template.New("ListWords.html")

        t = t.Funcs(template.FuncMap{"pinyin": templatefuncs.PinyinFormatter})
        t, err := t.ParseFiles("html/ListWords.html")

        if err != nil {
                fmt.Println("Parse error " + err.Error())
                http.Error(rw, err.Error(), http.StatusInternalServerError)
                return
        }
        err = t.Execute(rw, cards)
        if err != nil {
                fmt.Println("Execute error " + err.Error())
                http.Error(rw, err.Error(), http.StatusInternalServerError)
                return
        }
}
```

This sends the populated table to the browser, as shown in Figure 10-4.

The showFlashCards Function

The final function to complete the server is showFlashCards. This changes the default values of CardOrder and ShowHalf in the flashcard set based on the form submitted from the browser. It then applies the PinyinFormatter and sends the resulting document to the browser. I captured the output of a command-line session using the UNIX command script and then ran the command:

```
GET /flashcardSets?flashcardSets=Common+Words&order=Random&half=Chinese&submit=Show+cards+i
n+set HTTP/1.0
```

Part of the result is as follows:

```
<html>
  <head>
    <title>
      Flashcards for Common Words
    </title>

    <link type="text/css" rel="stylesheet"
          href="/html/CardStylesheet.css">
    </link>
```

```html
<script type="text/javascript"
        language="JavaScript1.2" src="/jscript/jquery.js">
  <!-- empty -->
</script>

<script type="text/javascript"
        language="JavaScript1.2" src="/jscript/slideviewer.js">
  <!-- empty -->
</script>

<script type="text/javascript"
        language="JavaScript1.2">
  cardOrder = "RANDOM";
  showHalfCard = "CHINESE_HALF";
</script>
</head>
<body onload="showSlides();">

  <h1>
    Flashcards for Common Words
  </h1>
  <p>

    <div class="card">
      <div class="english">
        <div class="vcenter">
          hello
        </div>
      </div>

          <div class="pinyin">
            <div class="vcenter">
              nǐ hǎo
            </div>
          </div>

          <div class="traditional">
            <div class="vcenter">
              你好
            </div>
          </div>

          <div class="simplified">
            <div class="vcenter">
              你好
            </div>
          </div>
```

```
<div class ="translations">
  <div class="vcenter">

    hello <br />

    hi <br />

    how are you? <br />

  </div>
  </div>

</div>
```

Presentation on the Browser

The final part of this system is how this HTML is shown in the browser. Figure 10-3 shows a screen of four parts displaying the English, the simplified Chinese, the alternative translations and the traditional/simplified pair. How this is done is by the JavaScript program downloaded to the server (this takes place using the FileServer Go object). The JavaScript slideviewer.js file is actually pretty long and is omitted from the text. It is included in the program files at http://www.apress.com/9781484226919.

Running the Server

This is the first program in this book that uses our own imported files. All the previous programs have just used a main file and the Go standard libraries. The imported files in the package's dictionary, flashcards and pinyin, need to be organized so that the go command can find them.

The environment variable GOPATH needs to be set to a directory with a subdirectory src containing the imported source files in the appropriate subdirectories:

```
src/flashcards/FlashCards.go
src/pinyin/PinyinFormatter.go
src/dictionary/Dictionary.go
```

The server can then be run on port 8000 (or other port) using a command such as this:

```
go run Server.go :8000
```

Conclusion

This chapter has considered a relatively simple but complete web server, using static and dynamic web pages with form handling and using templates for simplifying coding.

CHAPTER 11

HTML

The Web was originally created to serve HTML documents. Now it is used to serve all sorts of documents as well as data of different kinds. Nevertheless, HTML is still the main document type delivered over the Web.

HTML has been through a large number of versions, with the current version being HTML5. There have also been many "vendor" versions of HTML, introducing tags that never made it into the standards.

HTML is simple enough to be edited by hand. Consequently, many HTML documents are "ill formed," which means they don't follow the syntax of the language. HTML parsers generally are not very strict and will accept many "illegal" documents.

The HTML package itself only has two functions—EscapeString and UnescapeString. These properly handle characters such as <, converting them to < and back again.

A principal use of this might be to escape the markup in an HTML document so that if it is displayed in a browser, it will show all the markup (much like Ctrl+U in Chrome on Linux or Option+Cmd+U on Mac Chrome).

I'm more likely to use this to show the text of a program as a web page. Most programming languages have the < symbol and many have &. These mess up an HTML viewer unless escaped properly. I like to show program text directly out of the file system rather than copy and paste it into a document, to avoid getting out of synch.

The following program EscapeString.go is a web server that shows its URL in preformatted code, having escaped the troublesome characters:

```go
/*
 * This program serves a file in preformatted, code layout
 * Useful for showing program text, properly escaping special
 * characters like '<', '>' and '&'
 */

package main

import (
        "fmt"
        "html"
        "io/ioutil"
        "net/http"
        "os"
)
```

© Jan Newmarch 2017
J. Newmarch, *Network Programming with Go*, DOI 10.1007/978-1-4842-2692-6_11

```go
func main() {
        http.HandleFunc("/", escapeString)

        err := http.ListenAndServe(":8080", nil)
        checkError(err)
}

func escapeString(rw http.ResponseWriter, req *http.Request) {
        fmt.Println(req.URL.Path)
        bytes, err := ioutil.ReadFile("." + req.URL.Path)
        if err != nil {
                rw.WriteHeader(http.StatusNotFound)
                return
        }

        escapedStr := html.EscapeString(string(bytes))
        htmlText := "<html><body><pre><code>" +
                escapedStr +
                " </code></pre></body></html>"
        rw.Write([]byte(htmlText))
}

func checkError(err error) {
        if err != nil {
                fmt.Println("Error ", err.Error())
                os.Exit(1)
        }
}
```

When it runs, serving files from the directory including the EscapeString.go program, a browser will display it correctly using the URL localhost:8080/EscapeString.go.

Run the server with this command:

```
go run EscapeString.go
```

Run a client with this command, as an example:

```
curl localhost:8080/EscapeString.go
```

The Go HTML/Template Package

There are many attacks that can be made on web servers, the most notable being SQL-injection, where a user-agent enters data into a web form deliberately designed to be passed into a database and wreak havoc there. Go does not have any particular support to avoid this, since there are many variances among databases as to the SQL-injection techniques that can succeed. The SQL Injection Prevention Cheat Sheet (see https://www.owasp.org/index.php/SQL_Injection_Prevention_Cheat_Sheet) summarizes the defenses against such attacks. The principal one is to avoid such attacks by using SQL *prepared statements,* which can be done using the Prepare function in the database/sql package.

More subtle attacks are based on XSS—cross-site-scripting. This is where an attacker is not trying to attack the web site itself, but stores malicious code on the server, to attack any of the clients of that web site.

These attacks are based on inserting data into the database strings that, when delivered to a browser for example, will attack the browser and through it, attack the client of the web site. (There are several variants of this, discussed at "OWASP: Types of Cross-Site Scripting"—https://www.owasp.org/index.php/Types_ of_Cross-Site_Scripting.)

For example, JavaScript may be inserted where a blog comment was requested to redirect a browser to an attacker's site:

```
<script>
    window.location='http://attacker/'
</script>
```

The Go html/template package is designed on top of the text/template package. The assumption is made that whereas the template will be trusted, the data that it deals with may not. What html/template adds is suitable escaping of the data to try to eliminate the possibility of XSS. It is based on the document called "Using Type Inference to Make Web Templates Robust Against XSS" by Mike Samuel and Prateek Saxena. Read that paper at https://rawgit.com/mikesamuel/sanitized-jquery-templates/ trunk/safetemplate.html#problem_definition for the theory behind the package, and the package documentation itself.

In short, prepare templates as per the text/template package and use the html/template package if the resultant text is delivered to an HTML agent.

Tokenizing HTML

The package golang.org/x/net/html in the Go sub-repositories contains a tokenizer for HTML. This allows you to build a parse tree of HTML tokens. It is compliant with HTML5.

It can be used after running this:

```
go get golang.org/x/net/html
```

An example program using this is ReadHTML.go:

```
/* Read HTML
 */

package main

import (
        "fmt"
        "golang.org/x/net/html"
        "io/ioutil"
        "os"
        "strings"
)

func main() {
        if len(os.Args) != 2 {
                fmt.Println("Usage: ", os.Args[0], "file")
                os.Exit(1)
        }
```

```
        file := os.Args[1]
        bytes, err := ioutil.ReadFile(file)
        checkError(err)
        r := strings.NewReader(string(bytes))

        z := html.NewTokenizer(r)

        depth := 0
        for {
                tt := z.Next()

                for n := 0; n < depth; n++ {
                        fmt.Print(" ")
                }

                switch tt {
                case html.ErrorToken:
                        fmt.Println("Error ", z.Err().Error())
                        os.Exit(0)
                case html.TextToken:
                        fmt.Println("Text: \"" + z.Token().String() + "\"")
                case html.StartTagToken, html.EndTagToken:
                        fmt.Println("Tag: \"" + z.Token().String() + "\"")
                        if tt == html.StartTagToken {
                                depth++
                        } else {
                                depth--
                        }
                }
        }

}

func checkError(err error) {
        if err != nil {
                fmt.Println("Fatal error ", err.Error())
                os.Exit(1)
        }
}
```

When it runs on a simple HTML document such as this:

```
<html>
  <head>
    <title> Test HTML </title>
  </head>
  <body>
    <h1> Header one </h1>
    <p>
      Test para
    </p>
  </body>
</html>
```

It produces the following:

```
Tag: "<html>"
 Text: "
  "
 Tag: "<head>"
  Text: "
   "
  Tag: "<title>"
   Text: " Test HTML "
   Tag: "</title>"
  Text: "
   "
  Tag: "</head>"
 Text: "
  "
 Tag: "<body>"
  Text: "
   "
  Tag: "<h1>"
   Text: " Header one "
   Tag: "</h1>"
  Text: "
   "
  Tag: "<p>"
   Text: "
      Test para
   "
   Tag: "</p>"
  Text: "
   "
  Tag: "</body>"
 Text: "
 "
 Tag: "</html>"
Text: "
 "
```

(All the whitespace it produces is correct.)

XHTML/HTML

There is also limited support for XHTML/HTML in the XML package, discussed in the next chapter.

JSON

There is good support for JSON, as discussed in Chapter 4.

Conclusion

There isn't much to this package. The sub-package `html/template` was discussed in Chapter 9 on templates.

CHAPTER 12

XML

XML is a significant markup language mainly intended as a means of representing structured data using a text format. In the language we used in Chapter 4, it can be considered as a means of serializing data structures as a text document. It is used to describe documents such as DocBook and XHTML. It is used in specialized markup languages such as MathML and CML (Chemistry Markup Language). It is used to encode data as SOAP messages for Web Services, and the Web Service can be specified using WSDL (Web Services Description Language).

At the simplest level, XML allows you to define your own tags for use in text documents. Tags can be nested and can be interspersed with text. Each tag can also contain attributes with values. For example, the file person.xml may contain:

```
<person>
  <name>
    <family> Newmarch </family>
    <personal> Jan </personal>
  </name>
  <email type="personal">
    jan@newmarch.name
  </email>
  <email type="work">
    j.newmarch@boxhill.edu.au
  </email>
</person>
```

The structure of any XML document can be described in a number of ways:

- A document type definition DTD is good for describing structure

- XML schema are good for describing the data types used by an XML document

- RELAX NG is proposed as an alternative to both

There is argument over the relative value of each way of defining the structure of an XML document. We won't buy into that, as Go does not support any of them. Go cannot check for validity of any document against a schema, but only for well-formedness. Even well-formedness is an important characteristic of XML documents, and is often a problem with HTML documents in practice. That makes XML suitable for representation of even very complex data, while HTML is not.

Four topics are discussed in this chapter: parsing an XML stream, marshalling and unmarshalling Go data into XML, and XHTML.

© Jan Newmarch 2017
J. Newmarch, *Network Programming with Go*, DOI 10.1007/978-1-4842-2692-6_12

Parsing XML

Go has an XML parser that's created using NewDecoder from the encoding/xml package. This takes an io.Reader as a parameter and returns a pointer to Decoder. The main method of this type is Token, which returns the next token in the input stream. The token is one of these types—StartElement, EndElement, CharData, Comment, ProcInst, or Directive.

We will use this type:

```
type Name struct {
    Space, Local string
}
```

The XML types are StartElement, EndElement, CharData, Comment, ProcInst, and Directive. They are described next.

The StartElement Type

The type StartElement is a structure with two field types:

```
type StartElement struct {
    Name Name
    Attr []Attr
}
```

where

```
type Attr struct {
    Name   Name
    Value string
}
```

The EndElement Type

This is also a structure as follows:

```
type EndElement struct {
    Name Name
}
```

The CharData Type

This type represents the text content enclosed by a tag and is a simple type:

```
type CharData []byte
```

The Comment Type

Similarly for this type:

```
type Comment []byte
```

The ProcInst Type

A ProcInst represents an XML processing instruction of the form <?target inst?>:

```
type ProcInst struct {
    Target string
    Inst   []byte
}
```

The Directive Type

A Directive represents an XML directive of the form <!text>. The bytes do not include the <! and > markers.

```
type Directive []byte
```

A program to print out the tree structure of an XML document is ParseXML.go:

```
/* Parse XML
 */

package main

import (
        "encoding/xml"
        "fmt"
        "io/ioutil"
        "os"
        "strings"
)

func main() {
        if len(os.Args) != 2 {
                fmt.Println("Usage: ", os.Args[0], "file")
                os.Exit(1)
        }
        file := os.Args[1]
        bytes, err := ioutil.ReadFile(file)
        checkError(err)
        r := strings.NewReader(string(bytes))

        parser := xml.NewDecoder(r)
        depth := 0
        for {
                token, err := parser.Token()
                if err != nil {
                        break
                }
```

```
                switch t := token.(type) {
                case xml.StartElement:
                        elmt := xml.StartElement(t)
                        name := elmt.Name.Local
                        printElmt(name, depth)
                        depth++
                case xml.EndElement:
                        depth--
                        elmt := xml.EndElement(t)
                        name := elmt.Name.Local
                        printElmt(name, depth)
                case xml.CharData:
                        bytes := xml.CharData(t)
                        printElmt("\""+string([]byte(bytes))+"\"", depth)
                case xml.Comment:
                        printElmt("Comment", depth)
                case xml.ProcInst:
                        printElmt("ProcInst", depth)
                case xml.Directive:
                        printElmt("Directive", depth)
                default:
                        fmt.Println("Unknown")
                }
        }
}

func printElmt(s string, depth int) {
        for n := 0; n < depth; n++ {
                fmt.Print("  ")
        }
        fmt.Println(s)
}

func checkError(err error) {
        if err != nil {
                fmt.Println("Fatal error ", err.Error())
                os.Exit(1)
        }
}
```

Note that the parser includes all CharData, including the whitespace between the tags. If we run this program against the person data structure given earlier, as follows:

```
go run ParseXML.go person.xml
```

It produces the following:

```
person
  "
  "
  name
    "
    "
```

```
    family
       " Newmarch "
    family
       "
       "
    personal
       " Jan "
    personal
       "
  "
  name
  "
  "
  email
     "
    jan@newmarch.name
  "
  email
  "
  "
  email
     "
    j.newmarch@boxhill.edu.au
  "
  email
  "
"
person
"
"
```

Note that as no DTD or other XML specification has been used, the tokenizer correctly prints out all the whitespace (a DTD may specify that the whitespace can be ignored, but without it that assumption cannot be made).

There is a potential trap in using this parser. It reuses space for strings, so that once you see a token, you need to copy its value if you want to refer to it later. Go has methods such as func (c CharData) Copy() CharData to make a copy of data.

Unmarshalling XML

Go provides a function called Unmarshal to unmarshal XML into Go data structures. The unmarshalling is not perfect: Go and XML are different languages.

We consider a simple example before looking at the details. First consider the XML document given earlier:

```
<person>
  <name>
    <family> Newmarch </family>
    <personal> Jan </personal>
  </name>
```

```
    <email type="personal">
      jan@newmarch.name
    </email>
    <email type="work">
      j.newmarch@boxhill.edu.au
    </email>
</person>
```

We would like to map this onto the Go structures:

```
type Person struct {
        Name Name
        Email []Email
}

type Name struct {
        Family string
        Personal string
}

type Email struct {
        Type string
        Address string
}
```

This requires several comments:

- Unmarshalling uses the Go reflection package. This requires that all fields be public, i.e., start with a capital letter. Earlier versions of Go used case-insensitive matching to match fields such as the XML string "name" to the field Name. Now, though, *case-sensitive* matching is used. To perform a match, the structure fields must be tagged to show the XML string that will be matched against. This changes Person to the following:

  ```
  type Person struct {
          Name Name `xml:"name"`
          Email []Email `xml:"email"`
  }
  ```

- While tagging of fields can attach XML strings to fields, it can't do so with the names of the structures. An additional field is required, with the field name XMLName. This only affects the top-level struct, Person:

  ```
  type Person struct {
          XMLName Name `xml:"person"`
          Name Name `xml:"name"`
          Email []Email `xml:"email"`
  }
  ```

- Repeated tags map to a slice in Go.

- Attributes within tags will match to fields in a structure only if the Go field has the tag ,attr. This occurs with the field Type of Email, where matching the attribute type of the email tag requires xml:"type,attr".

- If an XML tag has no attributes and only has character data, then it matches a string field by the same name (case-sensitive, though). So the tag xml:"family" with character data Newmarch maps to the string field Family.

- But if the tag has attributes, then it must map to a structure. Go assigns the character data to the field with tag ,chardata. This occurs with the email data and the field Address with tag ,chardata.

A program to unmarshal the document above is Unmarshal.go:

```
/* Unmarshal
 */

package main

import (
        "encoding/xml"
        "fmt"
        "os"
)

type Person struct {
        XMLName Name      `xml:"person"`
        Name    Name      `xml:"name"`
        Email   []Email   `xml:"email"`
}

type Name struct {
        Family   string `xml:"family"`
        Personal string `xml:"personal"`
}

type Email struct {
        Type    string `xml:"type,attr"`
        Address string `xml:",chardata"`
}

func main() {
        str := `<?xml version="1.0" encoding="utf-8"?>
<person>
  <name>
    <family> Newmarch </family>
    <personal> Jan </personal>
  </name>
```

```
    <email type="personal">
      jan@newmarch.name
    </email>
    <email type="work">
      j.newmarch@boxhill.edu.au
    </email>
</person>`

        var person Person

        err := xml.Unmarshal([]byte(str), &person)
        checkError(err)

        // now use the person structure e.g.
        fmt.Println("Family name: \"" + person.Name.Family + "\"")
        fmt.Println("Second email address: \"" + person.Email[1].Address + "\"")
}

func checkError(err error) {
        if err != nil {
                fmt.Println("Fatal error ", err.Error())
                os.Exit(1)
        }
}
```

(Note that the spaces are correct.) The strict rules are given in the package specification.

Marshalling XML

Go also has support for marshalling data structures into an XML document. The function is:

```
func Marshal(v interface}{) ([]byte, error)
```

A program to marshal a simple structure is Marshal.go:

```
/* Marshal
 */

package main

import (
        "encoding/xml"
        "fmt"
)

type Person struct {
        Name   Name
        Email []Email
}
```

```
type Name struct {
        Family   string
        Personal string
}

type Email struct {
        Kind    string "attr"
        Address string "chardata"
}

func main() {
        person := Person{
                Name: Name{Family: "Newmarch", Personal: "Jan"},
                Email: []Email{Email{Kind: "home", Address: "jan"},
                        Email{Kind: "work", Address: "jan"}}}

        buff, _ := xml.Marshal(person)
        fmt.Println(string(buff))
}
```

It produces the text with no whitespace:

```
<Person><Name><Family>Newmarch</Family><Personal>Jan</Personal></Name><Email><Kind>home</Kind>
<Address>jan</Address></Email><Email><Kind>work</Kind><Address>jan</Address></Email></Person>
```

XHTML

HTML does not conform to XML syntax. It has unterminated tags such as <br>. XHTML is a cleanup of HTML to make it compliant with XML. Documents in XHTML can be managed using the techniques above for XML. XHTML does not appear to be as widely used as originally expected. My own suspicion is that an HTML parser is usually tolerant of errors and when used in a browser generally makes a reasonable job of rendering a document, XHTML parsers even in a browser tend to be more strict and often fail to render anything upon encountering even a single XML error. This is not generally appropriate behavior for user-facing software.

HTML

There is some support in the XML package to handle HTML documents even though they may not be XML compliant. The XML parser discussed earlier can handle many HTML documents if it is modified by turning off strict parse checking.

```
parser := xml.NewDecoder(r)
parser.Strict = false
parser.AutoClose = xml.HTMLAutoClose
parser.Entity = xml.HTMLEntity
```

Conclusion

Go has basic support for dealing with XML strings. It does not as yet have mechanisms for dealing with XML specification languages such as XML Schema or Relax NG.

CHAPTER 13

■ ■ ■

Remote Procedure Call

Socket and HTTP programming both use a message-passing paradigm. A client sends a message to a server, which usually sends a message back. Both sides are responsible for creating messages in a format understood by both sides, and in reading the data out of those messages.

However, most standalone applications do not use message passing techniques much. Generally the preferred mechanism is that of the *function* (or method or procedure) call. In this style, a program will call a function with a list of parameters, and on completion of the function call, will have a set of return values. These values may be the function value, or if addresses have been passed as parameters then the contents of those addresses might have been changed.

The remote procedure call is an attempt to bring this style of programming into the network world. Thus a client will make what looks to it like a normal procedure call. The client side will package this into a network message and transfer it to the server. The server will unpack this and turn it back into a procedure call on the server side. The results of this call will be packaged up for return to the client.

Diagrammatically it looks like Figure 13-1.

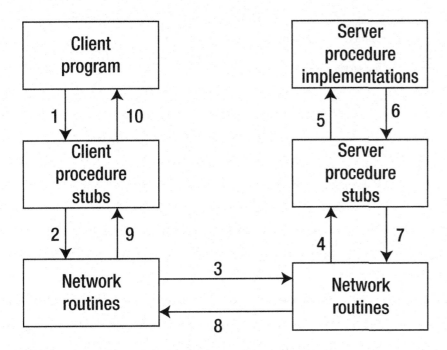

Figure 13-1. *The remote procedure call steps*

© Jan Newmarch 2017

J. Newmarch, *Network Programming with Go*, DOI 10.1007/978-1-4842-2692-6_13

The steps are as follows:

1. The client calls the client procedure stubs. The stub packages the parameters into a network message. This is called *marshalling*.

2. Networking routines in the O/S kernel are called by the stub to send the message.

3. The kernel sends the message(s) to the remote system. This may be connection-oriented or connectionless.

4. The server procedure stubs unmarshal the arguments from the network message.

5. The server procedure stubs execute server procedure implementations.

6. The procedures complete, returning execution to the server procedure stubs.

7. The server stubs marshal the return values into a network message.

8. The return messages are sent back.

9. The client procedure stubs read the messages using the network routines.

10. The message is unmarshalled and the return values are set on the stack for the client program.

There are two common styles for implementing RPC. The first is typified by Sun's ONC/RPC and by CORBA. In this, a specification of the service is given in some abstract language such as CORBA IDL (interface definition language). This is then compiled into code for the client and for the server. The client then writes a normal program containing calls to a procedure/function/method, which is linked to the generated client-side code. The server-side code is actually a server itself, which is linked to the procedure implementation that you write.

In this first way, the client-side code is almost identical in appearance to a normal procedure call. Generally there is a little extra code to locate the server. In Sun's ONC, the address of the server must be known; in CORBA, a naming service is called to find the address of the server; in Java RMI, the IDL is Java itself and a naming service is used to find the address of the service.

In the second style, you have to use a special client API. You hand the function name and its parameters to this library on the client side. On the server side, you have to explicitly write the server yourself, as well as the remote procedure implementation.

This second approach is used by many RPC systems, such as Web Services. It is also the approach used by Go's RPC.

Go's RPC

Go's RPC is so far unique to Go. It is different than the other RPC systems, so a Go client will only talk to a Go server. It uses the Gob serialization system discussed in Chapter 4, which defines the data types that can be used.

RPC systems generally make some restrictions on the functions that can be called across the network. This is so that the RPC system can properly determine which value arguments are sent, which reference arguments receive answers, and how to signal errors.

In Go, the restriction is that

- The method's type is exported (begins with a capital letter).

- The method is exported.

- The method has two arguments, both exported (or built-in) types. The first is for data passed into the method; the second is for returned results.

- The method's second argument is a pointer.

- It has a return value of type error.

For example, here is a valid function:

```
F(T1, &T2) error
```

The restriction on arguments means that you typically have to define a structure type. Go's RPC uses the gob package for marshalling and unmarshalling data, so the argument types have to follow the rules of Gob as discussed in an earlier chapter.

We will follow the example given in the Go documentation, as it illustrates the important points. The server performs two trivial operations—they do not require the "grunt" of RPC, but are simple to understand. The two operations are to multiply two integers and to find the quotient and remainder after dividing the first by the second.

The two values to be manipulated are given in a structure:

```
type Values struct {
    A, B int
}
```

The sum is just an int, while the quotient/remainder is another structure:

```
type Quotient struct {
    Quo, Rem int
}
```

We will have two functions, multiply and divide, to be callable on the RPC server. These functions need to be registered with the RPC system. The Register function takes a single parameter, which is an interface. So we need a type with these two functions:

```
type Arith int

func (t *Arith) Multiply(args *Args, reply *int) error {
        *reply = args.A * args.B
        return nil
}

func (t *Arith) Divide(args *Args, quo *Quotient) error {
        if args.B == 0 {
                return errors.New("divide by zero")
        }
        quo.Quo = args.A / args.B
        quo.Rem = args.A % args.B
        return nil
}
```

The underlying type of Arith is given as int. That doesn't matter—any type will suffice.

An object of this type can now be registered using Register, and then its methods can be called by the RPC system.

HTTP RPC Server

Any RPC needs a transport mechanism to get messages across the network. Go can use HTTP or TCP. The advantage of the HTTP mechanism is that it can leverage the HTTP support library. You need to add an RPC handler to the HTTP layer, which is done using HandleHTTP, and then start an HTTP server. The complete code is ArithServer.go:

```
/**
 * ArithServer
 */

package main

import (
        "fmt"
        "net/rpc"
        "errors"
        "net/http"
)

type Values struct {
        A, B int
}

type Quotient struct {
        Quo, Rem int
}

type Arith int

func (t *Arith) Multiply(args *Values, reply *int) error {
        *reply = args.A * args.B
        return nil
}

func (t *Arith) Divide(args *Values, quo *Quotient) error {
        if args.B == 0 {
                return errors.New("divide by zero")
        }
        quo.Quo = args.A / args.B
        quo.Rem = args.A % args.B
        return nil
}

func main() {

        arith := new(Arith)
        rpc.Register(arith)
        rpc.HandleHTTP()
```

```go
        err := http.ListenAndServe(":1234", nil)
        if err != nil {
                fmt.Println(err.Error())
        }
}
```

and it is run by

```go
go run ArithServer.go
```

HTTP RPC Client

The client needs to set up an HTTP connection to the RPC server. It needs to prepare a structure with the values to be sent, and the address of a variable in which to store the results. Then it can make a Call with these arguments:

- The name of the remote function to execute

- The values to be sent

- The address of a variable in which to store the result

A client that calls both functions of the arithmetic server is ArithClient.go:

```go
/**
 * ArithClient
 */

package main

import (
        "net/rpc"
        "fmt"
        "log"
        "os"
)

type Args struct {
        A, B int
}

type Quotient struct {
        Quo, Rem int
}

func main() {
        if len(os.Args) != 2 {
                fmt.Println("Usage: ", os.Args[0], "server")
                os.Exit(1)
        }
        serverAddress := os.Args[1]
```

```
            client, err := rpc.DialHTTP("tcp", serverAddress+":1234")
            if err != nil {
                    log.Fatal("dialing:", err)
            }
            // Synchronous call
            args := Args{17, 8}
            var reply int
            err = client.Call("Arith.Multiply", args, &reply)
            if err != nil {
                    log.Fatal("arith error:", err)
            }
            fmt.Printf("Arith: %d*%d=%d\n", args.A, args.B, reply)

            var quot Quotient
            err = client.Call("Arith.Divide", args, &quot)
            if err != nil {
                    log.Fatal("arith error:", err)
            }
            fmt.Printf("Arith: %d/%d=%d remainder %d\n", args.A, args.B, quot.Quo, quot.Rem)
}
```

When it runs:

```
go run  ArithClient.go localhost
```

It produces the following:

```
Arith: 17*8=136
Arith: 17/8=2 remainder 1
```

TCP RPC Server

A version of the server that uses TCP sockets is TCPArithServer.go:

```
/**
 * TCPArithServer
 */

package main

import (
        "fmt"
        "net/rpc"
        "errors"
        "net"
        "os"
)
```

```go
type Args struct {
        A, B int
}

type Quotient struct {
        Quo, Rem int
}

type Arith int

func (t *Arith) Multiply(args *Args, reply *int) error {
        *reply = args.A * args.B
        return nil
}

func (t *Arith) Divide(args *Args, quo *Quotient) error {
        if args.B == 0 {
                return errors.New("divide by zero")
        }
        quo.Quo = args.A / args.B
        quo.Rem = args.A % args.B
        return nil
}

func main() {

        arith := new(Arith)
        rpc.Register(arith)

        tcpAddr, err := net.ResolveTCPAddr("tcp", ":1234")
        checkError(err)

        listener, err := net.ListenTCP("tcp", tcpAddr)
        checkError(err)

        /* This works:
        rpc.Accept(listener)
        */
        /* and so does this:
         */
        for {
                conn, err := listener.Accept()
                if err != nil {
                        continue
                }
                rpc.ServeConn(conn)
        }

}
```

```
func checkError(err error) {
        if err != nil {
                fmt.Println("Fatal error ", err.Error())
                os.Exit(1)
        }
}
```

Note that the call to Accept is blocking and just handles client connections. If the server wants to do other work as well, it should call this in a go routine.

TCP RPC Client

A client that uses the TCP server and calls both functions of the arithmetic server is TCPArithClient.go:

```
/**
* TCPArithClient
 */

package main

import (
        "net/rpc"
        "fmt"
        "log"
        "os"
)

type Args struct {
        A, B int
}

type Quotient struct {
        Quo, Rem int
}

func main() {
        if len(os.Args) != 2 {
                fmt.Println("Usage: ", os.Args[0], "server:port")
                os.Exit(1)
        }
        service := os.Args[1]

        client, err := rpc.Dial("tcp", service)
        if err != nil {
                log.Fatal("dialing:", err)
        }
        // Synchronous call
        args := Args{17, 8}
        var reply int
```

```
        err = client.Call("Arith.Multiply", args, &reply)
        if err != nil {
                log.Fatal("arith error:", err)
        }
        fmt.Printf("Arith: %d*%d=%d\n", args.A, args.B, reply)

        var quot Quotient
        err = client.Call("Arith.Divide", args, &quot)
        if err != nil {
                log.Fatal("arith error:", err)
        }
        fmt.Printf("Arith: %d/%d=%d remainder %d\n", args.A, args.B, quot.Quo, quot.Rem)

}
```

When it's run:

```
go run TCPArithClient.go localhost:1234
```

It produces the following:

```
Arith: 17*8=136
Arith: 17/8=2 remainder 1
```

Matching Values

You may have noticed that the types of the value arguments are not the same on the HTTP client and HTTP server. In the server, we used Values, while in the client we used Args. That doesn't matter, as we are following the rules of Gob serialization, and the names and types of the two structures' fields match. Better programming practice would say that the names should be the same, of course!

However, this does point out a possible trap in using Go RPC. If we change the structure in the server to be this:

```
type Values struct {
        C, B int
}
```

then Gob has no problems. On the client side, the unmarshalling will ignore the value of C given by the server and use the default zero value for A. This could cause problems if, say, a divide by A (zero) was done.

Using Go RPC will require a rigid enforcement of the stability of field names and types by the programmer. We note that there is no version control mechanism to do this, and no mechanism in Gob to signal any possible mismatches. There is also no required external representation to act as a reference. If you are just adding fields then it may be okay, but it will still need control. Perhaps adding a version field to the data structure would help.

JSON

This section adds nothing new to the earlier concepts. It just uses a different "wire" format for the data, JSON instead of Gob. As such, clients or servers could be written in other languages that understand sockets and JSON.

JSON RPC Server

A version of the server that uses JSON encoding is JSONArithServer.go:

```
/* JSONArithServer
 */

package main

import (
        "fmt"
        "net/rpc"
        "net/rpc/jsonrpc"
        "os"
        "net"
        "errors"
)

type Args struct {
        A, B int
}

type Quotient struct {
        Quo, Rem int
}

type Arith int

func (t *Arith) Multiply(args *Args, reply *int) error {
        *reply = args.A * args.B
        return nil
}

func (t *Arith) Divide(args *Args, quo *Quotient) error {
        if args.B == 0 {
                return errors.New("divide by zero")
        }
        quo.Quo = args.A / args.B
        quo.Rem = args.A % args.B
        return nil
}

func main() {

        arith := new(Arith)
        rpc.Register(arith)

        tcpAddr, err := net.ResolveTCPAddr("tcp", ":1234")
        checkError(err)

        listener, err := net.ListenTCP("tcp", tcpAddr)
        checkError(err)
```

```
        /* This works:
        rpc.Accept(listener)
        */
        /* and so does this:
         */
        for {
                conn, err := listener.Accept()
                if err != nil {
                        continue
                }
                jsonrpc.ServeConn(conn)
        }

}

func checkError(err error) {
        if err != nil {
                fmt.Println("Fatal error ", err.Error())
                os.Exit(1)
        }
}
```

It is run by

```
go run JSONArithServer.go
```

JSON RPC Client

A client that calls both functions of the arithmetic server is JSONArithClient.go:

```
/* JSONArithCLient
 */

package main

import (
        "net/rpc/jsonrpc"
        "fmt"
        "log"
        "os"
)

type Args struct {
        A, B int
}

type Quotient struct {
        Quo, Rem int
}
```

```go
func main() {
        if len(os.Args) != 2 {
                fmt.Println("Usage: ", os.Args[0], "server:port")
                log.Fatal(1)
        }
        service := os.Args[1]

        client, err := jsonrpc.Dial("tcp", service)
        if err != nil {
                log.Fatal("dialing:", err)
        }
        // Synchronous call
        args := Args{17, 8}
        var reply int
        err = client.Call("Arith.Multiply", args, &reply)
        if err != nil {
                log.Fatal("arith error:", err)
        }
        fmt.Printf("Arith: %d*%d=%d\n", args.A, args.B, reply)

        var quot Quotient
        err = client.Call("Arith.Divide", args, &quot)
        if err != nil {
                log.Fatal("arith error:", err)
        }
        fmt.Printf("Arith: %d/%d=%d remainder %d\n", args.A, args.B, quot.Quo, quot.Rem)

}
```

It's run as follows:

```
go run JSONArithClient.go localhost:1234
```

It produces the following output:

```
Arith: 17*8=136
Arith: 17/8=2 remainder 1
```

Conclusion

RPC is a popular means of distributing applications. Several ways of doing it have been presented here, based on the Gob or JSON serialization techniques, and using HTTP and TCP for transport.

CHAPTER 14

REST

In previous chapters we looked at HTTP and gave an example of a web system. However, we didn't give any particular structure to the system, just what was simple enough for the problem. There is an architectural style developed by one of the key authors of HTTP 1.1 (Roy Fielding) called *REST* (REpresentational State Transfer). In this chapter we look at the REST style and what it means for building web applications. We have to go back to fundamentals for this.

REST has many components that have to be followed if the term REST can be properly applied. Unfortunately, it has become a buzzword, and many applications have "bits" of REST but not the full thing. We discuss the Richardson Maturity Model, which says how far along the path to RESTful-ness an API has gone.

In the last chapter, we looked at RPCs (remote procedure calls). This is a completely different style than REST. We also compare the two styles, looking at when it is appropriate to use each style.

URIs and Resources

Resources are the "things" that we want to interact with on a network or the Internet. I like to think of them as objects, but there is no requirement that their implementation should be object-based—they should just "look like" a thing, possibly with components.

Each resource has one or more addresses known as URIs (uniform resource identifiers).

Note The internationalized form is IRIs—internationalized resource identifiers.

These have this generic form:

```
scheme:[//[user:password@]host[:port]][/]path[?query][#fragment]
```

Typical examples are URLs (uniform resource locator), where the scheme is `http` or `https`, and the host refers to a computer by its IP address or DNS name, as follows:

```
https://jan.newmarch.name/IoT/index.html
```

There are non-HTTP URL schemes such as telnet, news, and ipp (Internet Printing Protocol). These also contain a location component. There are also others, such as URNs (uniform resource names), which are often wrappers around other identification systems, and they do not contain location information. For example, the IETF has a standard URN scheme for books identified by their ISBN, such as the ISBN for this book:

```
urn:ISBN:978-1-4842-2692-6
```

© Jan Newmarch 2017
J. Newmarch, *Network Programming with Go*, DOI 10.1007/978-1-4842-2692-6_14

CHAPTER 14 ■ REST

These URNs tend not to be widely used but still exist. A list is given by IANA Uniform Resource Names (URN) Namespaces at `https://www.iana.org/assignments/urn-namespaces/urn-namespaces.xhtml`. The original schemes, such as ISBN, are still in wider use.

A formal definition of a resource may be hard to pin down. For example, `http://www.google.com` represents Google in some sense (it is the scheme and the host part of an URL), but the host certainly isn't some fixed computer somewhere. Similarly, the ISBN for this book represents something about this book, but certainly not any extant copies (at the time this chapter was written, no copies existed even though the ISBN did!).

Nevertheless, we take the concept of resource as primitive, and URIs are identifiers for these resources. The IETF at Uniform Resource Identifier (URI): Generic Syntax (`https://www.ietf.org/rfc/rfc3986.txt`) is similarly vague: "the term "resource" is used in a general sense for whatever might be identified by a URI".

A resource may have more than one URI. As a person, I have a number of different identifiers: my tax file number refers to one aspect of me, my financial affairs; my Medicare number refers to me as a recipient of health treatments; my name (fairly unique) is often used to refer to different aspects of me. My URL of `https://jan.newmarch.name` refers to those aspects of me that I chose to reveal on my web site. And Google, LinkedIn, Facebook, Twitter, etc. also presumably have URIs of some kind that label those aspects of me that they have chosen to save.

What is agreed upon is that resources are *nouns* and not *verbs* or *adjectives*. An URL for a bank account that says `http://mybank/myaccount/withdraw` is not counted as a resource as it contains the verb `withdraw`. Similarly, `http://amazon.com/buy/book-id` would not label a resource as it contains the verb buy (Amazon does not have such an URL).

This is the first key to REST for HTTP: identify the resources in your information system and assign URLs to them. There are conventions in this, the most common one being that if there is a hierarchical structure then that should be reflected in the URL path. However, that isn't necessary as the information should be given in other ways as well.

The REST approach to designing URIs is still a bit of an art form. Legal (and perfectly legitimate) URIs are not necessarily "good" REST URIs, and many examples of so-called RESTful APIs have URIs that are not very RESTful at all. 2PartsMagic in RESTful URI design (`http://blog.2partsmagic.com/restful-uri-design/`) offers good advice on designing appropriate URIs.

Representations

A representation of a resource is something that captures some information about a resource in some form. For example, a representation of me from my Tax Office URI might be my tax returns in Australia. A representation of me from my local pizza cafe would be a record of pizza purchases. A representation of me from my web site would be an HTML document.

This is one of the keys to REST: URIs identify resources and requests for that resource return a representation of that resource. The resource itself remains on the server and is not sent to the client at all. In fact, the resource might not even exist at all in any concrete form. For example, a representation might be generated from the results of an SQL query that's triggered by making a request to that URI.

REST does not particularly talk about possibilities for negotiating the representation of a resource. HTTP 1.1 has an extensive section on how to do this, considering *server, client,* and *transparent* negotiation. The `Accept` headers can be used by a client to specify, for example:

```
Accept: application/xml; q=1.0, application/json; q=0.5
Accept-Language: fr
Accept-Charset: utf8
```

This states that it would prefer the `application/xml` format but will accept `application/json`. The server can either accept one of these or reply with the formats it will accept.

REST Verbs

You can make certain requests to a URI. If you are making an HTTP request to an URL, HTTP defines the requests that can made: GET, PUT, POST, DELETE, HEAD, OPTIONS, TRACE, and CONNECT, as well as extensions such as PATCH. There is only a limited number of these! This is very different than what we have come to expect from O/O programming. For example, the Java JLabel has about 250 methods, such as getText, setHorizontalAlignment, etc.

REST is now commonly interpreted as taking just four verbs from HTTP: GET, PUT, POST, DELETE. GET roughly corresponds to the getter-methods of O/O languages while PUT roughly corresponds to the setter-methods of O/O languages. If a JLabel were a REST resource (which it isn't), how would one single GET verb make up for the hundred or so getter-methods of JLabel?

The answer lies in the PATH component of URIs. A label has the properties of text, alignment, and so on. These are really sub-resources of the label and could be written as sub-URIs of the label. So if the label had a URI of http://jan.newmarch.name/my_label, then the subresources could have URIs:

```
http://jan.newmarch.name/my_label/text
http://jan.newmarch.name/my_label/horizontalAlignment
```

If you want to manipulate just the text of the label, you can use the URI of the text resource, not getter/setter-methods on the label itself.

The GET Verb

To retrieve a representation of a resource, you GET the resource. This will return some representation of the resource. There may be innumerable possibilities to this choice. For example, a request for this book's index might return a representation of the index in French, using the UTF-8 character set, as an XML document, or many other possibilities. The client and server can negotiate these possibilities.

The GET verb is required to be *idempotent*. That is, repeated requests should return the same results (to within representation type). For example, multiple requests for the temperature of a sensor should return the same result (unless of course the temperature has changed).

Idempotency by default allows for caching. This is useful for reducing traffic on the web, and may save battery power for sensors. Caching cannot always be guaranteed: a resource that returns the number of times it has been accessed will give a different result each time it is accessed. This is unusual behavior and would be signaled using the HTTP Cache-Control header.

The PUT Verb

If you want to change the state of a resource, you can PUT new values. There are two principal limitations to PUT:

- You can only change the state of a resource whose URI you know

- The representation you send must cover all components of the resource

For example, if you only want to change the text in a label, you send the PUT message to the URL http://jan.newmarch.name/my_label/text, *not* to http://jan.newmarch.name/my_label. Sending to the label would require all of the hundred or so fields to be sent.

PUT is idempotent, but is not *safe*. That is, it changes the state of the resource, but repeated calls change it to the same state.

PUT and DELETE are not part of HTML, and most browsers do not support them directly. They can be called in browsers with Ajax support. There are several discussions as to why they are not included. See for example "Why are there are no PUT and DELETE methods on HTML forms?" at http://softwareengineering. stackexchange.com/questions/114156/why-are-there-are-no-put-and-delete-methods-on-html-forms.

The DELETE Verb

This deletes the resource. It is idempotent but not safe.

The POST Verb

POST is the do-everything-else verb to deal with situations not covered by the other verbs. There is agreement about two uses of POST:

- If you want to create a new resource and you don't know its URI, then POST a representation of the resource to a URI that knows how to create the resource. The returned representation should contain the URI of the new resource. *This is important*. To interact with a new resource you must know its URI, and the return from POST tells you that.

- If a resource has many attributes, and you only want to change one or a few of them, then POST a representation with the changed values only

There is intense argument about the respective roles of PUT and POST in edge cases. If you want to create a new resource and *do* know the URI it will have, then you could use either PUT or POST. Which one you choose seems to depend on other factors...

SOAP was designed as an RPC system on top of HTTP. It uses POST for *everything*. HTML continues to use POST in forms when it should have the option of using PUT. For these reasons, I do not use POST unless I absolutely have to. I suppose others have their own principled reasons for using POST instead of PUT, but I have no idea what they might be :-).

Due to its open-ended scope, POST could be used for almost anything. Many of these uses could be against the REST model, as is amply illustrated by SOAP. But some of these uses could be legitimate. POST is usually non-idempotent and not safe, although particular cases could be either.

No Maintained State

Let's establish this up-front: cookies are out. Cookies are often used to track the state of a user through an interaction with a server, with a typical example being a shopping cart. A structure is created on the server side and a cookie is returned to be used to signal that this is the shopping cart to be used.

REST made the decision not to maintain any client state on the server. This simplifies interactions and also sidesteps the tricky issues of how to restore consistency after the client or server has crashed. If the server doesn't need to maintain any state then it leads to a more robust server model.

If you can't use cookies, what do you do? It's actually trivial: a cart is created on the server. Under REST, that can only happen in response to a POST request, which returns a new URI for the new resource. So that is what you use—the new URI. You can GET, PUT, POST, and DELETE to this URI, to do all things you want to do directly on the resource without having to do workarounds with cookies.

HATEOAS

HATEOAS stands for "Hypermedia as the Engine of Application State". It is generally recognized as an awful acronym, but it has stuck. The basic principle is that navigating from one URI to another, which is related in some way, should not be done by any out-of-band mechanism but that the new link must be embedded in some way as a hyperlink within the representation of the first URI.

REST does not state the format of the links. They could be given using the HTML link tag, by URLs embedded in a PDF document, or by links given in an XML document. Formats that do not have simple representations for URLs are not considered as hypermedia languages and are not contained in REST.

Also, REST also does not explicitly state the meanings of the links nor how to extract the appropriate links. Fielding states in his blog "REST APIs must be hypertext-driven" at `http://roy.gbiv.com/untangled/2008/rest-apis-must-be-hypertext-driven`:

> A REST API should be entered with no prior knowledge beyond the initial URI (bookmark) and set of standardized media types that are appropriate for the intended audience (i.e., expected to be understood by any client that might use the API). From that point on, all application state transitions must be driven by client selection of server-provided choices that are present in the received representations or implied by the user's manipulation of those representations.

IANA maintains a registry of relation types (IANA: Link Relations at `http://www.iana.org/assignments/link-relations/link-relations.xhtml`) which can be used. The Web Linking RFP5988 describes the web linking registry. The HTML5 specification has a small number of defined relations, and points to Microformats `rel` values at `http://microformats.org/wiki/existing-rel-values#HTML5_link_type_extensions` for a larger list.

Mechanisms such as cookies, or external API specifications such as WSDL for SOAP, are effectively excluded by REST. They are not hyperlinks contained in the representation of a resource.

Representing Links

Links are standardized in HTML documents. The `Link` tag defines an HTML element that can only appear in an HTML header section. For example, a book with chapters, etc., might look like this if the links were given as HTML `link` elements:

```
<html>
  <head>
    <link rel= "author" title="Jan Newmarch" href="https://jan.newmarch.name">
    <link rel="chapter" title="Introduction" href="Introduction/">
    ...
```

Link relations in HTML are of two types: those that are needed for the current document such as CSS files, and those that point to related resources, as above. The first type is generally downloaded invisibly to the user. The second type is generally not shown by browsers, but user agents following HATEOAS principles will use them.

XML has a variety of link specifications. These include XLink and Atom . Atom seems to be more popular.

Links based on XLink would appear as so:

```
<People xmlns:xlink="http://www.w3.org/1999/xlink">
 <Person xlink:type="simple" xlink:href="http://...">
   ...
 </Person>
   ...
</People>
```

Links based on Atom would appear as so:

```
<People xmlns:atom="http://www.w3.org/2005/Atom">
 <Person>
   <link  atom:href="http://..."/>
   ...
 </Person>
 ...
</People>
```

For JSON, the format is not normalized. The REST cookbook (http://restcookbook.com/Mediatypes/json/) notes the lack of standardization and points to the W3C specification JSON-LD 1.0: "A JSON-based Serialization for Linked Data" and to the HAL (Hypertext Application Language). Bodies such as the Open Connectivity Foundation seem to use their own home-grown format, but that is for CoAP, another REST-based system.

JSON-LD uses the term @id to signal an URL, as in:

```
{
  "name": Jan Newmarch:,
  "homepage": {"@id": "https://jan.newmarch.name/"}
}
```

It is worth noting in this regard that the W3C also has a specification of an HTTP Link header at https://www.w3.org/wiki/LinkHeader, which may be returned by a server to a client. This is used by JSON-LD, for example, to point to a specification of the JSON document contained in the body of an HTTP response.

This can affect the serialization method in passing link information from servers to user agents. The user agent and server must agree on the format to be used. For HTML (or XHTML), this is standardized. For XML, a reference can be made in the document to the linking system. For JSON-LD, this can be signaled in the Accept HTTP header as application/ld+json.

Transactions with REST

How does REST handle transactions and indeed any other processes? They were not discussed in the original thesis by Fielding.

The Wikipedia entry for HATEOAS gives a poor example of managing transactions. It starts from an HTTP request of this:

```
GET /account/12345 HTTP/1.1
Host: somebank.org
Accept: application/xml
 ...
```

Which returns an XML document as representation of the account:

```
HTTP/1.1 200 OK
    Content-Type: application/xml
    Content-Length: ...

    <?xml version="1.0"?>
    <account>
```

```
  <account_number>12345</account_number>
  <balance currency="usd">100.00</balance>
  <link rel="deposit" href="http://somebank.org/account/12345/deposit" />
  <link rel="withdraw" href="http://somebank.org/account/12345/withdraw" />
  <link rel="transfer" href="http://somebank.org/account/12345/transfer" />
  <link rel="close" href="http://somebank.org/account/12345/close" />
</account>
```

This gives the URIs of the related resources deposit, withdraw, transfer, and close. However, the resources are *verbs* not *nouns*, and that is not good at all. How do they interact with the HTTP verbs? Do you GET a withdraw? POST it? PUT it? What happens if you DELETE a withdraw—is that supposed to roll back a transaction or what?

The better way, as discussed in, for example, the Stackoverflow posting "Transactions in REST?" (see http://stackoverflow.com/questions/147207/transactions-in-rest) is to POST to the account asking for a new transaction to be created:

```
POST /account/12345/transaction HTTP/1.1
```

This will return the URL of a new transaction:

```
http://account/12345/txn123
```

Interactions are now carried out with this transaction URL, such as by PUTing a new value that performs and commits the transaction.

```
PUT /account/12345/txn123
<transaction>
  <from>/account/56789</from>
  <amount>100</amount>
</transaction>
```

A more detailed discussion of transactions and REST is given by Mihindukulasooriya et. al in "Seven Challenges for RESTful Transaction Models" (see http://ws-rest.org/2014/sites/default/files/wsrest2014_submission_4.pdf). Similar models are proposed for managing processes that aren't just single-step.

The Richardson Maturity Model

Many systems claim to be RESTful. Most are not. I even came across one that claimed that SOAP was RESTful, a clear case of a warped mental state. Martin Fowler discusses the Richardson Maturity Model, which classifies systems according to their conformance to REST. (See https://martinfowler.com/articles/richardsonMaturityModel.html.)

Level 0

> *The starting point for the model is using HTTP as a transport system for remote interactions, but without using any of the mechanisms of the web. Essentially what you are doing here is using HTTP as a tunneling mechanism for your own remote interaction mechanism, usually based on Remote Procedure Invocation.*

Level 1: Resources

> *The first step toward the Glory of Rest in the RMM is to introduce resources. So now rather than making all our requests to a singular service endpoint, we now start talking to individual resources.*

Level 2: HTTP Verbs

> *I've used HTTP POST verbs for all my interactions here in level 0 and 1, but some people use GETs instead or in addition. At these levels it doesn't make much difference, they are both being used as tunneling mechanisms allowing you to tunnel your interactions through HTTP. Level 2 moves away from this, using the HTTP verbs as closely as possible to how they are used in HTTP itself.*

Level 3: Hypermedia Controls

> *The final level introduces something that you often hear referred to under the ugly acronym of HATEOAS (Hypertext As The Engine Of Application State). It addresses the question of how to get from a list of open slots to knowing what to do to book an appointment.*

Flashcards Revisited

In Chapter 10, we considered a web system consisting of a server and HTML pages rendered in a browser, using JavaScript and CSS to control the browser-side interaction. There was no attempt to do anything particularly structured, rather just as a traditional web system.

■ *Recap* The web system of Chapter 10 was used to demonstrate language learning using so-called flashcards. The user is presented with a set of cards one at a time, showing a word in one language and then hopes to remember the translation, which is shown by "turning over" the card. The system presented a list of different card sets and then showed the cards one at a time in the selected set.

We now approach the same situation as a HTTP client-server system built using the REST approach. We will make a number of changes:

- URLs will be given appropriate to the situation. These will include the 'root' URL / as well as URLs for each flashcard set and in addition, an URL for each flashcard.

- All user interaction code (HTML, JavaScript, and CSS) is omitted. The server will be talking to an arbitrary user agent, and many will not understand the UI code.

- The server will not maintain or manage any client state. In the web example, form data was sent from the browser to the server, which promptly returned it in a slightly different form. A client that wants to maintain state should do so itself.

- The server will be set up to manage a number of different serialization formats and will deliver as appropriate after client-server negotiation.

- Heavy use will be made of HTTP mechanisms, particularly for error handling and content negotiation.

URLs

The URLs for this system and the actions that can be performed are as follows:

URL	Action	Effect
/	GET	Gets a list of flashcard sets
	POST	Creates a new flashcard set
/flashcardSets/<set>	GET	Gets a list of cards in the set
	POST	Creates a new card for the set
	DELETE	Deletes the flashcard set if empty
/flashcardSets/<set>/<card>	GET	Gets the contents of the card
	DELETE	Deletes the card from the set

This differs a little from the system described in Chapter 10. The main structural difference is that each card is given its own URL as a member of a flashcard set.

Example URLs that will be handled by the server include these:

Root URL	URL for Flashcard Set	URL for One Flashcard
/	/flashcardSet/CommonWords	/flashcardSet/CommonWords/你好

The Demultiplexer (Demuxer)

REST is based on a small number of actions applied to URLs. A system that attempts to use REST principles must be URL based.

A server demuxer will examine URLs requested by clients and call handlers based on the URL pattern. The standard Go demuxer ServeMux uses a particular pattern-matching mechanism: if an URL ends in / it denotes a subtree of URLs rooted at that URL. If it ends without a / it represents that URL only. An URL is matched against the handler with the longest pattern match.

We need a handler for the root URL /. That will also match any URL such as /passwords unless another handler catches it. In this system, no other handler will, so in the handler for / we need to return errors for such attempts.

A tricky part occurs because we used a hierarchical structure to our URLs. One particular flashcard set will be /flashcardSets/CommonWords. This will actually be a directory of the cards for that particular set. We have to register *two* handlers: one for the URL /flashcardSets/CommonWords, which is the flashcard set resource, and one for /flashcardSets/CommonWords/ (note the trailing /), which is the subtree containing the individual cards and their URLs.

The code in the main function to register these is as follows:

```
http.HandleFunc(`/`, handleFlashCardSets)
files, err := ioutil.ReadDir(`flashcardSets`)
checkError(err)
for _, file := range files {
        cardset_url := `/flashcardSets/` + url.QueryEscape(file.Name())
        http.HandleFunc(cardset_url, handleOneFlashCardSet)
        http.HandleFunc(cardset_url + `/`, handleOneFlashCard)
}
```

Note that we have the function QueryEscape. This is to escape any special characters that might occur in URLs. For example, a $ in a filename should be encoded as %44;. We *do* need to use such a function: our URLs will include Chinese characters, which need to be escape-encoded to be represented in URLs. This is done by QueryEscape, with one exception: a space in a path should be encoded as %20 but in form data should be encoded as +. The PathEscape function does this correctly, but is not available until Go 1.8. We will remove spaces from URLs to avoid this issue.

Content Negotiation

Any web user agent can try to talk to any web server. The typical case of a browser talking to an HTML server is what we are used to on the Web, but many will be familiar with using other user agents such as curl, wget, and even telnet! The browser and other tools will use the Content-Type in HTTP replies to work out what to do with content supplied.

With a Web application, the user agent must be able to understand what the server is delivering, because it is trying to play a part in an interaction that probably doesn't have a user to help. RPC systems often use an external specification that the client and server conform to. That is not the case here.

The solution is that both parties must agree on a content format. This is done at the HTTP level. A client will state that it will accept a range of formats. If the server agrees, then they carry on. If not, the server will tell the client which formats it can accept and the client can start afresh if possible.

The negotiation uses MIME types. There are hundreds of standard ones: text/html, application/pdf, application/xml, ... A browser can render any HTML document it receives. An HTTP-aware music player such as VLC can play any MP3 file it receives. But for the flashcard application it can't handle any general format, only messages that conform to an expected structure. These aren't any standard MIME types that would be suitable for negotiating a specialized protocol for this flashcard application. So, we make up our own. The client and the server have to know that they are dealing with a shared MIME type, or they can't talk properly.

There are rules from IANA for making up your own MIME types. I use the types application/x.flashcards. The server will be able to deliver JSON and XML, so the two acceptable MIME types are application/x.flashcards+xml and application/x.flashcards+json.

HTTP content negotiation says that the user agent can suggest a list of acceptable formats, weighted between zero and one, as follows:

```
Accept: application/x.flashcards+xml; q=0.8,
        application/x.flashcards+json; q=0.4
```

The server can examine the request and decide if it can handle the format. We use the following code in the server to determine for any type if the user agent has requested it, and with what weighting (zero means not requested):

```
const flashcard_xml string = "application/x.flashcards+xml"
const flashcard_json string = "application/x.flashcards+json"

type ValueQuality struct {
        Value   string
        Quality float64
}

/* Based on https://siongui.github.io/2015/02/22/go-parse-accept-language/ */
func parseValueQuality(s string) []ValueQuality {
        var vqs []ValueQuality
```

```
        strs := strings.Split(s, `,`)
        for _, str := range strs {
                trimmedStr := strings.Trim(str, ` `)
                valQ := strings.Split(trimmedStr, `;`)
                if len(valQ) == 1 {
                        vq := ValueQuality{valQ[0], 1}
                        vqs = append(vqs, vq)
                } else {
                        qp := strings.Split(valQ[1], `=`)
                        q, err := strconv.ParseFloat(qp[1], 64)
                        if err != nil {
                                q = 0
                        }
                        vq := ValueQuality{valQ[0], q}
                        vqs = append(vqs, vq)
                }
        }
        return vqs
}

func qualityOfValue(value string, vqs []ValueQuality) float64 {
        for _, vq := range vqs {
                if value == vq.Value {
                        return vq.Quality
                }

        }
        // not found
        return 0
}
```

If the server does not accept any of the types requested by the user agent, it returns an HTTP code of 406 "Not acceptable" and supplies a list of accepted formats. The code segment to do this in the server is as follows:

```
func handleFlashCardSets(rw http.ResponseWriter, req *http.Request) {

        if req.Method == "GET" {
                acceptTypes := parseValueQuality(req.Header.Get("Accept"))

                q_xml := qualityOfValue(flashcard_xml, acceptTypes)
                q_json := qualityOfValue(flashcard_json, acceptTypes)
                if q_xml == 0 && q_json == 0 {
                        // can't find XML or JSON in Accept header
                        rw.Header().Set("Content-Type", flashcard_xml + `, ` + flashcard_json)
                        rw.WriteHeader(http.StatusNotAcceptable)
                        return
                }
                ...
```

This illustrates a common REST pattern for HTTP servers: given an HTTP request, examine it to see if the server can manage it. If not, return an HTTP error. If okay, attempt to handle it. If the attempt fails, return an HTTP error. On success, return an appropriate HTTP success code and the results.

GET /

The flashcard sets are all stored in the directory /flashcardSets. The GET / request needs to list all those files and prepare them in a suitable format for the client. The format is a list of flashcard set names and *their URLs*. The URLs are required by HATEOAS: the list of names tell us what the sets are, but the client will need their URLs in order to move to the stage of interacting with one of them.

The data type for each FlashcardSet in the server contains the name of the set and its URL (as a string):

```
type FlashcardSet struct {
        Name string
        Link string
}
```

The set of flashcard sets on the server can be built from the directory of flashcard sets. The ioutil. ReadDir() will create an array of os.FileInfo. This needs to be converted to a list of filenames as follows:

```
files, err := ioutil.ReadDir(`flashcardSets`)
checkError(err)
numfiles := len(files)
cardSets := make([]FlashcardSet, numfiles, numfiles)
for n, file := range files {
        cardSets[n].Name = file.Name()
        // should be PathEscape, not in go 1.6
        cardSets[n].Link = `/flashcardSets/` + url.QueryEscape(file.Name())
}
```

This creates an array of filenames and relative links to the resource on the server as /<name>. For the CommonWords set, the relative link URL would be /flashcardSets/CommonWords. The scheme (http or https) and the host (e.g., "localhost") are left up to the client to work out.

Unfortunately, the filename may contain characters not legal in URL path names. The function url. PathEscape escapes them all correctly, but is not available until Go 1.8. The function url.QueryEscape gets everything right except for spaces in the filename, which it replaces with + instead of %20;.

Finally, the server figures out if JSON or XML is preferred and runs it through a template to generate the right output to the client. For XML, the template code is as follows:

```
t, err := template.ParseFiles("xml/ListFlashcardSets.xml")
if err != nil {
        // parse error occurred in the template. Our error
        http.Error(rw, err.Error(), http.StatusInternalServerError)
        return
}
rw.Header().Set("Content-Type", flashcard_xml)
t.Execute(rw, cardSets)
```

The XML template is as follows:

```xml
<?xml version="1.0" encoding="UTF-8"?>

<cardsets xmlns="http://www.w3.org/2005/Atom">
  {{range .}}
  <cardset href="{{.Link}}">
    <name>
      {{.Name}}
    </name>
  </cardset>
  {{end}}
</cardsets>
```

For a listing of only two sets, `CommonWords` and `Lesson04`, the content sent to the client is as follows:

```xml
<?xml version="1.0" encoding="UTF-8"?>

<cardsets xmlns="http://www.w3.org/2005/Atom">

  <cardset href="/CommonWords">
    <name>
      Common Words
    </name>
  </cardset>

  <cardset href="/Lesson04">
    <name>
      Lesson04
    </name>
  </cardset>

</cardsets>
```

POST /

Here a client is asking for a new flashcard set to be created. The expectation is that the client will supply the name of the flashcard set. We make it look like form submission data:

```
name=<new flashcard set name>
```

This is much simpler than GET in this case. Get the value out of the request as form data. Then check that the requested name doesn't have nasties in it like calling the flashcard set /etc/passwd. If it does, return 403 "Forbidden". If it appears to be okay, create a directory with that name. Return a 403 again if it fails (the directory may already exist). Otherwise, return 201 "Created" and the new relative URL:

```go
if req.Method == "POST" {
        name := req.FormValue(`name`)
        if hasIllegalChars(name) {
                rw.WriteHeader(http.StatusForbidden)
                return
```

```
}
// lose all spaces as they are a nuisance
name = strings.Replace(name, ` `, ``, -1)

err := os.Mkdir(`flashcardSets/`+name,
            (os.ModeDir | os.ModePerm))
if err != nil {
      rw.WriteHeader(http.StatusForbidden)
      return
}
rw.WriteHeader(http.StatusCreated)
base_url := req.URL.String()
new_url := base_url + `flashcardSets/` + name
rw.Write([]byte(new_url))
```

Handling Other URLs

We discussed the code for the server handling the / URL with GET and POST requests. There are two other types of URL for this application—handling the cards in a set and handling each individual card. In terms of the coding, though, this presents no new ideas.

- Getting a list of cards in a set is another directory listing.

- Posting a new card to a set means creating a file in the appropriate directory with content from the client.

- Deleting a set means removing a directory. This is okay if the directory is empty, creates an error otherwise.

- Getting a card means reading the card file and sending its contents.

- Deleting a card means removing a file.

There is nothing particularly new about any of these. We have not completed the code for some operations such as DELETE: these return the HTTP code 501 'Not implemented'. We also return the contents of individual cards as text/plain: they have a complex JSON/Go structure as used in Chapter 10, but that is not needed for discussion of the REST aspects of this system.

The Complete Server

The complete server to handle requests to / and from there to other URLs follows. It requires the flashcard sets and individual cards in order to run, and these are in the ZIP file at http://www.apress.com/9781484226919 in the Ch14 folder.

```
/* Server
 */

package main

import (
        "fmt"
        "html/template"
```

```
        "io/ioutil"
        "net/http"
        "net/url"
        "os"
        "regexp"
        "strconv"
        "strings"
)

type FlashcardSet struct {
        Name string
        Link string
}

type Flashcard struct {
        Name string
        Link string
}

const flashcard_xml string = "application/x.flashcards+xml"
const flashcard_json string = "application/x.flashcards+json"

type ValueQuality struct {
        Value   string
        Quality float64
}

/* Based on https://siongui.github.io/2015/02/22/go-parse-accept-language/ */
func parseValueQuality(s string) []ValueQuality {
        var vqs []ValueQuality

        strs := strings.Split(s, `,`)
        for _, str := range strs {
                trimmedStr := strings.Trim(str, ` `)
                valQ := strings.Split(trimmedStr, `;`)
                if len(valQ) == 1 {
                        vq := ValueQuality{valQ[0], 1}
                        vqs = append(vqs, vq)
                } else {
                        qp := strings.Split(valQ[1], `=`)
                        q, err := strconv.ParseFloat(qp[1], 64)
                        if err != nil {
                                q = 0
                        }
                        vq := ValueQuality{valQ[0], q}
                        vqs = append(vqs, vq)
                }
        }
        return vqs
}
```

```go
func qualityOfValue(value string, vqs []ValueQuality) float64 {
        for _, vq := range vqs {
                if value == vq.Value {
                        return vq.Quality
                }

        }
        return 0
}

func main() {
        if len(os.Args) != 2 {
                fmt.Fprint(os.Stderr, "Usage: ", os.Args[0], ":port\n")
                os.Exit(1)
        }
        port := os.Args[1]

        http.HandleFunc(`/`, handleFlashCardSets)
        files, err := ioutil.ReadDir(`flashcardSets`)
        checkError(err)
        for _, file := range files {
                fmt.Println(file.Name())
                cardset_url := `/flashcardSets/` + url.QueryEscape(file.Name())
                fmt.Println("Adding handlers for ", cardset_url)
                http.HandleFunc(cardset_url, handleOneFlashCardSet)
                http.HandleFunc(cardset_url + `/`, handleOneFlashCard)
        }

        // deliver requests to the handlers
        err = http.ListenAndServe(port, nil)
        checkError(err)
        // That's it!
}

func hasIllegalChars(s string) bool {
        // check against chars to break out of current dir
        b, err := regexp.Match("[/$~]", []byte(s))
        if err != nil {
                fmt.Println(err)
                return true
        }
        if b {
                return true
        }
        return false
}

func handleOneFlashCard(rw http.ResponseWriter, req *http.Request) {
        // should be PathUnescape
        path, _ := url.QueryUnescape(req.URL.String())
        // lose initial '/'
        path = path[1:]
```

```go
        if req.Method == "GET" {
                fmt.Println("Handling card: ", path)
                json_contents, err := ioutil.ReadFile(path)
                if err != nil {
                        rw.WriteHeader(http.StatusNotFound)
                        rw.Write([]byte(`Resource not found`))
                        return
                }
                // Be lazy here, just return the content as text/plain
                rw.Write(json_contents)
                return
        } else if req.Method == "DELETE" {
                rw.WriteHeader(http.StatusNotImplemented)
        } else {
                rw.WriteHeader(http.StatusMethodNotAllowed)
        }
        return
}

func handleFlashCardSets(rw http.ResponseWriter, req *http.Request) {
        if req.URL.String() != `/` {
                // this function only handles '/'
                rw.WriteHeader(http.StatusNotFound)
                rw.Write([]byte("Resource not found\n"))
                return
        }
        if req.Method == "GET" {
                acceptTypes := parseValueQuality(req.Header.Get("Accept"))
                fmt.Println(acceptTypes)

                q_xml := qualityOfValue(flashcard_xml, acceptTypes)
                q_json := qualityOfValue(flashcard_json, acceptTypes)
                if q_xml == 0 && q_json == 0 {
                        // can't find XML or JSON in Accept header
                        rw.Header().Set("Content-Type", flashcard_xml + `, ` + flashcard_json)
                        rw.WriteHeader(http.StatusNotAcceptable)
                        return
                }

                files, err := ioutil.ReadDir(`flashcardSets`)
                checkError(err)
                numfiles := len(files)
                cardSets := make([]FlashcardSet, numfiles, numfiles)
                for n, file := range files {
                        fmt.Println(file.Name())
                        cardSets[n].Name = file.Name()
                        // should be PathEscape, not in go 1.6
                        cardSets[n].Link = `/flashcardSets/` + url.QueryEscape(file.Name())
                }

                if q_xml >= q_json {
                        // XML preferred
```

```
                    t, err := template.ParseFiles("xml/ListFlashcardSets.xml")
                    if err != nil {
                            fmt.Println("Template error")
                            http.Error(rw, err.Error(), http.StatusInternalServerError)
                            return
                    }
                    rw.Header().Set("Content-Type", flashcard_xml)
                    t.Execute(rw, cardSets)
            } else {
                    // JSON preferred
                    t, err := template.ParseFiles("json/ListFlashcardSets.json")
                    if err != nil {
                            fmt.Println("Template error")
                            http.Error(rw, err.Error(), http.StatusInternalServerError)
                            return
                    }
                    rw.Header().Set("Content-Type", flashcard_json)
                    t.Execute(rw, cardSets)

            }
    } else if req.Method == "POST" {
            name := req.FormValue(`name`)
            if hasIllegalChars(name) {
                    rw.WriteHeader(http.StatusForbidden)
                    return
            }
            // lose all spaces as they are a nuisance
            name = strings.Replace(name, ` `, ``, -1)
            err := os.Mkdir(`flashcardSets/`+name,
                    (os.ModeDir | os.ModePerm))
            if err != nil {
                    rw.WriteHeader(http.StatusForbidden)
                    return
            }
            rw.WriteHeader(http.StatusCreated)
            base_url := req.URL.String()
            new_url := base_url + `flashcardSets/` + name
            // add handlers for the resources
            http.HandleFunc(new_url, handleOneFlashCardSet)
            http.HandleFunc(new_url + `/`, handleOneFlashCard)
            rw.Write([]byte(new_url))
    } else {
            rw.WriteHeader(http.StatusMethodNotAllowed)
    }
    return
}

func handleOneFlashCardSet(rw http.ResponseWriter, req *http.Request) {
    cooked_url, _ := url.QueryUnescape(req.URL.String())
    fmt.Println("Handling one set for: ", cooked_url)
```

```go
    if req.Method == "GET" {
            acceptTypes := parseValueQuality(req.Header.Get("Accept"))
            fmt.Println(acceptTypes)

            q_xml := qualityOfValue(flashcard_xml, acceptTypes)
            q_json := qualityOfValue(flashcard_json, acceptTypes)
            if q_xml == 0 && q_json == 0 {
                    // can't find XML or JSON in Accept header
                    rw.Header().Set("Content-Type", flashcard_xml + `, ` + flashcard_json)
                    rw.WriteHeader(http.StatusNotAcceptable)
                    return
            }

            path := req.URL.String()
            // lose leading /
            relative_path := path[1:]
            files, err := ioutil.ReadDir(relative_path)
            checkError(err)
            numfiles := len(files)
            cards := make([]Flashcard, numfiles, numfiles)
            for n, file := range files {
                    fmt.Println(file.Name())
                    cards[n].Name = file.Name()
                    // should be PathEscape, not in go 1.6
                    cards[n].Link = path + `/` + url.QueryEscape(file.Name())
            }

            if q_xml >= q_json {
                    // XML preferred
                    t, err := template.ParseFiles("xml/ListOneFlashcardSet.xml")
                    if err != nil {
                            fmt.Println("Template error")
                            http.Error(rw, err.Error(), http.StatusInternalServerError)
                            return
                    }
                    rw.Header().Set("Content-Type", flashcard_xml)
                    t.Execute(os.Stdout, cards)
                    t.Execute(rw, cards)
            } else {
                    // JSON preferred
                    t, err := template.ParseFiles("json/ListOneFlashcardSet.json")
                    if err != nil {
                            fmt.Println("Template error")
                            http.Error(rw, err.Error(), http.StatusInternalServerError)
                            return
                    }
                    rw.Header().Set("Content-Type", flashcard_json)
                    t.Execute(rw, cards)

            }
    } else if req.Method == "POST" {
            name := req.FormValue(`name`)
```

```
            if hasIllegalChars(name) {
                    rw.WriteHeader(http.StatusForbidden)
                    return
            }
            err := os.Mkdir(`flashcardSets/`+name,
                    (os.ModeDir | os.ModePerm))
            if err != nil {
                    rw.WriteHeader(http.StatusForbidden)
                    return
            }
            rw.WriteHeader(http.StatusCreated)
            base_url := req.URL.String()
            new_url := base_url + `flashcardSets/` + name
            _, _ = rw.Write([]byte(new_url))
    } else if req.Method == "DELETE" {
            rw.WriteHeader(http.StatusNotImplemented)
    } else {
            rw.WriteHeader(http.StatusMethodNotAllowed)
    }
    return
}

func checkError(err error) {
    if err != nil {
            fmt.Println("Fatal error ", err.Error())
            os.Exit(1)
    }
}
```

It is run as follows:

```
go run Server.go :8000
```

Client

The client is relatively straightforward, offering nothing really new. This client asks for the content only in XML format. A new part is that the content for the flashcard sets includes links as hypertext attributes within a cardset tag. This may be turned into a field of a struct by the tag label xml:"href,attr" in the Card struct.

This client gets the list of flashcard sets and their URLs in the getFlashcardSets() function (Step 1). This returns a FlashcardSets struct. This can be used to present a list to a user, say, for selection of a particular set. Once selected, the URL of that set can be used to interact with the resource.

This client then creates a new flashcard set with name NewSet in the createFlashcardSet() function (Step 2). The first time it is run, it will create the set and be returned the URL for that set. The second time it is run, it will get an error from the server as a prohibited operation, since the set already exists.

This client then takes the first set of flashcards from the URLs given by the server and asks for the set of cards it holds (Step 3). It then picks the first card from the set and gets its content (Step 4).

The client is Client.go:

```go
/* Client
 */

package main

import (
        //"encoding/json"
        "encoding/xml"
        "fmt"
        "io/ioutil"
        "net/http"
        "net/http/httputil"
        "net/url"
        "os"
        "strings"
)

const flashcard_xml string = "application/x.flashcards+xml"
const flashcard_json string = "application/x.flashcards+json"

type FlashcardSets struct {
        XMLName string `xml:"cardsets"`
        CardSet    []CardSet `xml:"cardset"`
}

type CardSet struct {
        XMLName string `xml:"cardset"`
        Name string `xml:"name"`
        Link string `xml:"href,attr"`
        Cards []Card `xml:"card"`
}

type Card  struct {
        Name string `xml:"name"`
        Link string `xml:"href,attr"`
}

func getOneFlashcard(url *url.URL, client *http.Client) string {
        // Get the card as a string, don't do anything with it
        request, err := http.NewRequest("GET", url.String(), nil)
        checkError(err)

        response, err := client.Do(request)
        checkError(err)
        if response.Status != "200 OK" {
                fmt.Println(response.Status)
                fmt.Println(response.Header)

                os.Exit(2)
        }
```

241

```
        fmt.Println("The response header is")
        b, _ := httputil.DumpResponse(response, false)
        fmt.Print(string(b))

        body, err := ioutil.ReadAll(response.Body)
        content := string(body[:])
        //fmt.Printf("Body is %s", content)

        return content
}

func getOneFlashcardSet(url *url.URL, client *http.Client) CardSet {
        // Get one set of cards
        request, err := http.NewRequest("GET", url.String(), nil)
        checkError(err)

        // only accept our media types
        request.Header.Add("Accept", flashcard_xml)
        response, err := client.Do(request)
        checkError(err)
        if response.Status != "200 OK" {
                fmt.Println(response.Status)
                fmt.Println(response.Header)

                os.Exit(2)
        }

        fmt.Println("The response header is")
        b, _ := httputil.DumpResponse(response, false)
        fmt.Print(string(b))

        body, err := ioutil.ReadAll(response.Body)
        content := string(body[:])
        fmt.Printf("Body is %s", content)

        var sets CardSet
        contentType := getContentType(response)
        if contentType == "XML" {

                err = xml.Unmarshal(body, &sets)
                checkError(err)
                fmt.Println("XML: ", sets)
                return sets
        }
        /* else if contentType == "JSON" {
                var sets FlashcardSetsJson
                err = json.Unmarshal(body, &sets)
                checkError(err)
                fmt.Println("JSON: ", sets)
        }
        */
        return sets
}
```

242

```go
func getFlashcardSets(url *url.URL, client *http.Client) FlashcardSets {
        // Get the toplevel /
        request, err := http.NewRequest("GET", url.String(), nil)
        checkError(err)

        // only accept our media types
        request.Header.Add("Accept", flashcard_xml)
        response, err := client.Do(request)
        checkError(err)
        if response.Status != "200 OK" {
                fmt.Println(response.Status)
                fmt.Println(response.Header)

                os.Exit(2)
        }

        fmt.Println("The response header is")
        b, _ := httputil.DumpResponse(response, false)
        fmt.Print(string(b))

        body, err := ioutil.ReadAll(response.Body)
        content := string(body[:])
        fmt.Printf("Body is %s", content)

        var sets FlashcardSets
        contentType := getContentType(response)
        if contentType == "XML" {

                err = xml.Unmarshal(body, &sets)
                checkError(err)
                fmt.Println("XML: ", sets)
                return sets
        }
        return sets
}

func createFlashcardSet(url1 *url.URL, client *http.Client, name string) string {
        data := make(url.Values)
        data[`name`] = []string{name}
        response, err := client.PostForm(url1.String(), data)
        checkError(err)
        if response.StatusCode != http.StatusCreated {
                fmt.Println(`Error: `, response.Status)
                return ``
                //os.Exit(2)
        }
        body, err := ioutil.ReadAll(response.Body)
        content := string(body[:])
        return content
}
```

```go
func main() {
        if len(os.Args) != 2 {
                fmt.Println("Usage: ", os.Args[0], "http://host:port/page")
                os.Exit(1)
        }
        url, err := url.Parse(os.Args[1])
        checkError(err)

        client := &http.Client{}

        // Step 1: get a list of flashcard sets
        flashcardSets := getFlashcardSets(url, client)
        fmt.Println("Step 1: ", flashcardSets)

        // Step 2: try to create a new flashcard set
        new_url := createFlashcardSet(url, client, `NewSet`)
        fmt.Println("Step 2: New flashcard set has URL: ", new_url)

        // Step 3: using the first flashcard set,
        //          get the list of cards in it
        set_url, _ := url.Parse(os.Args[1] + flashcardSets.CardSet[0].Link)

        fmt.Println("Asking for flashcard set URL: ", set_url.String())
        oneFlashcardSet := getOneFlashcardSet(set_url, client)
        fmt.Println("Step 3:", oneFlashcardSet)

        // Step 4: get the contents of one flashcard
        //          be lazy, just get as text/plain and
        //          don't do anything with it
        card_url, _ :=  url.Parse(os.Args[1] + oneFlashcardSet.Cards[0].Link)
        fmt.Println("Asking for URL: ", card_url.String())
        oneFlashcard := getOneFlashcard(card_url, client)
        fmt.Println("Step 4", oneFlashcard)
        os.Exit(0)
}

func getContentType(response *http.Response) string {
        contentType := response.Header.Get("Content-Type")
        if strings.Contains(contentType, flashcard_xml) {
                return "XML"
        }
        if strings.Contains(contentType, flashcard_json) {
                return "JSON"
        }
        return ""
}

func checkError(err error) {
        if err != nil {
                fmt.Println("Fatal error ", err.Error())
                os.Exit(1)
        }
}
```

It is run as follows:

```
go run Client.go http://localhost:8000/
```

Using REST or RPC

The primary difference between REST and RPC is the interaction style. In RPC, you are calling functions, passing objects or primitive types as arguments, and getting objects or primitive types in return. The functions are *verbs*: do *this* to *that*. REST, on the other hand, is about interacting with objects, asking them to show their state or to change it in some way.

The difference is shown by the Go RPC mechanism discussed in the last chapter and the REST mechanism of this chapter. In Go RPC over HTTP, the server registers *functions*, while in REST, the server registers handlers for *URLs*.

Which is better? Neither. Which is faster? Neither. Which is better for a controlled environment? Possibly RPC. Which is better for an open environment? Possibly REST.

You will see arguments based on speed and resource allocation. RPC based on binary systems will probably be faster than text-based HTTP systems. But SOAP is a text-based RPC system using HTTP and is probably slower than REST. HTTP2 uses a binary format and when conveying binary data such as BSON will probably be equivalent in speed to other binary systems. Just to confuse things further, the Apache Thrift RPC allows a choice of data formats (binary, compact binary, JSON, and text) and transports (sockets, files, and shared memory). One system demonstrates all options!

A more important factor might be how tightly controlled the operational environment is. RPC systems are tightly coupled, and a failure in one component could bring an entire system down. When there is a single administrative authority, a limited set of hardware and software configurations and a clear channel for fixing problems, then an RPC system can work well.

On the other side, the web is uncontrolled. There is no single authority—even such "universal" services such as DNS are highly distributed. There is a huge variety of hardware, operating systems, and software; there will be little prospect of enforcing any policies; and if something breaks then there is often no one who can be pointed at to fix it. In such a case, a loosely-coupled system may be better.

REST over HTTP is a good match for this. HATEOAS allows servers to be reconfigured on the fly, changing URLs as needed (even pointing to different servers!). HTTP is designed to cache results when it can. Firewalls are usually configured to allow HTTP traffic and block most other. REST is a good choice here.

It should be noted that REST is not the only HTTP-based system possible. SOAP has already been mentioned. There are many commercial and highly successful systems that are "almost" REST—Richardson levels 1 and 2. They do not enjoy the full benefits of the REST/HTTP match but still work.

No doubt in future other models will arise. In the IoT space, CoAP is popular for low-power wireless systems. It is also REST-based, but in a slightly different way than HTTP-REST.

Conclusion

REST is the architectural model of the web. It can be applied in many different ways, particularly as HTTP and CoAP. This chapter illustrated REST as applied to HTTP.

CHAPTER 15

■ ■ ■

WebSockets

The standard model of interaction between a web user agent such as a browser and a web server such as Apache is that the user agent makes HTTP requests and the server makes a single reply to each one. In the case of a browser, the request is made by clicking on a link, entering a URL into the address bar, clicking on the forward or back buttons, etc. The response is treated as a new page and is loaded into a browser window.

This traditional model has many drawbacks. The first is that each request opens and closes a new TCP connection. HTTP 1.1 solved this by allowing persistent connections, so that a connection could be held open for a short period to allow for multiple requests (e.g., for images) to be made on the same server.

While HTTP 1.1 persistent connections alleviate the problem of slow loading of a page with many graphics, it does not improve the interaction model. Even with forms, the model is still that of submitting the form and displaying the response as a new page. JavaScript helps in allowing error checking to be performed on form data before submission, but does not change the model.

AJAX (Asynchronous JavaScript and XML) made a significant advance to the user interaction model. This allows a browser to make a request and just use the response to update the display in place using the HTML Document Object Model (DOM). But again the interaction model is the same. AJAX just affects how the browser manages the returned pages. There is no explicit extra support in Go for AJAX, as none is needed: the HTTP server just sees an ordinary HTTP POST request with possibly some XML or JSON data, and this can be dealt with using techniques already discussed.

All of these are still browser (or user agent) to server communication. What is missing is server to browser communications where a browser has set up a TCP connection to a server and reads messages from the server. This can be filled by WebSockets: the browser (or any user agent) keeps open a long-lived TCP connection to a WebSockets server. The TCP connection allows either side to send arbitrary packets, so any application protocol can be used on a WebSocket.

How a WebSocket is started is by the user agent sending a special HTTP request that says "switch to WebSockets". The TCP connection underlying the HTTP request is kept open, but both user agent and server switch to using the WebSockets protocol instead of getting an HTTP response and closing the socket.

Note that it is still the browser or user agent that initiates the WebSockets connection. The browser does not run a TCP server of its own. While the specification as IETF RFC6455 is complex (see `https://tools.ietf.org/html/rfc6455`), the protocol is designed to be fairly easy to use. The client opens an HTTP connection and then replaces the HTTP protocol with its own WS protocol, reusing the same TCP or a new connection.

Go has some support for WebSockets in a sub-repository, but actually recommends a third-party package. This chapter considers both packages.

© Jan Newmarch 2017
J. Newmarch, *Network Programming with Go*, DOI 10.1007/978-1-4842-2692-6_15

WebSockets Server

A WebSockets server starts off by being an HTTP server, accepting TCP connections and handling the HTTP requests on the TCP connection. When a request comes in that switches that connection to being a WebSockets connection, the protocol handler is changed from an HTTP handler to a WebSocket handler. So it is only that TCP connection that gets its role changed, the server continues to be an HTTP server for other requests, while the TCP socket underlying that one connection is used as a WebSocket.

One of the simple servers discussed in Chapter 8, HTTP registered various handlers such as a file handler or a function handler. To handle WebSockets requests, we simply register a different type of handler—a WebSockets handler. Which handler the server uses is based on the URL pattern. For example, a file handler might be registered for /, a function handler for /cgi-bin/..., and a WebSockets handler for /ws.

An HTTP server that is only expecting to be used for WebSockets might run as follows:

```
func main() {
        http.Handle("/", websocket.Handler(WSHandler))
        err := http.ListenAndServe(":12345", nil)
        checkError(err)
}
```

A more complex server might handle both HTTP and WebSockets requests simply by adding more handlers.

The Go Sub-Repository Package

Go has the sub-repository package called golang.org/x/net/websocket. To use this, you must first download it:

```
go get golang.org/x/net/websocket
```

The package documentation states the following:

> *This package currently lacks some features found in an alternative and more actively maintained WebSockets package: https://godoc.org/github.com/gorilla/websocket*

This suggests that you might be better off using the alternative package. Nevertheless, we consider this package here in keeping with the rest of this book of using the packages from the Go team. A later section looks at the alternative package.

The Message Object

HTTP is a stream protocol. WebSockets are frame-based. You prepare a block of data (of any size) and send it as a set of frames. Frames can contain strings in UTF-8 encoding or a sequence of bytes.

The simplest way of using WebSockets is just to prepare a block of data and ask the Go WebSockets library to package it as a set of frame data, send it across the wire, and receive it as the same block. The websocket package contains a convenience object called Message to do just that. The Message object has two methods—Send and Receive—that take a WebSocket as the first parameter. The second parameter is either the address of a variable to store data in, or the data to be sent. Code to send string data looks like this:

```
msgToSend := "Hello"
err := websocket.Message.Send(ws, msgToSend)

var msgToReceive string
err := websocket.Message.Receive(conn, &msgToReceive)
```

Code to send byte data looks like this:

```
dataToSend := []byte{0, 1, 2}
err := websocket.Message.Send(ws, dataToSend)

var dataToReceive []byte
err := websocket.Message.Receive(conn, &dataToReceive)
```

An echo server to send and receive string data is given next. Note that in WebSockets, either side can initiate sending of messages, and in this server we send messages from the server to a client when it connects (send/receive) instead of the more normal receive/send server. The server is EchoServer.go:

```
/* EchoServer
 */
package main

import (
        "fmt"
        "golang.org/x/net/websocket"
        "net/http"
        "os"
)

func Echo(ws *websocket.Conn) {
        fmt.Println("Echoing")

        for n := 0; n < 10; n++ {
                msg := "Hello  " + string(n+48)
                fmt.Println("Sending to client: " + msg)
                err := websocket.Message.Send(ws, msg)
                if err != nil {
                        fmt.Println("Can't send")
                        break
                }

                var reply string
                err = websocket.Message.Receive(ws, &reply)
                if err != nil {
                        fmt.Println("Can't receive")
                        break
                }
```

```
                fmt.Println("Received back from client: " + reply)
        }
}

func main() {

        http.Handle("/", websocket.Handler(Echo))
        err := http.ListenAndServe(":12345", nil)
        checkError(err)
}

func checkError(err error) {
        if err != nil {
                fmt.Println("Fatal error ", err.Error())
                os.Exit(1)
        }
}
```

It is run as follows:

```
go run EchoServer.go
```

A client that talks to this server is EchoClient.go:

```
/* EchoClient
 */
package main

import (
        "fmt"
        "golang.org/x/net/websocket"
        "io"
        "os"
)

func main() {
        if len(os.Args) != 2 {
                fmt.Println("Usage: ", os.Args[0], "ws://host:port")
                os.Exit(1)
        }
        service := os.Args[1]

        conn, err := websocket.Dial(service, "", "http://localhost:12345")
        checkError(err)
        var msg string
        for {
                err := websocket.Message.Receive(conn, &msg)
```

```
                    if err != nil {
                            if err == io.EOF {
                                    // graceful shutdown by server
                                    break
                            }
                            fmt.Println("Couldn't receive msg " + err.Error())
                            break
                    }
                    fmt.Println("Received from server: " + msg)
                    // return the msg
                    err = websocket.Message.Send(conn, msg)
                    if err != nil {
                            fmt.Println("Couldn't return msg")
                            break
                    }
            }
            os.Exit(0)
}

func checkError(err error) {
        if err != nil {
                fmt.Println("Fatal error ", err.Error())
                os.Exit(1)
        }
}
```

It is run as follows:

```
go run EchoClient.go ws://localhost:12345
```

The output on the *client* side is what is sent by the *server*:

```
Received from server: Hello  0
Received from server: Hello  1
Received from server: Hello  2
Received from server: Hello  3
Received from server: Hello  4
Received from server: Hello  5
Received from server: Hello  6
Received from server: Hello  7
Received from server: Hello  8
Received from server: Hello  9
```

The JSON Object

It is expected that many WebSockets clients and servers will exchange data in JSON format. For Go programs, this means that a Go object will be marshalled into the JSON format, as described in Chapter 4 and then sent as UTF-8 strings, while the receiver will read this string and unmarshal it back into a Go object.

The websocket convenience object called JSON will do this for you. It has Send and Receive methods for sending and receiving data, just like the Message object.

We consider a case where a client sends a Person object to a server using WebSockets (which can send messages both ways). A server that reads the message from the client and prints it to the server's standard output is PersonServerJSON.go:

```go
/* PersonServerJSON
 */
package main

import (
        "fmt"
        "golang.org/x/net/websocket"
        "net/http"
        "os"
)

type Person struct {
        Name    string
        Emails []string
}

func ReceivePerson(ws *websocket.Conn) {
        var person Person
        err := websocket.JSON.Receive(ws, &person)
        if err != nil {
                fmt.Println("Can't receive")
        } else {

                fmt.Println("Name: " + person.Name)
                for _, e := range person.Emails {
                        fmt.Println("An email: " + e)
                }
        }
}

func main() {

        http.Handle("/", websocket.Handler(ReceivePerson))
        err := http.ListenAndServe(":12345", nil)
        checkError(err)
}

func checkError(err error) {
        if err != nil {
                fmt.Println("Fatal error ", err.Error())
                os.Exit(1)
        }
}
```

A client that sends a `Person` object in JSON format is `PersonClientJSON.go`:

```go
/* PersonClientJSON
 */
package main

import (
        "fmt"
        "golang.org/x/net/websocket"
        "os"
)

type Person struct {
        Name    string
        Emails []string
}

func main() {
        if len(os.Args) != 2 {
                fmt.Println("Usage: ", os.Args[0], "ws://host:port")
                os.Exit(1)
        }
        service := os.Args[1]

        conn, err := websocket.Dial(service, "",
                "http://localhost")
        checkError(err)

        person := Person{Name: "Jan",
                Emails: []string{"ja@newmarch.name", "jan.newmarch@gmail.com"},
        }

        err = websocket.JSON.Send(conn, person)
        if err != nil {
                fmt.Println("Couldn't send msg " + err.Error())
        }
        os.Exit(0)
}

func checkError(err error) {
        if err != nil {
                fmt.Println("Fatal error ", err.Error())
                os.Exit(1)
        }
}
```

The server is run as follows:

```
go run PersonServerJSON.go
```

The client is run as follows:

```
go run PersonClientJSON.go  ws://localhost:12345
```

The output on the *server* side is what is sent by the *client*:

```
Name: Jan
An email: ja@newmarch.name
An email: jan.newmarch@gmail.com
```

The Codec Type

The Message and JSON objects are both instances of the type Codec. This type is defined as follows:

```
type Codec struct {
    Marshal   func(v interface{}) (data []byte, payloadType byte, err error)
    Unmarshal func(data []byte, payloadType byte, v interface{}) (err error)
}
```

The Codec type implements the Send and Receive methods used earlier.

It is likely that WebSockets will also be used to exchange XML data. We can build an XML Codec object by wrapping the XML marshal and unmarshal methods discussed in Chapter 12 to give a suitable Codec object.

We can create a XMLCodec package in this way, called XMLCodec.go:

```
package xmlcodec

import (
        "encoding/xml"
        "golang.org/x/net/websocket"
)

func xmlMarshal(v interface{}) (msg []byte, payloadType byte, err error) {
        msg, err = xml.Marshal(v)
        return msg, websocket.TextFrame, nil
}

func xmlUnmarshal(msg []byte, payloadType byte, v interface{}) (err error) {
        err = xml.Unmarshal(msg, v)
        return err
}

var XMLCodec = websocket.Codec{xmlMarshal, xmlUnmarshal}
```

This file should be installed in the src subdirectory of GOPATH:

```
$GOPATH/src/xmlcodec/XMLCodec.go
```

We can then serialize Go objects such as a Person into an XML document and send them from a client to a server. The server to receive the document and print it to standard output is as follows:

```
/* PersonServerXML
 */
package main

import (
        "fmt"
        "golang.org/x/net/websocket"
        "net/http"
        "os"
        "xmlcodec"
)

type Person struct {
        Name    string
        Emails []string
}

func ReceivePerson(ws *websocket.Conn) {
        var person Person
        err := xmlcodec.XMLCodec.Receive(ws, &person)
        if err != nil {
                fmt.Println("Can't receive")
        } else {

                fmt.Println("Name: " + person.Name)
                for _, e := range person.Emails {
                        fmt.Println("An email: " + e)
                }
        }
}

func main() {

        http.Handle("/", websocket.Handler(ReceivePerson))
        err := http.ListenAndServe(":12345", nil)
        checkError(err)
}

func checkError(err error) {
        if err != nil {
                fmt.Println("Fatal error ", err.Error())
                os.Exit(1)
        }
}
```

The client sending the Person object in XML form is PersonClientXML.go:

```go
/* PersonClientXML
 */
package main

import (
        "fmt"
        "golang.org/x/net/websocket"
        "os"
        "xmlcodec"
)

type Person struct {
        Name    string
        Emails  []string
}

func main() {
        if len(os.Args) != 2 {
                fmt.Println("Usage: ", os.Args[0], "ws://host:port")
                os.Exit(1)
        }
        service := os.Args[1]

        conn, err := websocket.Dial(service, "", "http://localhost")
        checkError(err)

        person := Person{Name: "Jan",
                Emails: []string{"ja@newmarch.name", "jan.newmarch@gmail.com"},
        }

        err = xmlcodec.XMLCodec.Send(conn, person)
        if err != nil {
                fmt.Println("Couldn't send msg " + err.Error())
        }
        os.Exit(0)
}

func checkError(err error) {
        if err != nil {
                fmt.Println("Fatal error ", err.Error())
                os.Exit(1)
        }
}
```

The server is run as follows:

```
go run PersonServerXML.go
```

The client is run as follows:

```
go run PersonClientXML.go  ws://localhost:12345
```

The output on the *server* side is what is sent by the *client*:

```
Name: Jan
An email: ja@newmarch.name
An email: jan.newmarch@gmail.com
```

WebSockets Over TLS

A WebSocket can be built above a secure TLS socket. We discussed in Chapter 8 how to use a TLS socket using the certificates from Chapter 7. That is used unchanged for WebSockets. That is, we use `http.ListenAndServeTLS` instead of `http.ListenAndServe`.

Here is the echo server using TLS:

```go
/* EchoServerTLS
 */
package main

import (
        "fmt"
        "golang.org/x/net/websocket"
        "net/http"
        "os"
)

func Echo(ws *websocket.Conn) {
        fmt.Println("Echoing")

        for n := 0; n < 10; n++ {
                msg := "Hello  " + string(n+48)
                fmt.Println("Sending to client: " + msg)
                err := websocket.Message.Send(ws, msg)
                if err != nil {
                        fmt.Println("Can't send")
                        break
                }

                var reply string
                err = websocket.Message.Receive(ws, &reply)
                if err != nil {
                        fmt.Println("Can't receive")
                        break
                }
                fmt.Println("Received back from client: " + reply)
        }
}
```

```go
func main() {

        http.Handle("/", websocket.Handler(Echo))
        err := http.ListenAndServeTLS(":12345", "jan.newmarch.name.pem",
                "private.pem", nil)
        checkError(err)
}

func checkError(err error) {
        if err != nil {
                fmt.Println("Fatal error ", err.Error())
                os.Exit(1)
        }
}
```

The client is the same echo client as before. All that changes is the URL, which uses the wss scheme instead of the ws scheme:

```
EchoClient wss://localhost:12345/
```

That will work fine if the TLS certificate offered by the server is valid. The certificate I am using is not: it is self-signed, and that is often a signal that you are entering a danger zone. If you want to keep going anyway, you need to employ the same "remove the safety check" that we did in Chapter 8 by turning on the TLS InsecureSkipVerify flag. That is done by the program EchoClientTLS.go, which sets up a configuration using this flag and then calls DialConfig in place of Dial:

```go
/* EchoClientTLS
 */
package main

import (
        "fmt"
        "crypto/tls"
        "golang.org/x/net/websocket"
        "io"
        "os"
)

func main() {
        if len(os.Args) != 2 {
                fmt.Println("Usage: ", os.Args[0], "wss://host:port")
                os.Exit(1)
        }

        config, err := websocket.NewConfig(os.Args[1], "http://localhost")
        checkError(err)
        tlsConfig := &tls.Config{InsecureSkipVerify: true}
        config.TlsConfig = tlsConfig

        conn, err := websocket.DialConfig(config)
        checkError(err)
```

```go
        var msg string
        for {
                err := websocket.Message.Receive(conn, &msg)
                if err != nil {
                        if err == io.EOF {
                                // graceful shutdown by server
                                break
                        }
                        fmt.Println("Couldn't receive msg " + err.Error())
                        break
                }
                fmt.Println("Received from server: " + msg)
                // return the msg
                err = websocket.Message.Send(conn, msg)
                if err != nil {
                        fmt.Println("Couldn't return msg")
                        break
                }
        }
        os.Exit(0)
}

func checkError(err error) {
        if err != nil {
                fmt.Println("Fatal error ", err.Error())
                os.Exit(1)
        }
}
```

WebSockets in an HTML Page

The original driver for WebSockets was to allow full duplex interaction between an HTTP user agent such as a browser and a server. The typical use case is expected to involve a JavaScript program in a browser interacting with a server. In this section, we build a web/WebSockets server that delivers an HTML page that sets up a WebSocket and displays information from that server using WebSockets. We are looking at the situation illustrated in Figure 15-1.

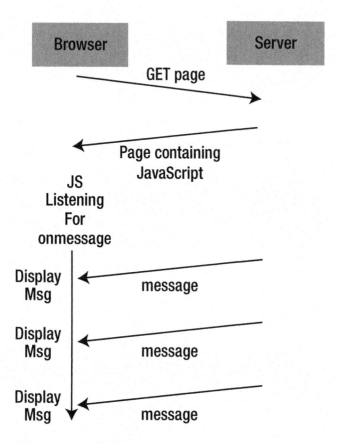

Figure 15-1. *Full duplex interaction situation*

The age of the Internet of Things (IoT) is coming. Consequently we can expect data from sensors and sensor networks to be used to drive actuators and to display information about an IoT network in browsers. There are innumerable books about using Raspberry Pi's and Arduinos for building sensor networks, but we will drastically simplify the situation by showing the CPU temperatures on a "sensor," updating in a web page every few seconds.

The Linux sensors command from the Debian package lm-sensors writes to standard output the values of sensors it knows about. The command sensors on my desktop machine produces output such as the following:

```
acpitz-virtual-0
Adapter: Virtual device
temp1:         +27.8°C  (crit = +105.0°C)
temp2:         +29.8°C  (crit = +105.0°C)

coretemp-isa-0000
Adapter: ISA adapter
Physical id 0:  +58.0°C  (high = +105.0°C, crit = +105.0°C)
Core 0:         +57.0°C  (high = +105.0°C, crit = +105.0°C)
Core 1:         +58.0°C  (high = +105.0°C, crit = +105.0°C)
```

On refresh, typically the temperature on Core 0 and Core 1 may change.
On Windows, a command to do the same is this:

```
wmic /namespace:\\root\wmi PATH MSAcpi_ThermalZoneTemperature get CurrentTemperature
```

When this runs, it has output such as

```
42.4° C
```

On the Mac, use the command osx-cpu-temp from https://github.com/lavoiesl/osx-cpu-temp.
If you don't want to go through these steps, just substitute a more mundane program such as the date.
We provide a Go program to deliver HTML documents from the ROOT_DIR directory and to then set up
a WebSocket from the URL GetTemp. The WebSocket on the server side gets the output from sensors every
two seconds and sends it to the client end of the socket. The web/WebSockets server runs on port 12345, for
no particular reason. This program will run under Linux after the lm-sensors package is installed. For other
systems, substitute any other interesting system call for the exec.Command call.
The Go server is TemperatureServer.go:

```go
/* TemperatureServer
 */
package main

import (
        "fmt"
        "golang.org/x/net/websocket"
        "net/http"
        "os"
        "os/exec"
        "time"
)

var ROOT_DIR = "/home/httpd/html/golang-hidden/websockets"

func GetTemp(ws *websocket.Conn) {
        for {

                msg, _ := exec.Command("sensors").Output()
                fmt.Println("Sending to client: " + string(msg[:]))
                err := websocket.Message.Send(ws, string(msg[:]))
                if err != nil {
                        fmt.Println("Can't send")
                        break
                }
                time.Sleep(2 * 1000 * 1000 * 1000)

                var reply string
                err = websocket.Message.Receive(ws, &reply)
```

```
                if err != nil {
                        fmt.Println("Can't receive")
                        break
                }
                fmt.Println("Received back from client: " + reply)
        }
}

func main() {
        fileServer := http.FileServer(http.Dir(ROOT_DIR))
        http.Handle("/GetTemp", websocket.Handler(GetTemp))
        http.Handle("/", fileServer)
        err := http.ListenAndServe(":12345", nil)
        checkError(err)
}

func checkError(err error) {
        if err != nil {
                fmt.Println("Fatal error ", err.Error())
                os.Exit(1)
        }
}
```

It is run as follows:

```
go run TemperatureServer.go
```

The top-level HTML file to kick this off is websocket.html:

```
<!DOCTYPE HTML>
<html>
  <head>

    <script type="text/javascript">
      function WebSocketTest()
      {
        if ("WebSocket" in window)
        {
          alert("WebSocket is supported by your Browser!");

          // Let us open a web socket
          var ws = new WebSocket("ws://localhost:12345/GetTemp");

          ws.onopen = function()
          {
            alert("WS is opened...");
          };
```

```
        ws.onmessage = function (evt)
        {
          var received_msg = evt.data;
          // uncomment next line if you want to get alerts on each message
          //alert("Message is received..." + received_msg);
          document.getElementById("temp").innerHTML = "<pre>" + received_msg + "</pre>"
          ws.send("Message received")
        };

        ws.onclose = function()
        {
          // websocket is closed.
          alert("Connection is closed...");
        };
      }

      else
      {
        // The browser doesn't support WebSocket
        alert("WebSocket NOT supported by your Browser!");
      }
    }
  </script>

</head>
<body>

  <div id="temp">
    <a href="javascript:WebSocketTest()">Run temperature sensor</a>
  </div>

</body>
</html>
```

The program uses JavaScript to open a WebSockets connection and to handle the onopen, onmessage, and onclose events. It reads and writes using evt.data and the send function. It presents the data in a preformatted element, exactly as the data above. It is refreshed every two seconds. The structure of the HTML document is based on HTML5 - WebSockets from TutorialsPoint (https://www.tutorialspoint.com/html5/html5_websocket.htm).

The Gorilla Package

The alternative package for WebSockets is the github.com/gorilla/websocket package. To use this, you will need to run the following:

```
go get github.com/gorilla/websocket
```

Echo Server

The echo server using this package is EchoServerGorilla.go. It makes the HTTP to WebSockets transition more explicit by introducing a call to a websocket.Upgrader object. It also more clearly distinguishes between sending text and binary messages.

```go
/* EchoServerGorilla
 */
package main

import (
        "fmt"
        "github.com/gorilla/websocket"
        "net/http"
        "os"
)

var upgrader = websocket.Upgrader{
        ReadBufferSize:  1024,
        WriteBufferSize: 1024,
}

func Handler(w http.ResponseWriter, r *http.Request) {
        fmt.Println("Handling /")
        conn, err := upgrader.Upgrade(w, r, nil)
        if err != nil {
                fmt.Println(err)
                return
        }

        for n := 0; n < 10; n++ {
                msg := "Hello  " + string(n+48)
                fmt.Println("Sending to client: " + msg)
                err = conn.WriteMessage(websocket.TextMessage, []byte(msg))

                _, reply, err := conn.ReadMessage()
                if err != nil {
                        fmt.Println("Can't receive")
                        break
                }
                fmt.Println("Received back from client: " + string(reply[:]))
        }
        conn.Close()
}

func main() {
        http.HandleFunc("/", Handler)
        err := http.ListenAndServe("localhost:12345", nil)
        checkError(err)
}
```

```
func checkError(err error) {
        if err != nil {
                fmt.Println("Fatal error ", err.Error())
                os.Exit(1)
        }
}
```

The server is run as follows:

```
go run EchoServerGorilla
```

Echo Client

The echo client using this package is EchoClientGorilla.go:

```
/* EchoClientGorilla
 */
package main

import (
        "fmt"
        "github.com/gorilla/websocket"
        "io"
        "net/http"
        "os"
)

func main() {
        if len(os.Args) != 2 {
                fmt.Println("Usage: ", os.Args[0], "ws://host:port")
                os.Exit(1)
        }
        service := os.Args[1]

        header := make(http.Header)
        header.Add("Origin", "http://localhost:12345")
        conn, _, err := websocket.DefaultDialer.Dial(service, header)
        checkError(err)

        for {
                _, reply, err := conn.ReadMessage()
                if err != nil {

                        if err == io.EOF {
                                // graceful shutdown by server
                                fmt.Println(`EOF from server`)
                                break
                        }
```

```
                        if websocket.IsCloseError(err, websocket.CloseAbnormalClosure) {
                                fmt.Println(`Close from server`)
                                break
                        }
                        fmt.Println("Couldn't receive msg " + err.Error())
                        break
                }
                //checkError(err)
                fmt.Println("Received from server: " + string(reply[:]))

                // return the msg
                err = conn.WriteMessage(websocket.TextMessage, reply)
                if err != nil {
                        fmt.Println("Couldn't return msg")
                        break
                }
        }
        os.Exit(0)
}

func checkError(err error) {
        if err != nil {
                fmt.Println("Fatal error ", err.Error())
                os.Exit(1)
        }
}
```

The client is run as follows:

```
go run EchoClientGorila ws://localhost:12345
```

Conclusion

The WebSockets standard is an IETF RFC, so no major changes are anticipated. This will allow HTTP user agents and servers to set up bidirectional socket connections and should make certain interaction styles much easier. Go has support from two packages for WebSockets.

Afterword

This book looked at the basics of distributed programming and how this can be done in Go. There are indefinite extensions to this. For example, you may be interested in how time is managed in distributed systems, or how replicated databases maintain consistency (or weaker, eventual consistency). You may be interested in algorithms for load balancing, or in techniques such as map-reduce, as is often used to process queries across distributed databases, or in how grid computing systems can span thousands of computers of different types, in different administrative domains. Or in how a dramatically simplified model is used for cloud computing.

Some of these are classic distributed system problems, and information may be found in books such as Andrew S. Tanenbaum and Maarten Van Steen's book, *Distributed Systems - Principles and Paradigms*. The fundamentals of grid computing may be found in the book by Ian Foster and Carl Kesselman, titled *The Grid: Blueprint for a New Computing Infrastructure*, while map-reduce is covered in books on Hadoop (for Java).

If you specifically want Go implementations of distributed frameworks, techniques, or algorithms not in the standard Go libraries, you should look at sites like Go Projects (see `https://github.com/golang/go/wiki/Projects`), which maintains a list of active third-party Go projects.

There are also other books dealing with topics in this area, such as *Web Development with Go* by Shiju Varghese, *Mastering Go Web Services* by Nathan Kozyra, and several others. A good site that lists many books is Golang books at `https://github.com/golang/go/wiki/Books`.

My own interests are increasingly in the IoT (Internet of Things) space. Here, you can see Go activity, with frameworks such as Gobot (`https://gobot.io/`) and Project Flogo (`https://dzone.com/articles/project-flogo-golang-powered-open-source-iot-integ`). The MQTT message passing protocol is getting some traction in the IoT space, and the Eclipse Paho MQTT Go client (see `https://github.com/eclipse/paho.mqtt.golang`) can partake in this. And of course, Go runs on the Raspberry Pi, which is a good starting point for experiments with the IoT. You can expect more activity in the IoT space using Go, as it can compile down to the native machine code on several processor types.

Enjoy your Go adventures!

© Jan Newmarch 2017
J. Newmarch, *Network Programming with Go*, DOI 10.1007/978-1-4842-2692-6

Index

A

Abstract syntax notation one (ASN.1)
  ASCII characters, 63
  Go asn1 package documentation, 62
  ASN1basic.go, 63–64
  character sets, 63
  character strings, 62
  data types and data structures, 61, 65
  daytime client and server, 66–67
  marshal and unmarshal data, 60
  marshal and unmarshal structures, 65
  pointers, 66
  pointer variable, 63
  PrintableString and IA5String, 63
  structured types, 62
  *time.Time, 63
  UTC time type, 63
Access transparency, 17
Apache, 247
Arrays, 22
ASCII, 107, 109, 111, 113
Asynchronous communication, 10
Asynchronous JavaScript and XML (AJAX), 247
Authenticating proxy, 151, 153

B

Block algorithms, 126
Body Area Network (BAN), 3
Browser files, 177
Browser site diagram, 175–177

C

Certificate authority (CA), 132
Character, 108
  ASCII, 109, 111
  code, 108
  encoding, 108
  ISO 8859, 111
  repertoire/set, 108

sets and Go, 119
transport encoding, 109
unicode, 111–112
UTF-8, 112
  ASCII client and server, 113
  client and server, 112
UTF-16, 113
  client and server, 114–116
  little-endian and big-endian, 113
Character-handling mechanisms, 107
CharData type, 200
Chinese dictionary, 181–182
Client
  Client.go, 241–244
  getFlashcardSets() function, 240
  XML format, content, 240
Client-server application, 8, 94
Client-server system, 7, 8
Client-side code, 210
Client state transition diagrams, 104
Codec type, 254, 256
Comment type, 200
Communication flows, 9
  asynchronous communication, 10
  publish/subscribe, 10
  streaming communication, 10
  synchronous communication, 10
Communications models, 5
  message passing, 5–6
  remote procedure call, 6–7
Complete server, 234, 236–240
Component distribution, 10
  application logic, 10
  data access, 10
  fat vs. thin, 14
  Gartner classification, 11–13
  presentation component, 10
  three-tier models, 13
Concurrency transparency, 17
Connection models, 5
  connectionless, 5
  connection oriented, 5

© Jan Newmarch 2017
J. Newmarch, *Network Programming with Go*, DOI 10.1007/978-1-4842-2692-6

Conn type
    interface, 50
    IPGetHeadInfo.go program, 50–52
    ThreadedIPEchoServer.go program, 52–53
    unix for UNIX sockets, 50
Conn.Write method, 53
Content negotiation
    acceptable formats, 230
    GET /, 232–233
    MIME types, 230
    POST /, 233–234
    range of formats, 230
    server, 230–231
    user agents, 230
CORBA, 210

D

Data format, 91–92
Data integrity, 124
Data serialization
    ASN.1 (see Abstract syntax
        notation one (ASN.1))
    Base64 encoding and decoding, 82
    external data representation
        (XDR), 59
    JSON (see JavaScript object
        notation (JSON))
    mutual agreement, 59
    protocol buffers
        binary encoding, 83
        compiled personv3.pb.go file, 84
        data types, 83
        installing and compiling, 84
        ONC RPC, 83
        personv3.proto, 83
        ProtocolBuffer.go, 85
    self-describing data, 59
    structured data, 57–58
Decryption key, 127
Default multiplexer, 158–159
Delay Tolerant
        Networking (DNT), 29
The Demultiplexer (Demuxer), 229–230
Directive type, 201–203
Distributed computing, fallacies, 18
    administrator, 19
    homogenous network, 20
    infinite bandwidth, 19
    reliable network, 18
    secure network, 19
    topology doesn't change, 19
    zero latency, 19
    zero transport cost, 20
Distributed computing models, 7

Distributed systems, 1
    acceptance factors, 16–17
    continuum of processing, 15
    points of failure, 16
Document Object Model (DOM), 247
Dynamic link libraries (DLLs), 6

E

EBCDIC, 107
Echo client, 265–266
Echo server, 264–265
EndElement type, 200
Error values, 26–27
External data representation (XDR), 59

F

Failure transparency, 18
Flashcard sets, 183–184
flashcards.ListFlashCardsNames(), 180
FlashCards struct, 187–189
Functions, 23–24

G

Gartner classification, 11
    distributed database, 11
    network file service, 12
    secure shell, 13
    terminal emulation, 12
    Web, 12
Gateways, 4
GET method, 143–145
Gob serialization, 59
Go language, 21
    character sets and, 119
    error values, 26–27
    functions, 23–24
    GOPATH, 25
    hashing algorithms, 125
    ISO 8859 and, 117–118
    maps, 24
    methods, 24
    multi-threading, 25
    packages, 25
    pointers, 23
    RPC
        HTTP client, 213–214
        HTTP server, 212–213
        restrictions, 210–211
        TCP client, 216–217
        TCP server, 214–216
    runes, 112
    running, 26

self-signed certificate, 133
slices and arrays, 22
Standard Libraries, 26
statements, 25
structures, 22–23
symmetric key encryption, 126
type conversion, 25
types, 22
UTF-16, 113–116
Gorilla package
    echo client, 265–266
    echo server, 264–265

■ H

Handler file, 248
Handler functions, 156
Hash, 124
Hashing, 124
Hash value, 124–125
HEAD method, 142–143
Homograph attacks, 138
HTML, 207
    EscapeString and UnescapeString, 193
    EscapeString.go, 193–194
    parsers, 193
    ReadHTML.go, 195–197
    template package, 194–195
    tokenizing, 195–197
    WebSockets, 259–263
HTTP 0.9, 138
HTTP 1.0
    request format, 139
    response format, 139–140
HTTP 1.1, 140–141, 247
HTTP/2, 141
HTTPS, 153
Hypermedia as the Engine of Application
    State (HATEOAS)
    appropriate links, 225
    cookies/external API specifications, 225
    IANA, 225
    link formats, 225
    principle, 224
Hypertext Application Language (HAL), 226
Hypertext Transport Protocol (HTTP)
    characteristics, 138
    client object, 147–148
    configure requests, 145–146
    connections by clients, 153–155
    HTTP 0.9, 138
    HTTP 1.0, 139–140
    HTTP 1.1, 140–141
    HTTP/2, 141
    i18n, 137
    proxy (*see* Proxy, HTTP)

RPC client, 213–214
RPC server, 212
servers (*see* Servers)
URLs and resources, 137
versions, 138

■ I

ICMP packet payload, 53
Increasing internationalization (i18n), 137
Internationalization (i18n), 107
Internet, 32-bit unsigned integer, 30
Internet Control Message Protocol (ICMP), 53
Internet of Things (IoT), 29, 260
Internet Printing Protocol (ipp), 221
Internet protocol (IP)
    defined, 32
    description, 30
    IPAddr type, 36–37
    IPv4 addresses, 31
    IPv6 addresses, 31
    LookupHost function, 37
    LookupHostname function, 38
    mask type, 33, 35–36
    process, 32–33
    ResolveIPAddr function, 37
    String() method, 32
ISO 8859, 111, 117–119
ISO security architecture
    functions, 122–123
    levels, 122–123
    mechanisms, 123–124

■ J

JavaScript object notation (JSON)
    array, 68
    client and server, 72–73
    Gob package
        circular structures, 75
        Decoder, 76
        Encoder, 76
        GobEchoClient.go, 78–79
        GobEchoServer.go, 80
        Gob marshalling and unmarshalling, 75
        Go data types, 75
        object, 251, 253
        pointer types, 75
        SaveGob.go, 76, 78
        X.509 serialization, 75
    JSONEchoServer.go, 73–74
    RPC client, 219–220
    RPC server, 218–219
    SaveJSON.go, 69–71
    string handling, 68
    type-dependent default encodings, 69

K

Keyed-Hash Message Authentication Code (HMAC), 125

L

Links
    defined, 225
    HTML types, 225
    user agent and server, 226
    W3C specification JSON-LD 1.0, 226
    XML specifications, 225
Linux, 260–261
listFlashCards function, 179, 180
Local area network (LAN), 3
Localization (l10n), 107
Location transparency, 17

M

manageFlashCards function, 181
Maps, 24
Marshalling, 210
Marshalling XML, 206–207
MD5 hashing, 125
Message
    format, 90–91
    object, 248, 250–251
    passing, 5–6
Methods, 24
Metropolitan Area Network (MANs), 3
Middleware model, 14
    examples, 14
    functions, 15
Migration transparency, 17
Multiplexer, 155
Multi-threading, 25

N

Networking, 3–4
404 not found messages, 156

O

Open systems interconnect (OSI), 29
    levels, 122
    protocol, 2
    seven-layer model, 122

P, Q

PacketConn interface, 53
Packet encapsulation, 4–5
PathEscape function, 230

Performance
    transparency, 18
Ping.go program, 53–55
PinyinFormatter, 189
PinyinFormatter.go, 184–187
Pipelines, 164
Pointers, 23
ProcInst type, 201
Protocol design
    client code, 99–100
    client-server application, 94
    client side, 94
    data format
        byte format, 91–92
        character format, 92
    issues, 87
    message format, 90–91
    server code, 97–98
    server side, 95
    standalone application, 93
    state information
        client state diagram, 104
        DCE file system, 102
        NFS file system, 102
        server pseudocode, 105
        server state diagram, 105
        state-transition
            diagram, 103
    text protocol, 96
    textproto package, 101
    version control, 90
Protocol layers, 1
    alternative protocols, 3
    ISO OSI protocol, 2
    OSI layers, 2
    TCP/IP protocols, 3
Proxy, HTTP
    authenticating, 151, 153
    simple, 149, 151
Public key encryption, 127
    decryption key, 127
    encryption key, 127
    RSA scheme, 127–128
Public Key Infrastructure (PKI), 129
Punycode, 137

R

Register function, 211
Remote procedure calls (RPCs), 6, 210,221.
    See also REST Verbs
    HTTP client, 213–214
    HTTP server, 212–213
    JSON client, 219–220
    JSON server, 218
    restrictions, 210–211

styles, 210
TCP client, 216–217
TCP server, 214–216
Replication transparency, 17
Representational State Transfer (REST)
    cards handling, 234
    definition, 221
    HTTP client-server system, 228
    HTTP verbs, 227
    interaction style, 245
    representation of, resources, 222
    resources, 221
    resourcesdefinition, 222
    resourcesnon-HTTP URL schemes, 221
    resourcesURLs, 221
    speed and resource allocation, 245
    tightly controlled and uncontrolled, 245
    URIs, 222
    URLs, 228–229
    URL transaction, 227
    Wikipedia entry, HATEOAS, 226
Request for Comments (RFCs), 29
REST verbs
    DELETE verb, 224
    description, 223
    GET verb, 223
    POST verb, 224
    PUT verb, 223
The Richardson Maturity
        Model, 227–228

S

Scalability transparency, 17
Secure Sockets Layer (SSL), 132
Self-signed certificate, 133, 135–136
Servers
    default multiplexer, 158–159
    distribution, 9
    file, 155–156
    handler functions, 156–157
Server-side code, 210
Server state transition diagrams, 105
Services
    host machines, 38
    ports, 38–39
    TCPAddr type, 39, 40
    TCP and UDP methods, 38
    types of, 38
SetKeepAlive method, 53
SetReadBuffer method, 53
showFlashCards function, 189–191
SimpleEchoServer.go program, 44–46
Simple proxy, 149, 151

Simple user agents
    GET method, 143–145
    HEAD method, 142–143
    response type, 141–142
Slices, 22
Standalone application, 93
StartElement type, 200
State transition diagram, 103
Stream Control Transmission
        Protocol (SCTP), 29
Streaming communication, 10
String, 107
Structured data, 57–58
Sub-repository package
    Codec type, 254, 256
    JSON object, 251, 253
    message object, 248, 250–251
    WebSockets in HTML page, 259–263
    WebSockets over TLS, 257–259
Sun's ONC, 210
Symmetric key encryption
    block algorithms, 126
    definition, 126
Synchronous communication, 10

T

TCP, 247
    connections
        staying alive method, 47
        timeout, 47
    RPC client, 216–217
    RPC server, 214–216
TCPConn type
    daytime server, 42–44
    description, 40
    TCP client, 40–42
TCP/IP protocols, 3
TCP/IP stack, 29
    connection-oriented protocol, 30
    IP datagrams, 30
    vs. OSI, 30
    RFCs, 29
    UDP, 30
    virtual circuit, 30
Templates
    conditional statements, 168–169, 171–173
    fmt package, 161
    functions defining, 165–166
    HTML package, 173
    object values inserting, 161–164
    parsing, process, 162–164
    pipelines, 164
    variables, 167

Text protocol, 96
ThreadedEchoServer.go program, 45
Three-tier models, 13
Transparency, 17
    access, 17
    concurrency, 17
    failure, 18
    location, 17
    migration, 17
    performance, 18
    replication, 17
    scalability, 17
Transport Layer Security (TLS), 153, 159
    basic client, 132–133
    self-signed certificate, 133, 135–136
Trivial File Transfer Protocol (TFTP), 4
Type conversion, 25

U

UDP datagrams
    functions, 47
    program, 47–49
    source and destination information, 47
Unicode, 108, 111–112
    Gotchas, 116–117
Uniform resource identifiers (URIs), 221, 222
Uniform resource locator (URLs), 137, 221
Uniform resource names (URNs), 221
Unmarshal function, 203–206
User Datagram Protocol (UDP), 30
UTF-7, 112
UTF-8, 112
    ASCII client and server, 113
    client and server, 112
UTF-16, 112–113
    client and server, 114–116
    little-endian and big-endian, 113
UTF-32, 112

V

Version control, 88–90

W

Web server
    accents fixing, 184–187
    browser pages, 175
    browser
        presentation, 191
    flashcards, 191
    flashcard sets, 183–184
    functions, URLs, 177
    pinyin, 191
    Server.go, 178
WebSockets
    HTML page, 259–263
    over TLS, 257–259
    server, 248
Wide area network (WAN), 3
World Wide Web, 137

X, Y, Z

X.509 certificates, 153, 159
    example, 129–131
    PKI, 129
XHTML, 207
XML
    marshalling, 206–207
    parser, 200
        CharData type, 200
        Comment type, 200
        Directive type, 201–203
        EndElement type, 200
        ProcInst type, 201
        StartElement type, 200
    unmarshalling, 203–206

Get the eBook for only $5!

Why limit yourself?

With most of our titles available in both PDF and ePUB format, you can access your content wherever and however you wish—on your PC, phone, tablet, or reader.

Since you've purchased this print book, we are happy to offer you the eBook for just $5.

To learn more, go to http://www.apress.com/companion or contact support@apress.com.

Apress®

CPSIA information can be obtained
at www.ICGtesting.com
Printed in the USA
BVOW04s1940231117
501135BV00007B/114/P